THE JET MAKERS

THE JET MAKERS

The Aerospace Industry
from 1945 to 1972

CHARLES D. BRIGHT

THE REGENTS PRESS OF KANSAS

Lawrence

Library of Congress Cataloging in Publication Data
Bright, Charles D.   1921-
The jet makers.
Bibliography: p.‑‑‑‑‑‑‑
Includes index.
1. Aerospace industries—United States—History.
I. Title.
HD9711.5.U6B74   338.4′7′62910973   78-2377
ISBN 0-7006-0172-4

TO

HEIDI WITH LOVE

AND TO

ROBIN HIGHAM WITH APPRECIATION

CONTENTS

LIST OF ILLUSTRATIONS

PREFACE

In 1945 a few jet fighters flew among thousands of piston-engined aircraft in the world's air forces and airlines. In 1972 fleets of jets were in the air around the world. At both periods American-built aircraft outnumbered those from any other country.

American leadership was not foreordained. Although the United States had long been the largest industrial country, it had not been preeminent in every major field of production. In shipbuilding, for example, after leading in the age of sail, the United States lagged behind despite government encouragement. One reason was the failure of American shipbuilders to convert early to the new technology of steam. A similar failure was possible in the American aircraft industry, for although foremost in the older technology of piston aircraft production in 1945, the United States was far behind in the development of the new jet technology.

There are some basic similarities between piston and jet engines, but the latter are simpler and more efficient. The piston engine's disadvantages are fourfold. First, it is "reciprocating": its pistons are accelerated in one direction, then braked to a stop, then accelerated again in the opposite direction, many times a second. By contrast, the jet engine's continuous rotary turbine operates with a far more efficient motion. The second disadvantage of the piston engine is its circuitous routing of the air used to generate power. This air must be turned as it flows through a supercharger, a carburetor, and a minor labyrinth called an intake manifold, then halted until a valve opens, accelerated along a nonlinear path into the combustion chamber, compressed again, burned, and finally exhausted through another valve and labyrinthine exhaust manifold. Large masses of air must also be routed to control engine temperatures. A centrifugal-compressor jet engine also turns masses of air around corners, and this is one reason it, too, is a limited use engine. The axial-flow type, on the other hand, moves its air almost perfectly straight from intake through compressor, burner chamber, and turbine to exhaust.

A third disadvantage is that the piston engine cannot stand being run for long periods at over about 60 percent of its maximum available power, while the turbine can be used continuously at about 90 percent of maximum power. The fourth disadvantage of the piston engine is its use of a propeller, whose tips reach the speed of sound at relatively few revolutions per minute, causing grave efficiency problems. The jet engine can also drive a propeller (it is then called the propjet or turbo-prop), or it can get all its thrust from the exhaust gases.

Even in its early stages the jet was competitive with the piston. Each of the two Junkers Jumo 004B's used in the twin-engine Messer-schmitt Me 262A, the first jet fighter, developed 1,980 pounds of thrust. At 540 miles per hour this was equivalent to about 2,800 horsepower. The American Republic P-47D, a contemporary fighter, had a 2,300 horsepower Pratt & Whitney R-2800 engine. Furthermore, the efficiency of the jet is underscored by comparing engine weights, a factor of importance in aircraft performance: the Jumo weighed only 1,850 pounds, and the Pratt & Whitney 2,350 pounds, so the Jumo produced about 50 percent more horsepower per pound.

In 1945 the jet engine was a new technology in design and manufacture. The German and British developments had taken years. Although the British helped the United States get established in jets during the war, and German equipment and information were seized, it was no small task for the Americans to catch up. Great Britain, a first-class nation in aviation design since the beginning of flight, hoped to translate its already lengthy and early jet engine lead into competitive advantage in both fighter and airliner production. The formidable nature of the British effort is shown by their achievements in the production of jet engines and turbine transports. In the fifties Britain was the leading producer; by 1960 Rolls Royce had supplied 60 percent of the turbines for airliners built or building in the West; by 1962 over 500 British turbine transports were in service in the world's airlines, and the Royal Air Force and other free-world air forces were using British jets. The Russians, too, were producing superb, if not superior, jet fighters, and they had a fleet of turbine bombers and airliners (about 400 of the latter by 1962). Over 130 turbine airliners of British, French, and Dutch design or manufacture were in use on American airlines in 1962. Yet in spite of these able competitors, America's leadership was restored beyond doubt during the early sixties.

American success in the new technology was not a result of default by the competition. Other explanations have been ventured. One Englishman attributes American airliner leadership to adaptation of military designs, but asserts the same lineage held back the British. He also credits American dominance in modern piston transports to the Americans' having been the first to build them, and the American pre-eminence in jets to their having been second and thereby having learned from the British.[1] Since one usually cannot have things both ways, it seems likely that American success with jet technology is a result of other causes.

Americans are not only tinkerers, they like the biggest and the best. The race for home and foreign markets was important to the United States and fit the American character, but more important was the concern for survival in military terms. Throughout the period of jet engine development Americans believed their security in the cold war rested upon a balanced mixture of technological and quantitative superiority over the Soviet Union in nuclear weapons and the associated delivery systems. The major share of this technological challenge fell upon the aircraft, or aerospace, industry. How did the United States, which was behind in the race in the forties, leap to the fore by the early sixties? It is to answer this question that this book has been written.

The approach has been to analyze the part of the American aero-space industry that manufactures the final product. For the purpose of this book the giants of the aerospace industry were chosen for analysis, those on the frontiers of technology who manufactured fixed-wing aircraft of their own design. This is the group that bore the brunt of adaptation to the jet age: Boeing, Curtiss-Wright, Douglas, Fairchild, General Dynamics, Grumman, Lockheed, Martin, McDonnell, North American, Northrop, and Republic. When appropriate, General Dynamics will be referred to by the name of its predecessor company, Convair, which is a contraction of Consolidated Vultee Aircraft. Martin is also known as Martin Marietta, and North American by its earlier name, North American Aviation, or its later, North American Rockwell (today it is part of Rockwell International). One giant, Vought, has been excluded because of the years in which it was a subsidiary of United, whose main concern was engines. Curtiss-Wright, although it was once United's main engine competitor, produced many aircraft types and was one of the larger manufacturers in the industry; therefore it has been included. Companies that have been short-lived or peripheral, such as Chase and Ryan, are excluded.

Because of the breadth of this work and the large number of sources, footnotes have been limited to special situations: quotations, and material and ideas of a remote nature.

ACKNOWLEDGMENTS

The generous guidance and encouragement of Professor Robin Higham was vital for writing this book. I am most grateful for his insights and efforts. Additional help was given by Professor E. J. Laughlin.

Important information was provided at some effort to themselves by The Boeing Company, General Dynamics Corporation, Lockheed Aircraft Corporation, and Trans World Airlines. Other contributors were Fairchild Industries, McDonnell Douglas Corporation, Martin Marietta Corporation, Northrop Corporation, and Rockwell International Corporation. Special help with photographs was given with enthusiasm by Bill Whisler, a design engineer with Boeing.

My clumsy style was improved greatly by Abigail Siddall. Much of the clerical labor was done by my wife, Heidi, whose contributions include patience, encouragement, and criticism.

Any errors are my responsibility alone.

I

WORLD WAR II:
AVIATION COMES OF AGE

The aerospace companies of the United States grew to maturity during the Second World War. By 1944 aircraft manufacturing was the largest industry in the country, and piston technology had been exploited nearly to its limits. On its basic structure, still visible today, have been superimposed the effects of postwar revolutionary technological developments.

PEACETIME EQUILIBRIUM

From the thirties to 1948 the industry conformed to the Wave Cycle of Development, a hypothesis worked out by Robin Higham that aircraft manufacturing follows a cyclical pattern of peacetime equilibrium, rearmament instability, wartime equilibrium, and demobilizational instability.[1] In the years before 1938 the United States was in that phase of the cycle called peacetime equilibrium, although during the thirties the airframe manufacturers had gone through a "monoplane revolution" which had called for radical changes in design and manufacture from the earlier biplanes. By 1938, however, the government was concerned with economy, and American airpower was at a low point. The Air Corps had only 1,401 planes, of which fewer than 900 were combat types, and many were obsolete. The Navy had over 800 planes that were called first-line, but their true worth is indicated by the fact that several hundred of them were biplanes. The market for transports was small, and in 1938 only 42 civilian aircraft were built that had a capacity for five or more passengers.

1

The export market was relatively good: in 1937 one-third of the U.S. aircraft production was exported at better prices than were obtained domestically, and exports were estimated to have produced half the industry's profits.

American rearmament began in early 1938 when President Roosevelt asked Congress for $800 million for the Navy. Most of it was to build ships, but the air arm's share was to be an increase in strength from 1,900 to 3,000 planes. The Army was to get a token $17 million, with none for aircraft. There was resistance to the request from some air-minded congressmen who believed that bombers would be a better investment than battleships. The president's reply, a clue to his attitude toward aviation at the time, was that torpedo boats, submarines, and aircraft had each led amateur strategists to declare battleships obsolete, but he, a professional strategist because he was a former assistant secretary of the Navy, knew that each weapon has its "antidote": for the airplane it was the antiaircraft gun. Congress passed a bill to expand the Navy, but the air arm's share, in line with its peripheral status, was only 950 aircraft. This was the last victory for the old order which had held the airplane in low esteem. There soon came a series of shocks that changed airpower's form and importance and created the modern aerospace industry.

THE SHOCKS OF WAR

The Munich Crisis over Sudeten Czechoslovakia in the late summer of 1938 drastically changed the president's views and started a period of rearmamental instability for aircraft manufacturing. Hitler was believed to have successfully threatened Great Britain with his bomber fleet; and, shortly after Pearl Harbor, Harry Hopkins wrote of the effect on Roosevelt: "The President was sure then that we were going to get into war and he believed that air power would win it."[2] Although expressing a desire for an Air Corps strength of 30,000 planes, Roosevelt called in January 1939 for only 3,000 more planes for the Air Corps; he made this modest request in accordance with what he regarded as political possibilities.

The president's new attitude broke the Army's resistance to the Air Corps' demands for bombers. Before the presidential move the Army had forbidden production or development of four-engine bombers for the immediate future; now there were procurement orders for B-17's beyond the thirteen that existed during Munich, and development of the B-24 was started. From this time forward throughout the war the four-engine big bomber had an established position in America's airpower. The size, complexity, and cost of this class would greatly alter an industry in which twin-engine aircraft had heretofore been the largest normal product.

Problems began immediately. Years of peace had led to impractical mobilization plans. The Army had expected, if war broke out, to grow to 4,000,000 men, including 200,000 in its Air Corps. There were to be 12,000 planes, around 4,400 of which were to be small observation craft. As it turned out, the Army grew to about 7,600,000 men, including Army Air Forces (AAF) of 2,372,292 by 1944. The maximum number of aircraft was 79,908, over 13,000 of which were four-engine bombers. The prewar plans were known to be inadequate as soon as they were seriously examined, because they called for an impractical freeze on designs so as to produce 12,000 combat and 2,000 training aircraft within six months. The projections had been drawn up without basic information about the capacity of the aircraft industry, and had been evaluated by war games without any test of their assumptions, a common failing of military exercises. In July 1939 the Air Corps called a conference of aircraft manufacturers to prepare for war production. The manufacturers recommended that the required basic information, missing in the old plans, be prepared before further steps were taken.

Fortunately, a plunge into production was made, but it was for exports rather than for the U.S. Air Corps. Rushing to rearm, the British and French turned to the American aircraft industry for fighters, bombers, and trainers. To spur American efforts, they not only paid high prices but were willing to finance plant expansions in 1939 and 1940. The British alone ordered supplies worth $2 billion and furnished $171 million for factories. The U.S. aircraft industry's total sales for 1939 were about $225 million, and the foreign business was thus very important in stimulating expansion in the industry, for the country as a whole still showed apathy until June 1940.

In the spring of 1940 Hitler launched his attack towards the west, spearheaded by tactical airpower and exploited by armor. The Luftwaffe made effective use of all elements of tactical airpower: air-superiority fighters, attack planes, and airborne forces. The impact on leaders is shown by French Premier Reynaud's desperate appeal for "clouds of warplanes" and Roosevelt's famous call to Congress for "the ability to turn out at least 50,000 planes a year."

As with Munich, this shock altered the composition of American airpower. In the thirties the Air Corps had believed the air-superiority fighter was obsolete. To correct this error, design was now started on the Republic P-47. The nucleus of American airborne forces, which would increase the importance and use of transports, was formed in June 1940.

3

Observation planes, which had been small, simple, low-powered airplanes, and which had formed a large part of Air Corps strength, were proven obsolete in the Battle of France. Their functions were now divided, to be carried out by high-performance "reconnaissance" planes and by light planes. As night bombardment increased in Europe during this period, the Americans began work on the Northrop P-61, their first night fighter designed as such. These were important shifts to higher-performance, larger aircraft using more complex equipment. The changes prevented the freezing of designs for production.

At the same time, bombers received renewed emphasis in numbers and types beyond the experimental XB-15 and XB-19. The Army airmen submitted specifications for the B-29 bomber generation in January 1940. As the possibility that Hitler would conquer Britain aroused interest in an intercontinental bomber, studies began which would lead to development of the giant six-engine XB-36. Again the trend was toward larger and more complex units, complicating the production problem.

As a start was made towards greater production, government management of aircraft manufacture began. Congress backed Roosevelt's "go-ahead" signal with emergency legislation which permitted placement of contracts without the time-consuming safeguards and red tape of peacetime. Congress also provided government funds for plant expansion and other capital investment needs for production, for the aircraft industry was concerned about overexpansion after its experience in World War I. In its desire to assure aircraft production, the government began enlistment of the automobile industry for additional capacity. Although the government cleared the way, the aircraft industry now faced its biggest challenge: to convert to line production from the only manufacturing system it had known, the job shop. This revolution was to influence every phase of the business, calling for new organization, additional plant space, and more production equipment.

Effective, directed mobilization of the aircraft industry thus began in June 1940. Although the president's initiative has been aptly called a get-rich-quick scheme, it provided a start, a goal, and the motivation needed at the time. Even so, it was still only an interim stage and was not the all-out effort that was to come later.

The Japanese attack on Pearl Harbor ended the period of partial mobilization. In January 1942, in response to the prospect of war on two fronts, the president again vastly increased aircraft production goals, asking that 125,000 planes be built in 1943.

After the destruction of American battleships at Pearl Harbor and British battleships off Malaya, the airplane became the striking arm of the Navy. This change from peripheral to central status revised the demands for aircraft, and the impact was not only in numbers. Although the Navy had traditionally used air-superiority fighters, and had striven to have the best, the Brewster F2A and Grumman F4F were out-classed by the Japanese Zero. New designs were called for, and modification of the old. Also, the vastness of the Pacific put renewed emphasis on long-range aircraft.

With American entry into the war, the German Navy started an offensive in the western North Atlantic. The U.S. Navy asked for help from the Army Air Forces and also from the Royal Air Force (RAF), who had wide experience fighting German submarines before America entered the war. The Navy adopted four-engine, land-based aircraft because of their range and their successful use by the RAF's antisubmarine Coastal Command, and this led to further pressures for quantity production of the big bombers. Effectiveness of the German drive also encouraged experiments on aircraft giantism as possible means of by-passing the high-risk surface transportation—and with an eye toward future peacetime airliners with low seat-mile-cost.

By this time enough progress had been made on mobilization for this shock to result primarily in problems of scale. But this period was one when shortages of raw material, purchased parts, and equipment were at their worst.

WARTIME EQUILIBRIUM

In 1943 comparative stability arrived. Plant expansion had taken place, material shortages were eased, and management had adjusted to quantity orders, subcontracting, licensing, line production, and large organizations. Designs could now be reasonably standardized, and 87 percent of the production from 1940 to 1944 was of only nineteen models. Plant layouts were changed to eliminate backtracking of components, and assembly lines were instituted: production was scheduled and controlled to produce the continuous, smooth processes necessary for quantity production; tool engineering was centralized, and manufacturing information was organized and coordinated even between companies. The automobile industry became a partner and contributed greatly to the use of line-production techniques. An example of their contribution is in B-24 fuselage fabrication: where Convair had assembled a shell and then installed equipment, Ford formed two half-shells, installed the equipment, and then united them. Since production becomes increasingly difficult as a product becomes more dense, a trend which has been characteristic

5

of aircraft design, this simple improvement was an important one. The usefulness of the automobile industry was greater in this period of wartime equilibrium than it was at earlier or later stages, for the car manufacturers' system emphasized elaborate and time-consuming tooling, which must have long production runs of fixed designs to be economical.

Rough spots remained. Spare parts were not ordered in a way to minimize the disruption of production. Labor turnover, shortages, and absenteeism were a problem. The aircraft industry recruited women, the aged, the disabled, high school boys, farmers, and workers from service businesses such as automobile salesmen for the labor force, but this did not relieve a shortage of skilled workers. For too long Convair was unable to make the transition to quantity production, and had a midwar reorganization of its management. The conflict between quantity production and design change was not fully resolved in any company. A compromise solution attempted to make the best of the situation: factory design changes were introduced less often than required for combat, safety, or efficiency, and finished aircraft were then reworked in a "modification center." In another kind of change, bigger bombers and transports continued to claim increasing emphasis through 1945.

The final production achievement was impressive by any measure, as shown by Table I-1. The trend in emphasis to large bombers and transports is clearly evident and presaged the coming of age of aviation.

GLOBAL TRANSPORTATION AND AERODYNAMICS

Increased production of transports reflects the growth in American use of air transportation in the war. During the world-wide conflict, there was a need to move men and cargo quickly and far, and the technology and productive capacity were available to meet the demands. The extreme example was the airbridge to China, where planes proved to be indispensable in supporting Chiang Kai-shek after all surface communication was cut off by the Japanese. This aspect of aviation was unplanned and unexpected, despite the expansion of the prewar airlines, which had approached global systems. Before the war the Air Corps had used air transport on only a small scale for the expeditious movement of supplies. The prewar transoceanic efforts, typified by the use of a few flying boats, were soon to be dwarfed by America's military airline fleets. At the end of the war the AAF's Air Transport Command (ATC) was operating 3,700 transports over transoceanic and transcontinental routes. Its airways spanned the North and South Atlantic, crossed Africa and India to China, went to Alaska, and reached across the Central and South Pacific

TABLE I-1
SELECTED PRODUCTION ACHIEVEMENTS IN WORLD WAR II

Production	1940	1943	1944
Pounds of airframe	20,336,000	597,358,800	915,047,900
Number of aircraft	5,982	85,363	95,274
Four-engine bombers	61	9,615	16,334
Large transports (25,000 lbs. and up, including C-46's and C-47's)	179	3,443	6,792

to Australia, the Philippines, and the Ryukyus. In July 1945 close to 275,000 passengers were carried, and 100,000 tons of mail and freight. The Naval Air Transport Service (NATS), which had 431 aircraft at the end of the war, flew routes running to the western Pacific, Alaska, South America, and West Africa. Commercial airlines augmented these activities, flying routes abroad under contract to the armed services, and Convair operated an air transport service (Consairways) to the South Pacific. The entire transport effort consisted of airliners, airliner designs converted to military use, bombers converted into air transports, and flying boats.

The dominant use of large, land-based aircraft, bombers and transports, required a revolution in airfields. The traditional sod fields were inadequate. Heavy take-off weight, tricycle landing gear, high speeds, high wing-loadings, and the resultant long take-off rolls demanded lengthy, level, high-load-bearing surfaces. A frenzy of runway construction by the AAF and Navy ensued to support the operations of thousands of four-engine bombers and transports around the world.

The major accomplishments in construction and manufacture obscured the lack of accomplishments in aerodynamics in America. In an earlier war, in 1917, the United States had found itself well behind other nations in aviation, and an agency had been created for the specific purpose of "regaining and then maintaining the lead in aeronautics which had been given to America by Orville and Wilbur Wright." The National Advisory Committee for Aeronautics (NACA, now the National Aeronautics and Space Administration, or NASA) was directed to "supervise and direct the scientific study of the problems of flight, with a view to their practical solution, and to determine the problems which should be experimentally attacked, and to discuss their solution and their application to practical questions."[3] Yet by World War II NACA's work consisted mainly of cleaning up drag and improving the structures of current designs. The nature of this work is refinement and the quick fix; it is not on the cutting edge of technology. The concentration on short-term,

7

"win-the-war" projects by NACA may have resulted in many accomplishments, but it did not substantially advance the field of aerodynamics. Ever since World War I American aerodynamic and structural design had been advanced primarily by German concepts supplemented by British, Italian, Japanese, and Russian research. With the advent of World War II German support had been removed, and by 1945 the United States was again well behind. Germany's lead in jet-engine development, shared by Britain, was the most serious problem left to American aeronautical designers at the end of the war, and they generally followed patterns already set by the Germans.

Although far behind, the United States did work hard to get a jet into the air during the war. Lockheed was engaged to build a jet fighter, using the British De Havilland Goblin engine. Speed was called for, and Lockheed gave Clarence L. "Kelly" Johnson full authority for the project. He set up his special unit, the famous "Skunk Works," with 23 engineers and 105 shop men, and he did 96 percent of his own fabrication and all inspection. Lockheed's normal development procedure of engineering conferences was by-passed; only 700 drawings were made; sometimes parts were made from a drawing, and sometimes the reverse was done: simplicity was Johnson's keynote. The XP-80 cost only 63 percent of the XP-38 prototype, which had been made by the customary system of development. It was accepted by the AAF only 143 days after the start of development, even though the engine had not been on hand until the 132nd day. After General Electric had designed an improved Whittle-type engine, the I-40 or J33, the XP-80A was designed around it: the United States had a jet fighter and one of the best aeronautical designs in its history by the end of 1945.

TERMINATING WAR PRODUCTION

Development of the XP-80A came in the final months of war, and at a period when economic instability was to be anticipated and avoided if possible. In World War I there had been no preparation for demobilization. Contracts were ended abruptly, resulting in chaos and bankruptcies. This time, as early as November 1943, government procurement agencies wisely began to prepare for the distant reductions. Recommendations were made to Congress, and the Contract Settlement Act was passed in July 1944. Terminations were to be negotiated procedures, orderly and as rapid as possible. They would be final save for fraud, so that contractors would be free to move directly into reconversion plans and not be forced to tie up their capital in reserves held against unexpected or

8

capricious governmental contract review. The program was carried out with apparent great success despite a reduction of $20 billion in contracts. Factories were disposed of as surplus, and litigation was avoided. The termination system may have contributed to the absence of a general postwar depression.

STATUS AT THE END OF THE WAR

The use of airpower on a grand scale in World War II ultimately produced an American demand for aircraft in the thousands each month. The general growth in aircraft size and complexity is illustrated by the weight changes between 1940 and 1945, shown in Table I-2.

In successfully responding to the challenge, the aerospace industry attained its modern shape. Its management now had experience with handcrafting as well as with serial production; with small as well as vast operations. Much of the management was young enough to remain in control for many more years, providing continuity, and there was a large pool of experienced engineering talent and workers.

There probably also was a general letdown, to be expected after the wartime exertions. At Lockheed, for example, after the hard-driving development of the XP-80, the project engineers had a sickness rate of 30 percent. Decreasing production requires adjustments in attitudes, just as increasing production does, and there was no experience in this kind of adjustment, necessarily critical in a competitive industry. In the aircraft industry particularly, because it had been "capital intensive" in human engineering resources, the natural reluctance to cut overhead tended to be intensified and delayed too long. The return to handcraft manufacturing quantities meant fewer production engineers, a cutback easily overlooked and omitted. During the war, costs had been of small importance compared to rapid production; in peace, the values had to be reversed.

TABLE I-2
GROWTH IN AIRCRAFT SIZE, 1940–1945

Aircraft	1940	1945
Army Fighter	5,376 lbs. (P-40)	7,920 lbs. (F-80A)
Army Fighter Bomber	5,376 lbs. (P-40)	9,900 lbs. (P-47D)
Army Heavy Bomber	24,458 lbs. (YB-17)	69,000 lbs. (B-29B)
Navy Fighter	4,036 lbs. (F4F)	9,205 lbs. (F4U)
Navy Bomber	5,903 lbs. (SBD-1)	10,589 lbs. (SB2C)
Transport	18,200 lbs. (C-47)	37,000 lbs. (C-54)

The industry's plant and equipment were adequate and not a burden, thanks to governmental willingness to furnish most of the war expansion facilities and then to sell them off cheaply. Prudent policies had created by the end of 1945 a financial reserve of $117 million available for reconversion and readjustment. There was a collective bank debt of only $13 million, and working capital of the fifteen main aircraft companies was over $620 million.

Government procurement practices had proven acceptable. Letters of intent were used to save time before formal contracts. The problem of costs and profit settlement where expenses were difficult to forecast—and nearly all aircraft production is of this sort because it involves new or evolving designs—had been met by the cost plus fixed fee (CPFF) contract arrangement according to which the government pays all reasonable costs and a fixed profit based upon the forecast cost. With this system aircraft costs and profits appeared to be acceptable because there were no violent objections to their level.

At the end of the war it appeared that, with the countries long regarded by Americans as the world's troublemakers in ruins, a long period of peace was assured. This prospect, plus the specter of the usual postwar depression, might have been frightening for the aircraft industry. Yet airpower had become so important it could reasonably be expected to receive a larger share of peacetime appropriations than it had before the war. Further, the jet revolution, obviously in its early stages, might mean extensive reequipping. The airlines had boomed in the war, and excellent transport designs were available for the postwar civilian systems. World-wide transport operations had become commonplace, and sales to airlines could make the difference between solvency and bankruptcy. The general public was much more airplane-conscious than before the war, and the millions of young men who had served in military aviation were a friendly constituency and potential customers. The large airplane, with its high unit-cost, might prove to be the industry's salvation even if unit sales were low. Worry over foreign competition was not in evidence.

The aircraft industry entered the postwar era with both concern and hope.

II

THE AEROSPACE INDUSTRY SINCE WORLD WAR II:
A BRIEF HISTORY

DEMOBILIZATIONAL INSTABILITY

After the war's end the American aerospace industry was quickly disabused of its hopes, finding itself in a classical situation of demobilizational instability. Government business was greatly reduced as the armed services returned to skeletal forces after the war. There was a catastrophic collapse of the AAF: from a high of 243 groups, or wings, in 1945 it shrank to such a degree that a few months after final victory there was not one completely ready squadron.

One small break in the demobilizational pattern was in the AAF's interest in jets. Shaken by the experience of meeting German jet fighters and bombers in battle, the AAF put eight jet fighters and seven jet bombers into development. This was a fair level of research and development work, but the facilities of the aircraft companies at the time were nearly all in production plant and equipment. Production orders were needed to stay out of the red, and only a trickle of Lockheed F-80's and, a little later, Republic F-84's made up the AAF's first postwar jet programs.

For the production-hungry aircraft industry there was also some hope of relief as a result of other AAF interests. The dream of a global bomber was still pursued, so prototype development of the Convair XB-36 and its flying-wing competitors, Northrop's XB-35 and YB-49, continued. The cutback in very heavy bombardment wings was smallest and, despite the thousands of B-29's built in the war, production continued on an improved B-29, which was redesignated B-50. The first

11

plane designed for military cargo needs, the Fairchild C-82, was put into production.

The Navy's immediate postwar effect on the aerospace industry was similar, but there was much less naval interest in jets. The Navy had not had the jolt of dealing with a jet-equipped enemy. Major technical problems in jet carrier operations loomed because of the low take-off acceleration and higher landing speeds of the new technology, and jets were not operational off American carriers until 1948. Secretary of the Navy James Forrestal believed jets were both unproven and overly expensive. The outcome was token production of the McDonnell FH and North American FJ jet fighters, and of the hybrid piston and jet Ryan FR.

The Navy ordered production of three piston fighters and of some other aircraft developed late in the war: the Douglas A-1, which was needed because earlier Navy bombers lacked punch, and the Lockheed P2V for antisubmarine warfare (ASW).

The industry had expected military business to be low, and hoped for orders for civil airliners. At first the airlines expected to buy many planes, but as traffic failed to continue to rise after an initial surge the purchase plans were cut back. Eight aerospace companies attempted to sell twenty-seven designs, ranging from those which never left the paper stage to serial production types, from feeder airliners to giants. Then there was the government, which was not only a poor customer for new aircraft, but was selling its surplus war transports at bargain-basement prices. Like the airline business, general aviation sales surged and then sickened. Money was lost on ventures like North American's Navion, which went $8 million into the red. The result during the demobilizational instability period was that nearly all airliner manufacturers lost money, although some probably contributed to their fixed costs including the vital retention of engineers.

Sales in the demobilization period were actually double those of 1939, but losses were heavy, apparently because of larger overhead. In 1946 twelve aerospace companies lost an aggregate $35 million, and in 1947, $115 million. This was before taxes, and carry-back provisions reduced these losses to $11 and $42 million.

The response of the companies at first took three forms. One company, Curtiss-Wright, husbanded its liquidity and took only minor risks because its president, Guy Vaughan, expected the usual postwar depression. Then there was a rash of merger discussions. Curtiss-Wright approached Lockheed, but negotiations broke down over the former's complicated capital structure. A proposed Convair-Lockheed merger was abandoned because of antitrust fears, an unsettled securities situation, and doubt by Convair over Lockheed's future when the Constellation airliners were grounded. A third response was diversification: aluminum canoes, kitchen appliances, buses, radio cabinets, toys, motor scooters, and other goods were made. With minor exceptions these attempts failed, although they may have contributed towards meeting fixed costs.

By the latter part of 1947 the industry had run out of money, ideas, courage, and hope. It sank to forty-fourth in rank among American industries in 1948. The war-built reserves were consumed, and there would be no more tax carry-backs. Diversification in civil and non-aviation markets had failed.

The industry turned to the government for relief.

SIGNIFICANT EVENTS DURING THE TRUMAN ERA

Appeals for help were made to the president's Air Policy Commission of 1947, the Finletter Commission, which was formed in response to the distress of the aircraft industry and dissension over the role of airpower in our national strategy. The commission listened favorably to the industry's plea and to the U.S. Air Force's (USAF) case for an airpower strategy. The Air Force presented to the commission a logical, comprehensive, specific system which seemed appropriate to the nascent Cold War, while the Navy's testimony was vague and chaotic. Eventually the commission accepted the Air Force's positions on strategy and strength, and also recommended planned procurement at a level calculated to sustain the aircraft industry and provide a base for mobilization. The findings of a congressional group called the Aviation Policy Board paralleled those of the Finletter Commission, and an air-nuclear-deterrent strategy was adopted.

Although the build-up was now under way towards the USAF's goal of seventy combat wings designed for an era of American nuclear monopoly, the goal was not attained before the Korean War. Meanwhile, an armada of big bombers and aircraft of a wholly new class—the aerial tankers—was being maintained, and the program therefore represented an increase to a higher level of military orders for a sustained period.

The Finletter Commission result was the first of five events that came in rapid succession, as had the shocks that transformed the aircraft industry during the Second World War. These events initially interrupted the Wave Development Cycle pattern, into which the American aerospace industry from 1948 to 1969 does not fit.

Russian postwar imperialism in Europe was increasingly recognized with alarm, and the cold war came into the open in 1948 when the Russians moved against Berlin and the Americans chose an airlift as the counter move. Thanks to the experience of the airlift to China in the war, and to the availability of the same leader, General William H. Tunner, the effort was improvised successfully. Lessons were learned that were to be valuable in later periods of dense airline traffic, and recognition of the importance of military air transport led to an expanding market for the aerospace industry.

Not only the United States but Western Europe was alarmed by Russia's actions, and the North Atlantic Treaty Organization (NATO) was formed in 1949 to halt the use of force to spread communism. The American contribution of forces to Europe and the equipping of allies lacking the capability to build modern aircraft enlarged our exports.

The third event that occurred to interrupt the wave cycle was the development of air coach, or tourist, transportation. Started by non-scheduled airlines which were hungry for business, it was adopted by Capital Airlines in 1948. Competition forced its spread to other domestic airlines and, in 1952, across the oceans. Commercial air transportation became truly mass transportation, and a demand was created for thousands of large airplanes.

In 1949 the Russians exploded a nuclear device, breaking the American monopoly, and the United States now had to provide for air defense against possible air-nuclear attack. A large interceptor force had to be built to defend the expanses of the air approaches to North America, as a result of this crucial postwar event.

Finally, in only another year the Korean War broke out, and the USAF was forced to revitalize and expand its tactical air power, which had been deliberately neglected in the peace years while priority had been given to bombers. Naval carrier aviation, too, got a new lease on life by demonstrating its usefulness in limited conventional war. The Navy encountered enemy jets in combat for the first time, and almost complete reequipment became necessary.

By the time the Korean War had ended in 1953, the aerospace industry had undergone a massive expansion and was restored to its World War II status as the largest American industry. The five events had caused an expansion in numbers of all categories of aircraft and added a massive new market, the tankers. In 1954 sales of ten aircraft companies totaled about $4.5 billion, nine times the 1947 level. Profits were around $170 million in 1954 in contrast with the heavy losses of 1947.

The recovery was not smooth, and there was one casualty and three near casualties. Curtiss-Wright failed to win contracts as a prime contractor and withdrew from aircraft design. A combination of little government business and early losses with its airliner brought Convair to a crisis, but it was saved by successful development of the B-36, which went into production in 1947; in 1954 Convair was merged into General Dynamics, becoming part of John Jay Hopkins' effort to build a General Motors of the defense industry. Martin's ill-fated attempts to build an airliner brought it to the brink of failure in 1947, from which it was rescued by a loan from the government's Reconstruction Finance Corporation (RFC); a second government rescue took place when Martin ran low on funds in a renewed airliner effort combined with expansion during the Korean War. The second transfusion was made mostly with wartime V-loans. Like Convair, Northrop was shaky when a design, the F-89 interceptor, was accepted for production in 1949; but this was a temporary reprieve, for the F-89 was soon made obsolescent by the F-102.

Unlike previous American wars, the Korean War was not followed by massive demobilization. Indefinite maintenance of large armed forces and the existence of a substantial air-transport industry appeared to have ended the boom-and-bust days of aircraft manufacture. The Truman level of defense spending, around $15 billion, was increased to the Eisenhower level of around $40 billion. Similar continuity was true of the aerospace industry as a whole, and production was fairly stable between the Korean War and the Vietnam War. But there was to be no routine peacetime equilibrium in the fifties, even though the hand-to-mouth existence had ended. The political, economic, and military events that had interrupted the wave cycle were followed by technological revolutions that were to keep the aerospace industry in ferment.

THE JETS TAKE OVER

The Korean War marked the watershed between piston and jet production. In 1950 more than half of production was piston; in 1953 this was reversed. By the end of the war, the aerospace industry had built 10,000 jets for the Air Force, 3,500 for the Navy, and 2,000 for export. Lockheed alone had built 5,000.

The reequipment of the Navy with jets as a result of the Korean War was the most conspicuous conquest by jet propulsion in the early fifties. As early as the spring of 1951, there were no Air Force or Navy development contracts for a piston aircraft. The Air Force, having already accepted the jet for fighters and short- and medium-range bombers, did not appear to reequip so broadly. Yet marked progress in jet engine efficiency and the introduction of thrust augmentation, or afterburning, meant

15

major changes that virtually eliminated an expected competitor in engines, the propjet. The main aerodynamic problems of high-speed flight had been resolved. The intercontinental jet bomber and supersonic fighters became feasible, and the Air Force started development of propjet transports, the last stand of this engine. With jet trainers developed from the F-80, it was moving rapidly towards an all-jet force.

British development of the first jet airliner, the De Havilland Comet, which began service in 1952, forced the hand of American aerospace manufacturers. The success of the Comet weakened the reluctance of the conservative American airlines to use jets and caused manufacturers to fear a loss of exports. Consequently, the aerospace industry began a race for the jet airliner market, and by the early sixties the jets, primarily the Boeing 707 and Douglas DC-8 families but also the turboprop Lockheed Electra, dominated the American airliner scene.

The jet's great advance over the piston in its power-to-weight ratio enabled aircraft to grow in size and weight, and this capability was accompanied by the parallel technological explosion in avionics for navigation, weapons control, and electronic warfare measures. Aircraft empty weights increased drastically, as can be seen in Table II-1.

Empty weights are given in the table because they best show the effects on design and manufacturing, but it should be noted that the impact of the jet's efficiency is sometimes even more dramatically evident from gross weights. For example, the gross weights for the B-50 and B-52 were 175,000 and 480,000 pounds, respectively.

The increased size and weight plus the need for strength in high-speed flight changed the production systems of the manufacturers. Instead of being primarily sheet metal processors, they became great machine shops and thus were even more capital-intensive than before. After the Korean War, especially in 1957, the government tried to reduce as much as possible its financing of the aerospace industry's plant, equipment, and inventories, and this forced the industry to further increase its own investment and, therefore, its financial risks.

Appalled during the Korean War by fast-rising costs, some manufacturers made efforts to reverse the trend by emphasizing light, simple aircraft. Only three such attempts succeeded. The Douglas A-4 attack plane, weighing 9,559 pounds, has been one of the most important and highly regarded naval aircraft since the war; it was in continuous production from 1954 into the seventies. The other two, the F-104 and the F-5, weighing 15,000 and 7,596 pounds, did not please the USAF, which has traditionally favored heavily equipped aircraft; but they found wide markets abroad and some limited adoption by the U.S. forces.

TABLE II-1
GROWTH IN AIRCRAFT SIZE, 1946–1960

Aircraft	1946	1954	1960
Air Force			
Fighter	9,538 lbs. (F-84)	21,000 lbs. (F-100)	15,000 lbs. (F-104)
Fighter Bomber	11,000 lbs. (P-47)	13,645 lbs. (F-84F)	27,500 lbs. (F-105)
Interceptor	22,000 lbs. (P-61)	25,194 lbs. (F-89)	26,000 lbs. (F-106)
Heavy Bomber	81,050 lbs. (B-50)	171,035 lbs. (B-36)	169,822 lbs. (B-52)
Medium Bomber	71,360 lbs. (B-29)	80,756 lbs. (B-47)	55,560 lbs. (B-58)
Transport	32,500 lbs. (C-82)	67,700 lbs. (C-130)	67,700 lbs. (C-130)
Navy			
Fighter	7,323 lbs. (F8F)	18,691 lbs. (F3H)	28,200 lbs. (F-4)
Light Bomber	9,583 lbs. (F4U)	10,470 lbs. (A-1)	9,559 lbs. (A-4)
Airliner	57,160 lbs. (Constellation)	78,750 lbs. (DC-7C)	137,000 lbs. (707)

The Eisenhower administration started with the intent to avoid what it believed was a Truman administration error: to stint on defense. Soon dismayed, however, by total budget costs and by accelerating cost increases per aircraft, the Eisenhower government shrank from its original intentions and sought to contain the defense budget within a fixed amount. By the sixties, the rises in real cost, inflation, and the emergence of a plethora of new defense systems meant disruptive cancellations and less prosperity than the aerospace industry had expected.

MISSILES AND SPACE

As the fifties began, small tactical missiles were ending development, and by 1955 six types were in service. In 1953 the Russians exploded a "dry" hydrogen bomb, a revolutionary development in explosives that meant that large, long-range missiles were practical. And those that were suborbital space vehicles made space flight possible.

Awareness of Russian missile possibilities led the government to give priorities to the development of intercontinental and intermediate range ballistic missiles (ICBM's and IRBM's). To ensure success, parallel development of the General Dynamics Atlas and the Martin Titan ICBM's were ordered. Similarly, the Douglas Thor and the Army-Chrysler Jupiter IRBM's competed. Later a breakthrough in solid propellant technology led to noncompetitive parallel development of the land-based Boeing Minuteman ICBM and the Lockheed Polaris IRBM, or Fleet Ballistic Missile (FBM). Because missiles were a natural outgrowth of aircraft technology, many believed that there would be a transitory stage of jet-powered guided missiles, sometimes called unmanned aircraft. But before these missiles of the fifties became operational in even limited quantities, they were found to be highly vulnerable to advances in air defense, and development and production ended.

Advances in technology made missiles practical across the whole spectrum: air-to-ground (or surface), ground-to-air, air-to-air, and ground-to-ground. The successes achieved, and the fact that missiles are cheaper to produce, led to the belief that manned combat aircraft would soon be made obsolete, or at least less important in sales volume, either because of missile effectiveness or perhaps because of cost. In this break with the past, firms such as Hughes and Chrysler, which had not participated earlier in aerospace prime contracts, began to bid for and get programs.

Some of the traditional aerospace companies began to have difficulty getting contracts for military aircraft. Boeing feared the end of its tradi-

18

tional, heavy-bomber business. Boeing and Douglas began producing relatively more and more commercial, not military, aircraft. Fairchild never found a successor to its C-119, the "dollar nineteen," which ceased production in the midfifties. Grumman lost ground in competing with McDonnell in fighters and sought to carve a new niche in specialty aircraft such as rescue, utility, antisubmarine warfare planes, and so forth. Martin gradually lost out on the production of types other than flying boats. When the dead-end was reached in flying boats, Martin "withdrew" from aircraft manufacture, although it has tried to reenter since, without success. North American's last important production aircraft was the F-100, and most of its airplane business since has been developmental or of minor types.

In the late fifties there was widespread concern over these developments. If a company was down to one or two products, sudden cancellation, a common occurrence, could cause bankruptcy. A new wave of diversification swept the industry, for the most part pushing the trend towards missiles and space. Another direction was to invade the avionics market, just as the avionics companies had entered the missile business. Because the aerospace companies already had a minimal avionics capability as prime contractors, it was simply a matter of expansion rather than entry into a new market. Lockheed emulated General Dynamics and tried to become more of a general defense contractor, while General Dynamics and Martin entered the construction business through merger, because construction was expected to be countercyclical to defense.

A large new market, comparable to missiles in sales, was space vehicles. Russia's skillful exploitation of space with its first Sputnik satellites shattered America's confidence and world prestige and led to a national convulsion as the United States launched a massive effort to catch up with the Soviets. American frustration at the Russian lead is illustrated by a note which appeared on a Pentagon bulletin board: "Although Soviet Russia leads the U.S. in rocket propulsion, the U.S. maintains its lead in such vital areas as miniaturization. Otherwise it would not have succeeded in building a space program so much smaller than the one Russia has."[1] At first it appeared that there would soon be major military activities in space, but these prospects faded and the main activity became the race for the moon. This new market was large for the aerospace manufacturers who successfully bid to build boosters and spaceships, but it was also a crash program which emphasized speed in development and manufacturing and disregarded cost. And at its peak it did not equal military aircraft sales.

THE JETS ARE CONFIRMED: THE VIETNAM WAR

Just as Eisenhower had criticized the level of defense spending under Truman, so did Kennedy react to his predecessor. The new administration doubled the defense budget, expanding conventional arms. At the same time, a major effort was made to reduce governmental costs, and management and procurement formulas were sought which would drastically reduce government costs while improving company profits.

Costs had continued to skyrocket with the technological developments of the fifties. The piston DC-7 of 1955, which had cost $1.9 million, was replaced by the jet DC-8, whose price was around $5 million by 1960. The DC-8 was more productive than the DC-7, however, and was actually cheaper when all costs and income were figured. Its speed, capacity, and useful life meant the capital cost per unit of output was 43 percent less than the DC-7C, and 20 percent less than the DC-6B. Similar advancement in the efficiency of new designs enabled Defense Secretary Robert S. McNamara to reduce the number bought. He also sought to reduce the degree of aircraft specialization into different types, and he deliberately increased the contractors' business risks so as to encourage vigorous cost-reduction efforts on their part.

After the first big missiles were in place, production of the Minuteman and Polaris/Poseidon continued as improved models replaced earlier versions. The experience in Vietnam, and the accumulation of several years of missile service, led to some disenchantment with missile capability. Earlier expectations were not fulfilled, although it was evident that missiles had a major role, and models that had become obsolete for military uses were kept in service in the space program.

The overall outcome was a rough plateau of sales for the industry at around $16 billion from 1962 until the Vietnam War in 1965, but financial crises occurred throughout the period. General Dynamics lost a crushing $425 million, mostly in 1960 and 1961, in its efforts with the 880/990 airliners to hold or expand its commercial business. Lockheed and Fairchild took severe losses in 1960 in similar attempts. The three companies were driven out of competition by Boeing and Douglas, the main commercial transport survivors in the early sixties. Both of the latter, however, were faced with a steady decline in their government business, a serious development for an aerospace firm. Essentially these five companies, against their will, were becoming increasingly concentrated in their markets despite their desire for diversification.

McNamara's drive to reduce specialization meant that the Navy's McDonnell F-4 became a biservice fighter, putting an unexpected early

20

end to Republic's F-105 production. Republic limped along on its sub-contracting and other business for a while and was then absorbed by Fairchild in 1965. Fairchild itself had to struggle to survive with a short-range airliner, the FH-227, subcontracting, and other minor business. McDonnell sought diversification into the commercial field by merging with Douglas in 1963, but Douglas rejected the proposal. North American sought diversification beyond the broad aircraft-missile-space activities it had developed and merged with Rockwell Standard, primarily in the automotive business, in 1967.

The Vietnam War increased military aircraft purchases, and at the same time there was a renewed wave of airline buying. The war did not actually increase sales proportionally as much as earlier wars had, because of the government's efforts to economize and because of a low loss rate. But prospects for continued use of piston aircraft were apparently ended, as Secretary McNamara came to the conclusion that piston aircraft were not as cost-effective as jets. The leading piston attack plane, the A-1, was estimated to cost $800,000 in 1965, a fourfold to five-fold increase over the late 1940's. The jet revolution for military aircraft was complete.

The number of airliners produced doubled from 1964 to 1966, and doubled again by 1968, and total sales of the aerospace industry rose by over half from 1965 to 1968, the peak year up to that time. Douglas benefited little from Vietnam War orders but had a great surge in the airliner business, and found itself with a massive financial problem because of expansion. Despite its success in getting several large loans,

A highly successful design, the F-4 contributed greatly to the rise of the McDonnell company. *Courtesy McDonnell Douglas Corporation.*

21

its capital needs outran the impaired confidence of its creditors, and Douglas had to seek a merger in 1966; it was absorbed in 1967 by McDonnell, which was still desirous of diversifying.

When the Nixon administration began disengaging from Vietnam in 1969, the race for the moon was over and won, and airline buying was also slackening off. Sales fell again, and Boeing entered a period of doldrums when the supersonic transport was abandoned. General Dynamics had a third period of crisis in 1969 and 1970, as a result of F-111 costs and of trouble in its diversified lines. But the most spectacular crisis was Lockheed's. In the midst of a renewed diversification attempt with a new airliner, the L-1011 TriStar, costs drove the engine supplier, Rolls Royce, into bankruptcy in 1971. Having already undergone a government-ordered loss of $200 million on the C-5A, and cancellation of the Cheyenne helicopter program, Lockheed faced bankruptcy, a situation it had diversified to prevent. Lockheed's crisis was unique because it had simultaneous, multiple-program difficulties, and the government came to the rescue with guarantees on private loans, in the fourth large-scale attempt to save an aerospace company since World War II.

Costs continued to skyrocket, plaguing manufacturer and customer alike. The Lockheed TriStar, weighing 240,000 pounds empty, was selling for $15 million in 1968, in contrast to the DC-8 price, at roughly half the weight, of $5 million in 1959. The small airliners were up in price also.

By 1972 a sort of profitless survival appeared to have set in. Total aerospace industry sales seemed to have leveled off at around $20 billion, including business aviation. The peak had been reached in 1968 with sales of nearly $30 billion. The sales of military aircraft and missiles paralleled the total, leveling at around $8 billion and $5 billion, respectively. Space sales appeared to be in a steady decline from their 1966 peak of $6 billion and were down to around $3 billion. Commercial transport sales, after a peak of $4 billion in 1968, seemed to be holding at well under $3 billion. It seems evident there was overcapacity.

The aerospace industry since World War II, then, is the story of an increasingly capital-intensive business whose manufacturing function has steadily declined, and its product cost has risen so high that it has almost priced itself out of its market. It is an industry which has, perhaps with the sole exception of North American, not been able to diversify adequately to shelter itself against its captive status in relation to its dominant customer, the government. Its crises have shrunken the numbers, but there may still be too many units for all to survive. In the United States the government has discouraged merger, in contrast to British policy; but there has been some temporary associating, as in the

F-111, which was a General Dynamics–Grumman project, and even on an international basis, between Lockheed and Rolls Royce, for example. The industry has thrived on successive waves of favorable political, economic, and technological revolution. If these frequent growth surges have now stopped, the industry faces a precarious future with its high overhead and its expensive, efficient, and durable product.

Perhaps Lockheed, suffering simultaneous disasters in different activities, is a dramatic prototype of the whole of today's aerospace industry. If it does face little growth in its military, space, and commercial markets, the industry appears to have returned to the interrupted wave cycle pattern: it has gone through demobilizational instability as Nixon wound down the Vietnam War, and it is now in peacetime equilibrium.

III

THE NATIONAL MILITARY STRATEGY: BACKGROUND FOR THE GOVERNMENT MARKETS

The controlling element behind the fluctuations within the American aerospace industry has been the national military strategy. There was no such strategy immediately following World War II. Some Air Force generals expected a resurgence of Germany and Japan, but the postwar condition of the losers must have made those ideas seem ludicrous. Navy Secretary James Forrestal and AAF Intelligence accurately assessed the possibilities for a Russian threat, but the top AAF generals believed the Red Air Force was so backward technologically that it would be unable to catch up for at least twenty years. Further, to them, the Red Army and Navy were unimportant in modern war: there was no conceivable enemy with a navy that could seriously threaten the United States. Perhaps most important, the United Nations (UN) was expected to prevent war, and the formation of a UN permanent international police force to enforce peace was anticipated. U.S. military strategy would be simply to contribute to the international body.

Other circumstances delayed formation of a military strategy. The effort to prevent chaos during massive demobilization demanded so much attention that little effort was given to strategy: the world situation of the time appeared stable enough that the government could defer the problem of military planning. The available service energies were consumed in the intense political struggle over the autonomy of air forces, which was called a struggle over unification. The Army Air Forces saw autonomy as necessary for survival, fearing that continued subordination to the Army would result in renewed neglect of airpower. The Navy saw autonomous airpower as a threat to its own survival as a major force because of the popular support for airpower concepts. The Army regarded air autonomy as inevitable. The concern over survival by two parties accounts for the intensity of the controversy. President Truman shared the AAF's fears over the possibility of neglect, and his views were decisive. The AAF became the USAF in 1947; and subsequently, with demobilization and autonomy no longer overriding issues, and with the emergence of a distinguishable postwar international framework, more attention was given to a national military strategy.

THE ONE-WAR STRATEGY

The immediate postwar years witnessed growing concern over Russian noncooperation with American international concepts. Simultaneously, the prospects of an effective UN international police force faded. As awareness grew of the need for a national military strategy, two proposals became major contenders. Both accepted military preparedness as the means to deter armed aggression. President Truman, General George C. Marshall, and Secretary Forrestal advocated strength through the Army, in the continental European tradition: there would be universal military training (UMT), and the associated masses of reserve forces would be ready for national mobilization. The competing proposal was to adopt an airpower strategy according to which a strategic bombing force would be assembled which could destroy the economic fabric of Russia with atomic bombs. The Navy would keep the seas open, and allies would furnish the bulk of land forces. Since America had a monopoly of the bombs and was believed to be technologically superior to Russia, the forces in being could be small, and of course a force capable of dealing with Russia could crush lesser powers. The airpower proposal, resting upon technology rather than upon masses of men in a compulsory system, and costing less, had a far greater appeal to Americans than did universal military training. UMT failed in Congress and, after the Finletter Commission action, the USAF concept was adopted.

The Navy's status in either proposal was to keep the seas open, primarily an antisubmarine mission. The Navy had hoped, instead, to dominate or at least to share in the air strategy, regaining the primacy in defense it had held before the war. And when the Navy's main means to achieve a strategic bombing role, the U.S.S. *United States*, was canceled while under construction, the Navy believed it was faced with a renewed threat to its survival. It took drastic action, a "revolt of the admirals," to upset the dominant position of the Air Force and restore a future for carrier aviation. Its course was to challenge the Air Force's main means to implement its air-nuclear strategy, the B-36. Claims were made that the B-36 could not execute its mission, and that strategic bombing and nuclear weapons were ineffective and their use immoral. Later the Navy reversed its position on strategic nuclear attack and weapons, and in the meantime it did achieve its objective of getting carriers suitable for long-range bombardment.

LAND WAR IN ASIA

The one-war, air-atomic strategy did not survive the opening of the Korean War. The circumstances of that war had been partially foreseen by General Carl Spaatz, chief of staff of the Air Force from 1946 to 1948, who had expected that the most likely form that Red aggression would take in the face of American air-atomic strategy would be a limited attack on the communist periphery. Spaatz further believed that the American response would be implementation of the air-atomic strategy against the source of power: Russia.

Faced with the awful situation come true, the U.S. did not strike with atomic weapons, either at Russia as the supposed principal, or at North Korea or its armies as the proxy. The reasons are manifold. The commander in chief, Truman, shrank from using nuclear bombs in a peripheral war and deferred a decision on the matter; General Hoyt Vandenberg, Air Force chief of staff, believed it would impair his capability to handle Russia if American nuclear bombs were expended in the Far East; and for a while Truman feared that the Korean aggression might be only a first step in a series of attacks which would culminate in general war. Finally, the United States wanted to keep its allies, and there was opposition among the latter to the use of atomic bombs.

THE ONE-AND-ONE-HALF-WAR STRATEGY

The end of the Korean War came soon after Eisenhower took office, and he and John Foster Dulles believed that his threat to use nuclear weapons against Chinese sources of power was the reason that the Communists suddenly accepted terms they had rejected for two years. New developments in nuclear weapons increased their importance in strategy as well. The Russians exploded a nuclear bomb in 1949 and a thermonuclear one in 1953, so the United States now faced a nuclear-armed potential enemy with the ability to build long-range, aerospace delivery systems. Tactical nuclear weapons were being developed, and the Korean War had shown that the Russians were not technologically inferior to the United States in aircraft equipment.

The product of these circumstances was a "one-and-one-half-war" strategy. The United States was to be ready to fight a sudden air-nuclear general war with Russia, and also be ready to fight a short, sharp, limited nuclear war. Because the military forces now had no choice but to provide an air defense, a larger strategic air force to ensure crushing a competent Russian defense, the tactical nuclear forces to prevent a Russian overrun of Western Europe, and a limited-war force, as well as keep up with rapidly advancing technology, the total costs were much higher than in the Truman era. Eisenhower's fiscal conservatism and his belief in the efficacy of swift atomic strikes as a deterrent led to a nuclear strategy for limited war; and the United States, for a relatively small sum, established small, fast, mobile forces equipped with tactical nuclear weapons and little conventional armament. Nuclear weapons, strategic and tactical, gave, in common phrases of the time, "more bang for the buck" and promised "massive retaliation."

The Air Force dominated the general war air-nuclear strategy, with the Navy as a junior partner. Development of the ICBM and IRBM did not change this relationship, as the Navy's Polaris system supplemented the Air Force's Atlas, Titan, Thor, and Jupiter. All services shared the limited mission, however. The Air Force was able to move its tactical airpower and Army strike forces nearly globally by air refueling and airlift. At least two international crises, at Lebanon and Quemoy, occurred during the period of this strategy, and it was believed that they could result in limited war. The three services put into action the proposed swift deployment of small, nuclear-equipped forces, and the United States appeared both able and willing to use nuclear weapons. The crises evaporated, and it appeared that this strategy had kept peace, but an all-nuclear concept was never popular.

THE TWO-AND-ONE-HALF-WAR STRATEGY

President Kennedy, like Eisenhower before him, came to office with the belief that his predecessor had neglected defense, especially the ICBM. His strategy called for expanded forces which could take care of a nuclear general war, or a limited conventional war with a simultaneous second crisis: a "two-and-one-half-war" strategy. Under Eisenhower the conventional forces had been our shield, and the aerospace-nuclear forces our sword. Kennedy reversed the functions.

The aerospace-nuclear general war forces, also called strategic retaliatory forces, were enlarged by 100 percent in deliverable weapons. Secretary of Defense Robert S. McNamara believed that the growing Russian air-defense strength, which was further augmented by an increasing superiority of the fighter over the bomber and the better effectiveness of missiles over flak, greatly reduced the usefulness of bombers. He expected a bomber loss rate of 75 percent per mission. As a result, the Strategic Air Command's (SAC) bomber force was reduced, and the aircraft-carrier strategic bombers converted to reconnaissance aircraft.

The major increase came in Army and Navy forces for conventional war. Kennedy believed that a limited-war capability which depended on nuclear weapons did not give sufficient flexibility, and more versatile limited-war elements, called general-purpose forces, were prepared. As it turned out, as soon as the buildup of conventional forces was completed, they were committed to a new land war in Asia: Vietnam. In contrast to the swift-strike concept of Eisenhower, the forces were committed piecemeal in a strategy called gradual response. Also in contrast, nuclear weapons were spoken of in such a way as to indicate they would never be used, as in the Johnson presidential campaign in 1964. In carrying out this new strategy and war, Kennedy and Johnson spent over half of the $1 trillion expended for the military from 1946 to 1969, and the aerospace industry was a major recipient.

POST-VIETNAM STRATEGY

A new era in national military strategy began with Nixon and the disillusionments of the Vietnam War. Improvements in the aerospace-nuclear strategic forces continued, but in the new era, unlike previous periods, there was an unwillingness to compete with Russia for superiority and a tendency to settle for "sufficiency." The distaste for nuclear weapons became more pronounced, and the fact they have not been used, even in the difficult Vietnam War, casts doubt on the likelihood of their use ever in a limited war. Enthusiasm for conventional war, furthermore, was reduced to a low ebb by the Vietnam War.

The national military strategy after the Vietnam phasedown was not clear-cut, although it appeared to be the same as during the Kennedy-Johnson era but on a reduced scale. The aerospace-nuclear strategy for general war continued. The limited-war strategy appeared to be to use conventional forces only, and to prefer to use tactical airpower rather than ground forces. Also apparent was a partial return to Eisenhower's desire to use U.S. airpower together with allied armies.

IV

THE PRINCIPAL GOVERNMENT MARKET: THE UNITED STATES AIR FORCE

Since World War II the Air Force has been the largest customer for the aerospace industry. It has also been the principal instrument of American national military strategy, and its primary emphasis has been on grand-strategic attack.

THE STRATEGIC AIR COMMAND

It has already been shown in Chapter I that the Army Air Forces emphasized long-range, four-engine strategic bombers, a policy which did much to make airplanes more generally useful and which brought them to their postwar size. The AAF emerged from World War II believing that the efficacy of its concepts of grand-strategic bombing had been confirmed, and this belief provides the key to Air Force actions throughout the entire postwar period. Air Force leadership has always argued that grand-strategic attack is the most efficient means to conduct war, and that the heavy, or big, bomber was the best or at least necessary means to carry it out. All other functions and activities of airpower have, therefore, generally received only secondary attention. During the postwar years, the USAF continued development of its ideal aircraft, the bomber with global range, mainly on the strength of its strategic conceptions. When Russia emerged as the most likely enemy, the Air Force's predilections fit neatly into the one-war, air-nuclear military strategy.

The chosen instrument at first was the giant B-36, with its six piston

31

engines and four jet engines. Its design was set by the desire for a 10,000-mile range with 10,000 pounds of bombs, so that it could reach any significant global target and return to an American base. After some design difficulties were solved, the intercontinental B-36 exceeded expectations and was in practical use by 1949, thanks to the hybrid addition of more power through its jet engines.

There were two means other than the intercontinental bomber for the Air Force to reach a target in the enemy's homeland. One was to use overseas bases for its aircraft, and some were regained when Western Europe became frightened about Russian intentions. The second way was to use aerial refueling. The Air Force had experimented with the idea between the wars, but the attempts were crude. After the war, the British developed the probe-and-drogue system, which used a flexible hose, and the Americans adopted it and used it for smaller aircraft. The Americans developed the flying-boom method, which transfers large quantities of fuel quickly, for large aircraft. Two schools of thought emerged in the Air Force on the form the aerial tanker would take. One believed in using a transport aircraft to double as a tanker; the other preferred to convert bombers as both more efficient, because of the ability to use the same plane as a bomber, and cheaper. The transport advocates won.

The adoption of aerial refueling was a key development. It greatly expanded the aerospace business from 1951 on, for it added a whole new class of airplanes whose numbers would run around two-thirds of the bomber force, plus tankers for tactical airpower. The tankers proved useful in enabling aircraft to reach targets, and in ferrying aircraft, but the tanker was always regarded as an expedient, and the ideal solution for combat was thought to be the big bomber with requisite range.

Tankers speeded the development of jet bombers, for they circumvented the problem of high fuel consumption, which was a limitation of the early jet engines. And the Air Force wanted jet bombers badly because jet fighters had done well against the relatively slow piston bombers of World War II. Also, bomber men believed the jet bomber would be invulnerable to the fighter. If the bomber flew just below the speed of sound, the time available to intercept would be greatly reduced; and if the fighter did catch the bomber, it would be forced to maneuver and fire its guns while going back and forth between subsonic and supersonic conditions. The bomber people hoped this would present insoluble problems to the fighter.

Work on the XB-47 medium bomber had begun in the autumn of 1943. Initial investigations were done on four configurations, two jet and two propjet. The design first chosen resembled the B-29, with four jets in two wing nacelles. In an attempt to reduce nacelle drag, the four jet engines were moved into the body; side intakes were provided, and exhaust was discharged from the top of the straight wing's center section. This second design, which resembled a flying boat, was firm by December 1944. When knowledge of the German swept wing was received, a new version of the XB-47 incorporating the development was started. It was finished by September 1945. The four jet engines had been moved forward, to use nose intakes; exhaust was over the top of the wing; and two additional jet engines were added at the tail. This design was again changed to incorporate the German idea of engine pods under the wings: four of the engines were put into two pods, and two were mounted on the wing tips. The last change was to move the two outboard engines from the tips and suspend them in pods like the other engines. In December 1947 the XB-47 as we know it was flying, and Boeing engineers knew they had a winner, claiming that it was as revolutionary a design as the B-17 had been.

The design history of the XB-52 heavy bomber is linked to that of the XB-47 because of the incorporation of development experience. It

A stage in the design of the Boeing XB-47 with jet engines inside the body, side intakes, and exhausts over the wing center section. This photo is of wind tunnel model FR65 (FR for Flight Research), design model 432. It was taken 17 July 1945. *Courtesy The Boeing Company.*

began in April 1945, when the AAF asked for a long-range, turbine bomber design. The first Boeing configuration was ready for a June 1946 design competition. It won. This first model resembled the B-36, with six propjet engines, and it was expected to weigh 350,000 to 400,000 pounds. Range projections of this model were unsatisfactory, however. When Wright thought that they could produce a more powerful engine, the design was shrunk in late 1946 to a four-propjet version, but it still was short on range and speed. To get better performance, aerial refueling was accepted as necessary, and in early 1948 the wings were swept gently and contrarotating propellers were used. By the summer, propjet engine development for the XB-52 was in trouble, and prospects for the power plant to be ready in less than four years were dim. Wright Field proposed conversion to jet engines. Boeing's solution, resulting in part from the success of their B-47, was to use eight jet engines in four pods and to increase wing sweep; and the XB-52 evolved into a scaled-up B-47.

Boeing's B-17 had established the form of the large four-engine piston airplane, and Boeing engineers had now spent eight intensive years on the design and development of big turbine aircraft. Almost every conceivable turbine engine combination and mounting had been tried, and every style of nondelta wing had been examined. The design possibilities were manifold, but in the end Boeing knew they had found an effective

Another photo of wind tunnel model FR65 with jet engine installation under the wing tips. This picture was taken 22 August 1945. *Courtesy The Boeing Company.*

Another investigation of engine location is shown in this wind tunnel model. The engines were to be mounted at the ends of the horizontal tail surface. The photo was taken 22 August 1945. *Courtesy The Boeing Company.*

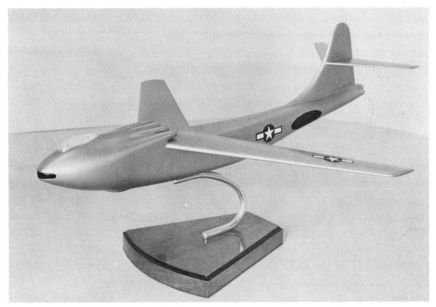

This is a 1/80 scale display model of Boeing type 448. It has a nose engine intake and incorporates the German swept airfoil concept for its wings and tail. This photo was taken 15 September 1945. *Courtesy The Boeing Company.*

Two historic aircraft: the Boeing B-52 and B-47. Their swept airfoils and suspended engines are the hallmark of the modern large jet airplane. Contrast their lines with those of the B-45, which used traditional piston-era approaches in its straight wing and tail and engines integral with the wing. *Courtesy The Boeing Company.*

combination for the big airframe. It has served them for a quarter of a century in the B-47, B-52, 707, 720, 727, 737, and 747 families and has been generally adopted throughout the world.

As the Boeing jet bombers neared operational service, the Korean War demonstrated that jet bombers were not just an idealistic improvement: they had become necessary for bombardment aviation. The MiG-15's superb performance destroyed the American illusion of Russian technical inferiority. Designed to destroy a possible successor to B-29's, it was able to slaughter the B-29. The Superfortress, still used in quantity by the Strategic Air Command, fled to the cover of darkness in 1951. What was even more shocking, the MiG's were masters of the jet RB-45, which the bomber enthusiasts had expected to be practically invulnerable against any fighter. The RB-45, as well as the B-29, had to be withdrawn from daylight operations. Faced with the prospect of future improved enemy fighters, fourteen of the B-36's guns were removed and other weight eliminated so it could operate at 50,000 feet and above, to redress the odds. When the B-47 jet bombers finally became operational in 1951 their speed, as had been hoped, was a problem to the fighters.

The bomber was soon in difficulty again, however, as technology advanced. With jet-thrust augmentation, or afterburning, faster climb rates and supersonic level flight to over Mach 2 were attained. The

36

America's first jet bomber was the North American B-45. The Air Force believed its speed would make it nearly invulnerable to fighters. The MiG-15 quickly disabused the Air Force of this wishful thinking. *Courtesy Rockwell International Corporation.*

missile, with conventional or nuclear warhead and terminal guidance, was developed for use by the fighter, and weapon aiming was made simpler by avionics. By the midfifties the fighter had once more attained a marked superiority over the bomber, and the development of excellent antiaircraft missiles at the same time compounded the bomber's problem.

Vigorous efforts were made to restore the bomber's viability. The Strategic Air Command had long planned to use fighter escort systems, but the extreme range of Soviet targets made traditional escorts difficult even with aerial refueling. An attempt was made to adopt the B-36 into a flying aircraft carrier to solve this problem, while fighters were modified to be carried in the bomb bays or on the wing tips. Some fighters were to do the bombing, thus creating a stand-off bombing system for the B-36. The B-58 of 1957 and the XB-70 were developed to give the bomber supersonic speeds to limit the fighter's advantage, but the B-58 had only a supersonic dash, and that was at high altitudes. The XB-70 had continuous supersonic flight, but the speed generated enough heat to make the bomber a dream target for missiles using heat-seeking guidance, and it was easy for radar to find. McNamara called it a strategic dinosaur. For years intensive efforts to provide the bomber with an air-to-air missile defense against fighters failed technologically.

In the end the only practical courses of action were development of stand-off air-to-ground missiles, such as Hound Dog and Skybolt, to be used against surface air-defense installations as the bomber flew towards

The North American XB-70 could be described in superlatives for most of its properties. Unfortunately, two disadvantages were cost and expected vulnerability to air defense weapons developed by the sixties. It was not a total loss, however, because of the technology learned in its design. *Courtesy Rockwell International Corporation.*

A Republic F-48F on its trapeze being retracted into the bomb bay of an RB-36F carrier aircraft. *Courtesy General Dynamics Corporation.*

the target; use of electronic countermeasures (ECM); and flying just above the ground so as to hide from radar. New models, the 1959 B-52G and 1961 H, had to be developed for the low-altitude tactic.

The heavy losses to be expected from grand-strategic operations against a competent enemy, with the highest loss estimates at a rate of 75 percent to 90 percent, reduced the bomber in the sixties to an auxiliary weapon. The bomber-oriented Air Force refused to accept this as a permanent condition, and renewed development proposals for heavy bombers followed each defeat of an earlier attempt, until the B-1 project was successfully implemented in 1970. The Air Force even, in desperation, sought to reopen assembly lines for the B-47, B-52, and B-58. A measure of the intensity of the desire for more manned bombers is shown by the B-58's inclusion in this list, for its production was ended early, in 1962, because of Air Force distaste for such a small bomber.

The twilight of both heavy and medium bombers as well as the auxiliary tankers, which started in the late fifties, resulted in the loss of a major market to the aerospace industry. This was the first large sales loss to the industry as a whole, and it was of special importance to Boeing, which had dominated both strategic and tanker markets. Boeing was able to partially offset the steep decline in its sales to the government by having the foresight to take over the Air Force strategic-missile business with the Minuteman.

The beautiful General Dynamics B-58 high-performance bomber. *Courtesy General Dynamics Corporation.*

General of the Air Force H. H. Arnold accurately predicted in 1945 that the missile would displace the grand-strategic bomber. His vision, together with a resolve that American aeronautical inferiority should not be repeated, led to the creation of two agencies to advise the AAF on directions to take in research and development (R&D). One was RAND (Research and Development Corporation), which soon proposed an earth-satellite project. The AAF did not follow this advice, but it did accept that of the other agency, the Scientific Advisory Group, led by Dr. Theodore von Karman. This second advisory group made proposals intended to establish a foundation for future development. One was to emulate the German organization for research and development, wherein all technical disciplines pertinent to a project had been brought together into a unit. Today this is called a "systems" approach. Other recommendations emphasized air supremacy in the near future and downgraded advanced missiles. It is ironic that, to avoid repetition of the earlier technological lag caused by short-term development, the group appointed to advise the Air Force was now recommending a similar short-term approach. RAND, whose advice was initially rejected, did better.

Nevertheless, some work did begin on intercontinental guided missiles although the emphasis was on two unmanned aircraft, successors to the German V-1: the Northrop Snark and the North American Navaho. The Snark was to be jet powered and subsonic, the Navaho to be ramjet powered and supersonic. There were years of struggle and failures with the Snark. The missile ultimately became operational only at squadron strength because it was vulnerable. The Mach 3 Navaho also went through years of difficulties and was successfully fired only after it had been canceled in 1957. Two other unmanned aircraft were developed, the Fairchild Goose, intended to divert air defenses from bombers, and the Boeing Bomarc interceptor. The Goose was canceled for the same reasons as the Snark and Navaho: too vulnerable. Bomarc alone became operational in significant, although small, numbers. Curiously, production was continued at this time on the big subsonic manned bombers, which were twenty times as expensive and not much less vulnerable—an inconsistency which can only be explained by a "battleship general" outlook: dogged clinging to a weapon for itself.

The unmanned aircraft, a guided missile, was for years believed to be easier to develop than the ballistic missile, and it was expected to be a bridge to the latter. As it turned out, the ballistic missile was less difficult to achieve than the unmanned intercontinental aircraft because the guidance was easier. But the technological relationships, the aero-

For a few years it was believed that the unmanned aircraft would bridge the operational gap between bomber and ballistic missile just as it did the technological. However, it proved to be vulnerable. Shown here is the launch of a Northrop Snark, which was put into service in small numbers. *Courtesy Northrop Corporation.*

dynamics, were linked as if development were to progress from jet aircraft to unmanned aircraft, then to missile.

Work on the ballistic missile began early. The V-2 and the atomic bomb inspired a contract between the AAF and Convair in April 1946 for Project MX-774, ancestor of the Atlas ICBM. The work did not enjoy a high priority because the expected accuracy, together with the yield and weight of the atomic weapon, appeared to render the missile impractical. In June 1947 MX-774 was canceled, yielding to more immediate SAC concerns during an economy drive. To put MX-774 into perspective as a program, about $465 million were spent for all research and development purposes in fiscal years 1946 through 1948, but only $2.25 million had been devoted to MX-774. In one of those fortunate cases of vision, Convair continued limited work on the ICBM with its own funds. When the dry hydrogen bomb was achieved in 1953, the yield-weight-

The mighty General Dynamics Atlas ICBM at launch. *Courtesy General Dynamics Corporation.*

accuracy combination changed to favor the ICBM. It assumed top priority in 1954 as knowledge of its feasibility and Russian development efforts combined to dictate urgency. To assure success, not only was General Dynamics' Atlas put in development but a competitor, the Martin Titan, was sponsored as well. As concern deepened over Russian progress, especially after Khrushchev "rattled his rockets" during the 1956 Suez crisis, it was realized that an IRBM could be made operational earlier because its shorter range meant simpler solutions. The Air Force produced its Thor in the late fifties in competition with the Army's Jupiter. Before these liquid-fueled missiles were successful, a solid fuel engine practical for big rockets was developed. Boeing realized this early and, concerned over future prospects for its bombers, worked hard in 1958 to win the Air Force solid-fuel ICBM competition.

Successful development of the ICBM and IRBM came during the

crisis of the bombers, and the missiles assumed the main aerospace-nuclear strategic role. Cheaper than bombers, they were invulnerable after launch. They had relatively short production runs, but production

Launch of a Martin Marietta Titan ICBM. *Courtesy Martin Marietta Corporation.*

did not end when the missile silos were filled, for improvements called for replacements. In addition, the ICBM and IRBM were useful as boosters for the space program.

PERSISTENCE: OTHER COMMANDS

The Tactical Air Command (TAC) was the Air Force's orphan combat command until conventional warfare was reemphasized under President Kennedy. Its initial existence was entirely the result of a suggestion by Eisenhower: the AAF organized TAC to ensure Ike's support in the autonomy struggle. Never very powerful in the early years, it expired before the Korean War. Limited war restored it, however, and tactical airpower specialists in the Air Force attempted to gain a stronger voice; but they did not get far, and an effort to simplify and lighten tactical aircraft failed. In the fifties TAC sought to support the new Eisenhower concept of limited war by organizing, together with Army elements, a highly mobile strike force called the Composite Air Strike Force (CASF). Aerial refueling was to be the key to achieving a global force to head off or fight small wars. Supersonic fighters, nuclear weapons, and a greatly improved tactical transport—the propjet Lockheed C-130 Hercules—gave the concept promise, and the CASF performed adequately when needed. It was cheaper to operate than the Navy's equivalent force, the carriers; but because of the emphasis on strategic air, TAC operated with low priority for everything. For example, its tankers were cast-offs from SAC. In the late fifties the smaller missiles led some to believe that tactical aircraft were obsolete, except for the transports, and concern for the continued existence of TAC as late as 1959 led its commander, General F. F. Everest, to conceive of the F-111 (TFX). He hoped the F-111 could compete with missiles and also serve as a junior strategic bomber. How he could believe the latter function could be included without TAC's being organizationally swallowed by SAC is puzzling.

Kennedy's conventional-warfare emphasis put TAC on an assured footing, although it has not become much larger. For the aerospace industry, TAC's story has meant that the jet fighter business has been good in war but poor in peace. Fighters have continued to be cyclical; no company has done well with USAF fighters for the whole period, 1945 to 1972, and the one company that specialized in Air Force fighters, Republic, failed. Yet, unlike the bomber, the fighter still appears to have a future with the Air Force and for export. And the fighter, along with the transport, is one of the best possibilities for the long serial production that spells profits. Fairchild had good business with the C-119 for tactical airlift, but that business was lost to the C-130. Then Lockheed had a large market in supplying transports for our Air Force and for exports. The 1949 piston C-119 never had the usefulness and reliability of the 1954 propjet C-130, a design which was still in production two decades later. For over a quarter of a century the workhorse jet engine created a continuing market for its services in tactical airpower.

The air-defense market, on the other hand, proved temporary. Before there was a discernible Russian air threat the Air Defense Command (ADC) was formed. Lacking resources of consequence it was virtually a phantom command, resting primarily upon the concept of big-bomber primacy, which in turn bestowed some status on the counterweapon. Emergence of a Russian air-nuclear capability in the early fifties, followed by the USAF miscalculation that the Soviet Air Force was building a massive grand-strategic bombing force, caused a mushrooming growth of ADC in the midfifties. Growth stopped with successful development of the ICBM, and with the eventual realization in the late fifties that Russia was emphasizing grand-strategic missiles and not bombers, as had been believed. It appears the American miscalculation and redirection was a mixture of being hoodwinked by the Russians, the self-deception of top Air Force generals in imputing their own intentions to others, and a change in plans as technology solved the feasibility problems of the ICBM.

The Russians did build a small force of 840 jet bombers, and together with nuclear weapons it remains a threat to the continental United States. Although the mechanics of air-defense demand almost as great a force to combat a small bomber fleet as a large one, it has been possible to reduce the U.S. interceptor force from its peak. The stable nature of the Soviet bomber force means that the existing interceptor force will continue to be serviceable. Thus, although the interceptor market rose rapidly in the fifties, it has been almost nonexistent since. The emergence of the ICBM as the main threat has not provided a market for an antiballistic missile (ABM), however. The technological problems of the ABM have not been simplified, its costs have been appalling, and the hypothesis has been generally accepted that defenselessness will preserve the balance of terror and, therefore, peace.

The third command, the Military Airlift Command (MAC), has, like the Tactical Air Command, grown in recognition. MAC performs strategic —that is, international or global—airlift functions, hauling large payloads for long distances in short times. As with commercial air transport, the power-to-weight efficiency of the jet engine has made strategic airlift increasingly effective and important. Repeated attempts to achieve that goal with piston engines met with moderate success. Of the giants that were built in this effort at the end of World War II, the Douglas C-74 Globemaster I, Lockheed R60 Constitution, and Convair XC-99, derived from the B-36, were unsuccessful. The Douglas C-124 Globemaster II of 1949, informally called "The Aluminum Cloud" and "The Flying Reynolds-Wrap," and the semigiant Boeing C-97 Stratofreighter of the end of World War II were the best of the large piston transports. Propjet efforts were made with the canceled Douglas C-132 and the 1957 C-133 Cargomaster. Progress towards jets and modern aircraft was not as fast as the Military Air Command wanted and technology permitted. The command had no jet transport until ten years after jet bombers were in service, and in 1963 the piston transport was still the backbone of the fleet. One of the rationalizations put forth by the bomber generals, a claim which sounds strange coming from the Air Force, was that speed was unimportant in a transport. This idea was not shared by those in the transport business: the airlines and the airlift command.

The C-133 was followed by a major step: the C-130 Hercules concept was enlarged and equipped with jet engines, and the result was a greatly improved strategic transport: the 1964 Lockheed C-141 StarLifter. Its success encouraged belief that the ultimate size could be achieved. The Lockheed C-5A Galaxy, also called "The Aluminum Overcast" or "Fat Albert," was built next; and the apparent commercial success of the C-5A's airliner counterparts—the Boeing 747, Lockheed L-1011 TriStar, and McDonnell DC-10—indicates that the jet engine has made the giant air transport, and therefore large-scale strategic airlift, feasible. General Arnold, in 1945, not only prophesied the ICBM, he also forecast an air capability to deliver ground forces, completely equipped, at any point in the world within hours. Such strategic airlift should have as bright a future as its commercial counterpart, and be an additional continuing market for the aerospace industry.

V

THE OTHER GOVERNMENT MARKETS:
THE AEROSPACE NAVY, THE AIR ARMY, AND NASA

THE JET AND THE AIR NAVY

The naval air arm has a history as long as that of the Air Force, and its demands have been large enough to support aerospace companies which specialized in meeting its particular needs, such as Grumman and, for a time, McDonnell. But immediately after World War II the Navy was in strategic and technological trouble.

Traditionally, the U.S. Navy believed that its purpose was to fight other navies. But from 1945 to 1947 America's only apparent potential enemy was Russia, a vast landpower which did not need the sea and was the antithesis of seapower in the geopolitics of Halford John Mackinder and Karl Haushofer. The battleship had been thought to be the main striking power before the war, but now all surface ships were in a supporting role; and it was believed by many that surface ships could no longer discharge even this role because nuclear weapons would easily destroy them. Furthermore, with large aircraft ranges becoming feasible, the usefulness of even the carrier was in question. The advent of the jet engine for aircraft made carrier operations difficult if not doubtful because jets accelerate and decelerate more slowly than piston planes. The agency which seemingly benefited from these developments was the Air Force, and therefore its struggle for survival through autonomy became a direct threat to the Navy's existence, or so the Navy believed. The Navy found it impossible to prevent the attainment of autonomy by the AAF in 1947. The sea service was able to keep its own air arm, and this ensured its organizational survival as a large service, but the Navy did lose to the Air Force the primacy in American defense that it had had before the war.

A partial response was the rise of a new Navy, different in leadership, strategy, and technology: an air navy. During the war naval fliers had come to the fore in operations, but command and administration were still vested in the "black-shoe Navy" or "Gun Club," nicknames for the battleship officers. At the end of the war Forrestal advanced young aviators to greater power because of their ability and as a counter to the AAF. The Navy deliberately included in its leadership young "brownshoe" aviators, and air officers came largely to dominate the Navy, although powerful ship and submarine factions continued to vie with the airmen for control.

The naval fliers broke with tradition by believing in both strategic bombing and the Air Force global view of air operations. They had not arrived at these views through deliberation or conscious imitation of the AAF, but the concepts had evolved in the course of conducting war. After destroying the Japanese Navy in a tactical role, the fliers looked for new targets, and among the new objectives chosen were Japan's industry and land bases. The fliers' experience against the Japanese homeland convinced them that they could operate in the face of land-based airpower; until this success they had feared such a method of operation and had been reluctant to support the concept of strategic bombing. The air Navy did not fully agree with the AAF on the usefulness of strategic bombing, however. The AAF viewed long-range bombardment as the most economic and effective way to destroy an enemy's source of power. The air Navy, on the other hand, thought that war *could* be conducted in this manner, but that it might not prove feasible in all cases. A war might still have to be won by attrition and mass assault using all military means, including strategic bombardment as just one style of attack. The new air Navy recognized, however, that adoption of the technique would be politically desirable in its struggle with the Air Force, should strategic bombing prove to be the main punch in war. When the air Navy openly adopted strategic bombing after World War II, and claimed it could perform the function better than the AAF, the latter in turn became alarmed for its own survival. The stage was set for years of bitter struggle because each service believed its continued existence was at stake.

Carrying out its new strategic concepts demanded technological change in the air Navy. The radius of action of Navy bombers in the "Marianas Turkey Shoot" was only 200 miles, appropriate for fleet actions between battleship or carrier lines. The 1946 Douglas A-1 Skyraider, the first attempt to increase range drastically, raised the radius of action to 700 miles. If Russia was to be considered as the potential enemy, this was marginal to inadequate. The radius-of-action requirement against Russia was 2,000 miles, and the air Navy in the immediate postwar years began thinking in terms of carrier-based strategic bombers on the order of the AAF's XB-47, which grossed 125,000 pounds. The adoption of nuclear weapons at this time also meant larger aircraft than those that had been carrier based. The North American AJ with two piston engines and one jet engine, under design for preatomic bombing, was adapted to carry a nuclear weapon. In the interim the Lockheed P2V was to be launched off carriers without a carrier recovery capability, an awkward, makeshift arrangement. A third technological demand was to adapt jet aircraft and carriers to each other. This was not only difficult technically but it was not given priority by the Navy's top leadership, which was cool to jets. The Navy did achieve an operational carrier-based jet squadron in 1948. After cancellation of the U.S.S. *United States* and the B-36 controversy, a supercarrier was finally built, and with the adoption of three British developments—the canted deck, the mirror landing system,

The Navy's makeshift attempt at a strategic bomber included use of Lockheed P2V's launched from aircraft carriers. The P2V could not be recovered on carrier decks. *Courtesy Lockheed Aircraft Corporation.*

and the steam catapult—the technological problems of operating jets from carriers were fully solved.

Other solutions to the problem of aircraft range were available to the Navy. A second possibility was to build a force of flying-boats for strategic bombing. For long-range operations the flying-boats would be serviced by submarine and surface tenders at changing sheltered locations. It was believed that the flying-boats would have the performance of land-based bombers, and their tender system would avoid carrier vulnerability and carrier dependence on overseas bases. Proponents believed this would make the system better than the Air Force's. Development of this concept included the Martin P6M Sea Master as the bomber, begun in 1948, and the General Dynamics XF2Y Sea Dart as a fighter, begun in 1952. Despite years of effort, however, the technology of this system was never mastered. In 1959, when supremacy of the fighter over the bomber had clearly been established, and ballistic missiles were becoming operational, work was finally abandoned on the flying-boat strategic-bomber project, and those few which had been built were destroyed.

The Martin P6M Sea Master was the key aircraft in the Navy attempt to create an ocean-based grand-strategic attack force. *Courtesy Martin Marietta Corporation.*

The fighter part of the Navy's water-based strategic force was to be General Dynamics' XF2Y. *Courtesy General Dynamics Corporation.*

A more successful method to extend range was found in refueling. The small Douglas A-1's and A-4's were nuclear armed in the fifties but lacked range. With the jet reequipping following Korea, an aircraft was designed especially to be the carrier's nuclear strategic bomber: the medium size Douglas A-3. A supersonic successor was also developed, the 1958 North American A-5. To help with the persistent range problem of these aircraft, aerial refueling was adopted, and the Navy chose to mainly rely on the method the Air Force had rejected: the "buddy system" in which like aircraft serve as tankers. A Navy version of the transport C-130 served as a tanker as well.

This line of carrier strategic bombers ended quietly in the sixties. In 1963 Secretary McNamara witnessed carrier maneuvers and promptly challenged the Navy to justify the ships. In the ICBM era, and with the vulnerability of large aircraft, McNamara was still critical of continued strategic operations after the Navy had made its case. The A-5's were converted to reconnaissance aircraft, and the Navy dropped its strategic bomber role. The ease and quietness of this move indicates no great stress. The Navy had by this time an assured grand-strategic role with its submarines; the carrier long-range bombers had never been more than a small operation compared with Air Force capability; the Navy no longer feared that strategic airpower would make naval power obsolete; and the Navy was still not of one mind.

There had always been officers who believed that the need for tactical airpower was enough to assure continuance of a large carrier force. The limited conventional war in Korea gave this group strong reinforcement despite the problems the war uncovered for the Navy. The shocking realization that its fighters were unable to contest the MiG-15 meant that development of modern fighters and attack aircraft had to be pushed, and the reluctance of senior officers to accept jet performance was overcome. This meant extensive naval conversion to jets during and after the Korean War, although only 16 percent of the inventory in jets had been achieved by mid-1953. Since then, the air Navy has concentrated on the role of fighting limited wars in the same way as the Tactical Air Command's Composite Air Strike Force. Its excellent performance in the international crises since Korea has reinforced it in this role, and in Vietnam the tactical airpower supporters in the Navy found justification in the circumstance that the carrier's tactical forces were used for strategic purposes. Maintenance of a large naval tactical air force seems assured. It has been, and should continue to be, a substantial market for the aerospace companies.

The Marines have specialized within tactical airpower in their almost exclusive concern with close support of ground forces. Since this function can be and usually has been performed by obsolescent aircraft, and since the Navy does procurement for the Corps, the Marines have had little direct effect on the aerospace industry. The principal influence has been to promote the helicopter as a short-haul tactical air transport.

THE AEROSPACE NAVY

The Navy, like the Air Force, worked on missiles in the postwar years. As with the jets, taking the technology to sea was a problem. The early missile fuels posed huge safety and control problems in shipboard use. Confined quarters, the unstable launching site of the surface of the sea, spillage, and pinpointing the ship's position led the Navy temporarily to abandon big missiles except for the Vought Regulus, an unmanned airplane. Regulus went into shipboard and submarine service on a small scale in the fifties but had the same limitations as the Air Force unmanned aircraft. As in the Air Force and Army, smaller solid missiles were widely used by the Navy.

When it became apparent that the ICBM was feasible, the Navy joined the scramble to exploit the new technology. To save money Defense Secretary Charles E. Wilson directed the Navy in 1956 to combine its development with that of the Army's. Since the Army was already well along with its program, the Navy was faced with adapting the Jupiter to shipboard use if it wanted an IRBM. The liquid-fueled Jupiter had been developed for land use, however, and it posed grave handling problems to the Navy. While attempting to solve these problems, the Navy also sought to make solid fuels useful in big missiles. Just when systems had been evolved which appeared to make the Jupiter acceptable, the solid-fuel technical problems were solved. Admiral William Raborn, head of the Special Project Office for the IRBM, asked Secretary Wilson for independence from the Army system, basing his argument on cost reduction, and approval in late 1956 led to development of the Lockheed Polaris and Poseidon systems for submarines.

The presently invulnerable nature of the submarine-launched ballistic missile has made it a desirable weapon despite lower accuracy. With the Polaris system the Navy finally moved into unquestioned partnership with the Air Force in contributing a grand-strategic system to U.S. defense. The Navy's strategic and tactical aerospace power has been a continuous major market for the aerospace industry, and should continue to be one.

THE AIR ARMY

Autonomy for the Air Force did not eliminate the Army as a customer of the aerospace industry. Out of a combination of Army concern, logic, and the Air Force's willingness to compromise to achieve autonomy, the ground service kept an air arm. To the aerospace industry this was advantageous, for it added a customer that could be expected to compete with the other air services, as boundaries between missions and roles are seldom clear-cut or absolute. But the Army also presented a potential threat to the future survival of the aerospace industry and the Air Force. In the immediate postwar period the threat was little more than a cloud on the horizon, but the industry was conscious of it.

Artillery had apparently reached the practical limits of its range, and a return to rocketry was a natural solution. To the soldier, the missile was a continuation of the function of artillery. To the airman, the missile was an extension of aerodynamic technology. They were both right; technology was leading to a confluence of weaponry. The concern of the aerospace industry arose from the fact that the Army had a government arsenal system in existence with a long tradition behind it. Since the Air Force believed until 1947 that missiles would make bombers obsolete, it was faced with yet another threat to its survival besides lack of autonomy and the air Navy's strategic interests. At this early indefinite stage a clash of the Air Force with the Army over missile roles and missions could be postponed, but its eventuality, plus the technical possibilities of winged missiles, led the Air Force to start research programs with its ally, the aerospace industry. In the past the companies had done some

The Fleet Ballistic Missile gave the Navy an assured grand-strategic attack role. Here is the launch of a Lockheed Poseidon. *Courtesy Lockheed Aircraft Corporation.*

research, but principal reliance had been placed upon NACA's leadership. Now the advanced technology of the jet-propelled, winged missile and the possible Army threat to its survival spurred an important new departure in the aerospace industry: major research contracts.

When in the early fifties it was apparent that the ICBM/IRBM was feasible, the interservice rivalry for possession became strong. Each service believed that its future role and, therefore, its size depended on being selected to employ the new weapon. The pressure for rivalry grew when these glamorous potential weapons were funded far more generously than other weapons systems. The intercontinental-minded USAF worked from the beginning directly on the ICBM. The Army hoped to gain the advantage by working up to the ICBM in steps. It believed its arsenal, using the German veterans of the rocket center at Peenemünde, could develop a better missile earlier than the Air Force's industrial contractors could. But when Russian advances became alarming, the Air Force, in scaling down to an IRBM (Douglas' Thor) from its ICBM (General Dynamics' Atlas), was able to produce a missile comparable to the Army's Jupiter in roughly the same time. The Air Force now had a psychological advantage: it had long espoused strategic attack and was popularly associated with it, and it had now proved capable of matching the Army's primary weapon. Army failure to achieve an IRBM of unquestioned superiority to the Air Force's Thor effectively blocked the Army from starting the next step to the ICBM, which was imminent for the Air Force by the time Jupiter was finished. A decision in 1956 in favor of the Air Force ended the Army effort on long-range missiles, and operation of the Jupiter was given to the airmen. However, a market for Army shorter-range missiles, like the Martin Pershing, continues for the aerospace industry. Loss of the German team to NASA, together with Army experience in the fifties, led to increasing adoption of Air Force procurement systems, including the substitution of industrial contractors for the arsenal system, a most welcome development to the aerospace industry.

Thwarted in its aerospace ambitions, the ground service did develop into an air Army. The Army and Air Force have long found their tactical views difficult to reconcile, with the Army seeking to use airpower for frontal attack on the battlefield and the Air Force claiming that it is more effective support to clear the air of enemy aircraft and to attack the enemy in his rear. Even on shared ground—the desirability of tactical airlift—contentions have risen because, until the administration of President Kennedy, the Air Force stinted on air transport so as to give funds to the bomber force. The Army's recourse has been to try repeatedly to gain the close air support and tactical airlift missions. Aside from the overt attempts, there has been the natural evolution of arming helicopters and moving to aircraft with greater payloads, including twin-engine aircraft. Starting with small numbers of very light aircraft, the air Army has become a significant customer of the large aerospace companies. The Army's airmobile division concept, its confirmation that helicopters can go anywhere a truck can and perform more effectively, and its Vietnam experience have meant a rapid growth of an air Army, a valuable customer for the aerospace industry.

THE NEW MARKET: NASA

The Army's evolution into a significant customer of the aerospace industry parallels that of another governmental unit, the National Aeronautics and Space Administration. Created in 1958 to close the wide technological gap opened by the Russians, NASA had an explosive growth that far overshadowed the air Army. NASA's formation around the cadre of NACA, its absorption of the Army's German missile team, the use of military boosters, and the circumstance that the aerospace companies won the big contracts demonstrated that the space program was the conclusion of a technical progression of airplane to missile to space vehicle.

The dominant portion of NASA's effort in the first ten years was the manned program, the race to the moon. North American, the biggest contract winner for the race, had sales of over $2 billion in 1964. Of this business, 40 percent was for space—for North American's Apollo spaceship and Saturn's second stage. Big business, too, were McDonnell's Mercury and Gemini spaceships, Boeing's Saturn first stage, and Douglas' Saturn third stage.

With the culmination of Apollo, space has ceased to be a priority, crash program. Like the missile programs from the midfifties to the midsixties, the space program produced a warlike business surge for the aerospace industry. Like the missile business, it will continue but at a level lower than that of its earliest years.

NASA's share of the government markets for aerospace has been about one-sixth of the recent total; the Air Force has received about one-half; the Navy, one-fourth; and the Army, one-tenth. During the entire period of this study the Air Force market was roughly twice as large as that of the Navy.

The agencies are, in the sense of different demands, distinct markets; yet the government also can be considered as a single market, since procurement procedures are basically uniform.

The military ballistic missile has been adapted for use as a space booster. This vehicle is a Martin Marietta Air Force Titan III with a General Dynamics Centaur upper stage. *Courtesy Martin Marietta Corporation.*

VI

FASHIONS IN GOVERNMENT PROCUREMENT

Nearly as important as *why* and *what* the government bought, is *how* it was done, or the mechanics of buying. The first two are concerned with product differentiation, and the last with the vital matter of price. Despite the presence of airline and foreign customers, there is no practical existence of a market to set the price for aerospace products. They are expensive, even for the United States government. They must be sold before they are made or, often, even designed, because the industry works on the frontiers of technology. The government reserves the right to break its contracts—including price agreements—so it is hardly a normal buyer, aside from its special relationships with the industry as financier and regulator. Pricing is therefore critical and difficult. A price which is too low could bankrupt the manufacturer if that were politically realistic; one which is too high is politically unacceptable. The desired product is often beyond the technological state of the art, and the costs of design and development thus depend upon technical unknowns. This includes "unk-unks," unknown-unknowns, or the unexpected. In addition, complex fabrication and assembly lead to difficulty in forecasting initial production costs, although once the first few models have been made, usually fifteen to thirty-five, production costs are usually predictable.[1] Forecasts are based upon learning, or logistic, curves developed from years of previous results, and the aerospace industry expects that costs will drop to 80–85 percent of the first lots' cost after the production quantity has doubled.[2]

The history of government procurement policies for aerospace goods since World War II is a series of attempts to grapple with this problem of price where neither market nor specific product is in existence. As purchaser of most of the industry output, the government has tried to avoid using its powerful position to drive the price down as far as possible. The reasons have been both altruistic and practical. If the companies were driven to bankruptcy, a source of indispensable and irreplaceable material would be gone—irreplaceable because there is doubt that government arsenals could deliver as much of the product in comparable quality and as quickly as private firms; the government must seek to get "the most for its money the soonest," since aerospace articles not only wear out but often become useless because of rapid technological advance. Too, as the recent Lockheed crisis has shown, the government shrinks from the economic dislocations of a large bankruptcy. So the government has sought, through its procurement system, to provide a reasonable profit to the firms while providing a contract that will both help and motivate the industry to cut its costs. In the quarter of a century after World War II there were recurrent company crises and some failures, and there were serious complaints about high profits, waste, and procurement practices themselves.[3]

THE PERIOD OF CALM: 1946–1950

In the postwar years, profits and prices were not a great issue in government procurement. As a whole the industry was profitless, and prices for aircraft, although regarded as high, were not considered excessive. There was no strong dissatisfaction with the contract system that continued to operate after World War II. The cost plus fixed fee (CPFF) had worked well compared to World War I's cost plus percentage of cost (CPPC). After the war, intentions were to start with a CPFF contract early in a program, when the costs were so uncertain that they could not be estimated closer than plus or minus 30 percent, and then use negotiated fixed price contracts for subsequent production lots, when the learning curve was a fairly reliable basis for setting costs. The fixed price contract need not be as fixed as its name implies; it could be very flexible, in practice, because it could call for periodic "redetermination" points at which the price could be adjusted as experience indicated. Such contracts can, in fact, be regarded as a variation in the cost reimbursement method. Despite the obvious potential problem that the higher the estimated costs the higher the percentage profit, or fee, the Air Force learned with time that the CPFF contracts often proved to be the cheapest kind, and that a specific situation determined the most favorable contract form. The

World War II procurement practices were thus generally carried forward into the postwar period, and although the Armed Services Procurement Act of 1947 specified that advertised bids were to be used, most aerospace contracts were negotiated under exceptions allowed by the act.

The Navy preferred a type of contract it had initiated in 1942, the "incentive" type, although it also used the other kinds of contracts. If the incentive program went as expected, the fee would be the same as for CPFF; if costs varied from the original estimate, the government and the firm would share in the savings or cost overrun, except that beyond a certain preset level all increased costs were borne by the company. This form of contract, by its very nature, demanded more elaborate cost accounting, but the Navy hoped the incentive form would motivate cost cutting by the contractor. The Air Force included it as a contract type in 1955.

The service organizations doing aerospace procurement were the Air Force's Air Materiel Command (AMC) and the Navy's Bureau of Aeronautics (BuAer) and Ordnance Bureau (BuOrd). AMC was in decline as a procurement agency from the end of World War II until its dissolution in 1961. An important step in its slide was the formation in 1947, by General Curtis E. LeMay, of the Aircraft and Weapons Board, which was set up to make the final decisions on procurement. In 1948 this board's duties were taken over by the Senior Officers Board, whose name was later changed to the Air Council. These boards were composed of selected top generals; and since adherence to and experience with the big bomber doctrine has been important to promotion to that level, Air Force decisions on all aerospace procurement have reflected the outlook of that group. It is difficult to exaggerate the importance of this parochialism in Air Force procurement and the combat capability of the service itself, aside from the delays caused by high-level review.

THE MISHANDLED MOBILIZATION: 1950–1953

Planning for mobilization was important in the postwar years. On the eve of the Korean War there were seventy-five aircraft plants in reserve and a large government stockpile of machine tools and materials. Contracts for wartime production had already been prepared. Yet the plans were found to be nearly as useless as those for the Second World War, for they were based on mobilization for total war, reflecting the one-war national military strategy of the time.

At first it was decided simply to double aircraft production, a procedure which was within the existing capacity of the industry. Related to the war was concern for NATO strength, and production was accelerated for 1,600 fighters for Britain, France, and Italy. Guided missile development also received attention; a central agency, the Office of Guided Missiles, was established in 1950 to expedite the services' thirty-five missile projects. Production of missile material was to double by fiscal year 1952 and undergo a further 50 percent increase by 1954. K. T. Keller, president of Chrysler, was named as director of the missile agency, reporting only to the secretary of defense and the Armed Forces Policy Council. Financing was needed immediately for the programs; the Federal Reserve consequently reactivated the V-loan program, which had provided $2 billion to the aircraft industry in World War II, and the General Services Administration provided government-owned machinery for lease.

The entry of China into the war in October 1950 again altered the course of events sharply. Afraid that the intervention was part of an escalation to World War III, Truman declared a war emergency and emulated Roosevelt by making an unrealistic call for 15,000 planes together with a $17 billion supplemental defense appropriation. This meant a fivefold increase in production in one year. World War II's best growth was only threefold and with simpler aircraft. Congress was willing to provide funds almost for the asking, yet the Joint Chiefs of Staff were unable to present a program immediately even though plans had been worked out in the spring for full mobilization. Evidently, as happens frequently, the plans were unacceptable to superiors when the applicable situation arose. The Air Force program costing $4.5 billion was settled in an all-night session of its Senior Officers' Board on 5 January 1951, a circumstance hardly conducive to effective decision making. General Electric's president, Charles E. Wilson, became head of the new Office of Defense Mobilization, which had been formed in December 1950 and immediately faced shortages in men, materials, and machine tools. Not all the stockpiled tools, many of which were left from World War II, were suitable for changed production methods. In this frenzied atmosphere the auto industry again entered into aircraft production.

Not surprisingly, the aerospace companies willingly embraced subcontracting to avoid overexpansion in those uncertain times. Before this period, subcontracting had been done reluctantly and at government urging. During World War II Lockheed had subcontracted only 18 percent; in 1951 it was 40 percent.[4] Lockheed's attitude toward subcontracting at this time is illustrated by the fact that in 1952 its Constellation airliner, whose sales did not depend on the zigzags of government buying, used practically no subcontracting. By contrast, subcontracting on its military aircraft ranged from 31 percent on the F-94 to 51 percent on the P2V.[5] This time the rise of subcontracting marked a permanent change in attitude in the aerospace industry, and subcontracting became an accepted, routine practice.

It was a wise move for the firms. As the months passed without renewed crises, there was a gradual relaxation of efforts to achieve emergency goals. But it was relaxation, not reversal, and action to further production continued: the Aircraft Production Resources Agency was established in 1951 to solve a war materials problem which had arisen; an attempt was made by the Air Force to freeze designs; and the World War II Boeing-Douglas-Lockheed cooperative arrangement for building B-17's was revived in 1951 to mass-produce B-47's.

The material and tools shortages continued to limit production, with tool problems alone estimated to reduce output by 20 percent in the early part of 1951. As in World War II, combat forced reequipping with more modern aircraft designs. There were strikes against materials suppliers, and the increased labor turnover and the absenteeism that go with a manpower shortage. Probably most important, the attempt to increase production occurred at the same time that the transition to jet aircraft manufacturing techniques was at its height. At the end of 1951 the production rate was 450 aircraft per month, which was not even twice the December 1950 rate of 250. The total production was roughly 5,000 aircraft, far short of Truman's goal of 15,000, although it is not clear whether he wanted his aim to be achieved in 1951. There was a mild shake-up of top mobilization managers at the end of 1951, and new goals were set that acknowledged the existing bottlenecks—which were primarily in engine production—and tried to reduce the sting of rising costs.

By the summer of 1952 jet engines were still the bottleneck, but attention was diverted when W. L. Campbell, acting chairman of the Defense Production Administration's Aircraft Production Board, dropped a bombshell. Either he alone saw the truth, or no one else was willing to act. He told the Defense Department that it was needlessly producing obsolescent aircraft as well as too many different types for each purpose. Campbell's list of obsolescent or redundant aircraft which he said should be terminated or cut back included twelve types, some produced for the Air Force and some for the Navy. There was an instant rebuttal which defended production of the older types, but some of Campbell's recommendations were soon quietly put into effect. More cutbacks followed but only because of the insistence of Defense Secretary Robert Lovett. The next year, in the late spring of 1953, a scandal broke when Congress learned of the slow production and high cost of C-119's built by Kaiser-

Frazer at Willow Run. Kaiser's aircraft cost almost three times those of Fairchild. The Air Force canceled Kaiser's contract a few days after the matter exploded in Congress. It was revealed in congressional investigations that General Motors' contract negotiators had got the better of an Air Force team and won windfall profits from building Republic F-84F's, and that the Navy persisted in ordering McDonnell F3H fabrication with a deficient engine against the manufacturer's advice, until the fighter had taken several lives. Perhaps an estimate of the efficiency of the period can be made from the fact that it sometimes took the services two years to convert a letter of intent to a contract; it should be done in less than ninety days.

Almost at the same time as the Campbell affair the qualitative procurement of missiles came under attack. Although the missiles' "czar," K. T. Keller, had gotten them into quantity production with a "brute-force" approach, he either lacked authority or had been unable to use it to force coordination among the services in missile development. Missiles were in production which could be shot down by obsolete piston fighters. Antiaircraft missiles were being developed without any reference to the air defense radar and control system, and were even being designed for altitudes lower than aircraft operational levels.

In September 1952 the secretary of defense was given legal authority to run all armed services procurement, while the war emergency machinery was being slowly phased out. This was an important step towards separating the services from their procurement powers. It appears that the services have only themselves to blame, for the Campbell, Keller, and other incidents demonstrated inefficiencies in service procurement both in weapon quality and cost consciousness.

The production record of the Korean War, shown in Table VI-1, demonstrates one important thing: production rose in spite of some governmental mismanagement and the fact that this was the principal period of conversion from piston to jet propulsion, which requires somewhat different production methods. Otherwise the record is blurred because

TABLE VI-1
AIRCRAFT PRODUCTION FOR THE KOREAN WAR

Calendar Year	Military Aircraft Produced
1949	2,600
1950	3,000
1951	5,000
1952	9,000
1953	12,000

the period of frantic effort did not begin until six months after the war began in June 1950, and the steam went out of the effort six months after the panic of December 1950.

INNOVATION: 1953–1960

The end of the Korean War brought not only the realization that the jet age had arrived, but also some shock at the costs associated with it. Consequently, military procurement in the Eisenhower era was dominated by the clash between desire for the new technology and its derivatives, missiles and space, and their costs. There were not only the natural responses of stretching out programs, of trying to transfer the expense to industry, and of attempting closer controls; there was also imaginative innovation in procurement and management, mostly by the Air Force.

Defense Secretary Charles E. Wilson, not the same man as the director of Defense Mobilization, set the tone for the administration in 1953. He announced that government commitments would be for shorter terms, and that failures to meet schedules would mean cancellation even if the contractor was not at fault. The industry was told its inventories were excessive and would be reduced by 30 percent, for the Defense Department was not going to finance all of them. In addition, there would be cuts in progress payments, program cuts, and stretchouts.

In 1954 and 1955 similar steps were taken to cut procurement costs. Spares were to be reduced by 25 percent in a renewed emphasis on inventory costs, and there was to be more testing before a decision to manufacture. Penalties for failure to perform were threatened. Fixed price and incentive contracts were to be emphasized, and in 1955 those contract types were in fact dominant. But as the fifties went on, with lowered production runs and more development, the CPFF contract rose in use again until it alone formed, in 1961, 38 percent of all awards. At the same time, incentive contracts became more popular despite the concern of influential Congressman Carl Vinson, who saw that one of the major problems with the incentive contract form was that it motivated a contractor to inflate initial cost estimates. It has had other basic problems: in many cases the contractor would be better off if he raised his direct costs; this would increase the overhead paid, assigned as a percentage of direct costs, and he would benefit more from this gain than he would lose from the reduced profit fee which declined on a sliding scale as his expenses rose. Finally, because estimating costs on unknowns is difficult, the incentive contractor knows he may be penalized after excellent performance or may gain a windfall on a job poorly done. As late as 1969 no one could produce evidence that incentive contracts accomplished their purpose.

In the summer of 1957 there was another major effort by the Defense Department to cut costs. Besides program cancellations and stretchouts, limits were placed on overtime and progress payments were reduced. There was also a drive to reduce the proportion of government-owned facilities. Government stockpiling of tools was abandoned, as were mobilization plans, for the Air Force's belief in a short nuclear war—and, hence, no need for mobilization—fit in neatly with the desire to cut government expenditures. In 1960 the Navy launched its own renewed effort along lines which were now familiar: penalties for contractor failure to meet a schedule, an aversion to cost reimbursement contracts which was so strong that attempts were even made to end them on research and development projects, and a reduction in government-owned plant and equipment. The repetitive nature of these drives to reduce costs with the same formulas indicates that the measures were palliatives.

Several more imaginative efforts were made. The most conspicuous were organizational changes. For the crash development of ballistic missiles, each service established a specialized agency with top priority. The Air Force led with its Ballistic Missile Division in 1954, followed by the Army Ballistic Missile Agency and the Navy's Special Projects Office in 1956. These Manhattan-Project–like agencies operated effectively but continued to undergo modification. In 1951 the Air Research and Development Command (ARDC) had been established both to recognize the growing role of R&D and to procure it more effectively. Previously, R&D had been bought by the Air Materiel Command within the Air Force, but in the fifties the Air Materiel Command had a tendency to concentrate on traditional buying patterns; and the Air Force became disappointed with the Defense Department's Research and Development Board, unofficially called the "Retardation and Delay Board," which lost itself in a maze of 16 committees, 174 panels, 284 subpanels, and 3,000 special consultants. The Air Research and Development Committee, chaired by H. Guyford Stever of the Massachusetts Institute of Technology (MIT), reported that the problem lay in the Air Force's tendency to keep decision-making at excessively high levels, a not-surprising conclusion in light of the Air Council discussed above.[6] The Air Force, however, believed its problem lay in having split its procurement function between the Air Materiel Command and the Air Research and Development Command. Its solution was to move all procurement in 1961 to a successor organization, the Air Force Systems Command (AFSC), named for the weapons systems concept. The Navy had already merged its Bureau of Aeronautics and Bureau of Ordnance into a Bureau of Weapons in 1959, a reflection of the convergence of aerodynamics and weaponry. The new organizational form was soon adopted by the Army, which abolished its traditional technical services and set up a Materiel Development and Logistics Command (MDLC) in 1962.

The weapons system concept was first presented to the Air Force by the AAF Scientific Advisory Group, which recommended that this German method be adopted. Air Force custom had formerly been to buy its engines, armament, radios, and so forth directly and then present them to an aircraft manufacturer for inclusion in an airplane design. These items were called government furnished equipment (GFE) or GFP ("P" for parts) or GFAE ("A" for aircraft). This method of buying has obvious advantages in equipment standardization and quantity-purchase savings, and in addition it had a special attraction to government as another means to use procurement to achieve socioeconomic goals, because the government dealt with more companies this way. However, as aircraft became more complex, and also denser with additional equipment, it became increasingly difficult for the aerospace firms to accommodate their designs to "off-the-shelf" parts without a loss in performance. Even when this was done, the newer electronics parts demanded avionics skill in aerospace designers. Avionics proved to be the precipitating factor for change. Under the weapons system concept one agency became responsible for assuring that all functions, except engines, became an integrated whole with optimum performance. Since the aerospace companies were already using this approach in their airliner products, the new concept was not a sharp break for them. Also, the Air Force intended to use the new method only where it was better. The first contract using the weapons system procurement concept went in 1950 to an airliner manufacturer, Convair, for the F-102; but this first step was a halfway move, because Hughes Aircraft provided the armament. The first complete use of the system again went to Convair, this time in 1952 for the B-58. Soon the Navy adopted the method, and then the Army, dealing a blow to its arsenal system. By 1958 90 percent of Army R&D was being done by industry. Adoption of the weapons system concept had the effect of further centralizing procurement decisions in the services and of greatly enlarging the aerospace firms' managerial and technical staffs, their overhead. It also enlarged the scope of make or buy decisions by the aerospace companies, especially for avionics.

The F-102 was not only the pioneer aircraft for the weapons system concept, it was also the first to fully test another Air Force effort to cut costs. This attempt was precipitated by three aircraft development

67

events which had occurred: a medium bomber was put in production before it could be made combat ready, and the modifications on the finished aircraft equaled the original production cost; a fighter was ordered into production after two hours of flight tests, but later structural failure required extensive rebuilding and made junk of a large supply of spare parts; and another fighter demonstrated major problems in flight test after 300 production models had been built. The new idea was to start production at a slow rate while testing up to fifty models. In the past, three aircraft had been considered to be enough for test, but months of testing had been required; the increased number was intended to reduce the length of the testing period while still accumulating sufficient flying hours. The aircraft would be production models and not prototypes. This plan was called the "development-production" or "concurrency" system, and it was copied by the Navy. The F-102 proved to be a disaster for this concept, however. Forty-two aircraft for test were ordered and slow production began, but on the first flights in 1953 and 1954 the F-102 performed far below expectations with its traditionally streamlined fuselage. Richard Whitcomb's area rule formula with its "Coke-bottle"–shaped fuselage was then tried as a solution and it worked. This change required a second production tooling and the scrapping of ten aircraft. Subsequently, the second design was given up as too heavy, after another four had been built. There was a third tooling-up before an acceptable, highly successful aircraft was produced. Thirty million dollars in tooling had become scrap, and more money was lost on reworked or scrapped planes.

The concurrency plan appears to have been successful in the Air Force's development of the ICBM, where it was regarded as a necessary gamble to hasten operational readiness in the missile race, but it was ill-conceived for both production and testing of manned military aircraft. The preceding, long-successful system of testing three fighters for a total of 1,000 hours meant about 350 hours for each model. The concurrency method was to test fifty aircraft. This would amount to only 20 hours of test per aircraft, assuming no increase in total hours and equal time per aircraft, assumptions which are probably unwarranted, especially because the aircraft would be built in sequence. Nevertheless, it still appears the plan cut testing hours too short. Kelly Johnson thought twenty test aircraft was excessive for military aircraft, and believed less than twelve would do for most programs.[7] For the Lockheed L-1011 jetliner, flight tested in 1970 to 1971, it was planned to use six aircraft for 1,695 hours; the least time on a test aircraft would be 240 hours, and the most 395, times which accord well with the original, preconcurrence system.[8]

In the late fifties the Navy, together with Lockheed and Booz, Allen,

These photos clearly show the extensive fuselage changes made in the development of the General Dynamics F-102. The later aircraft using Richard T. Whitcomb's area rule is at bottom. *Courtesy General Dynamics Corporation.*

and Hamilton, worked out a development tool subsequently adopted not only by the Air Force but by much of industry. This was Program Evaluation Review Technique (PERT), in the Air Force called PEP (Program Evaluation Procedure), a computer aid for monitoring the progress of a project. Used with the highly successful Polaris program, it seemed to offer exciting possibilities as a management tool. It has since, with expanded applications, been used on many programs, and it has proved to be useful but not the panacea or substitute for managerial ability that some hoped it would be.

THE McNAMARA REGIME, 1961–1968

While PERT expanded, the cost reimbursement contract went into a sharp decline, for it was anathema to Defense Secretary Robert S. McNamara, who has had a greater impact on defense procurement than any other individual. Perhaps he has also had the greatest individual impact on the aerospace companies as well, for the contract formula he devised brought the giant Lockheed and the long-sturdy Grumman to the brink of ruin.

When McNamara became secretary of defense he undertook to make the Defense Department more efficient. The primary means by which he sought to do this was by tightly centralized decisions using the technique of managerial economics. He employed the economists' cost-benefit analysis which he called cost-effectiveness, and opportunity cost, which compares the cost-benefits of alternative courses of action. In procurement, implementation of McNamara's ideas took place in three stages: first, there were interim, quick-action changes; second was seizure of detailed control of procurement from the military, and introduction of the economics viewpoint; and third came a shift to procurement contracting in the form he envisioned as the best.

McNamara's immediate actions started with a drive to stop cost-based contracts and use fixed-price and incentive ones instead. The new Defense Department leadership believed the cost contract encouraged waste, because profits are not directly linked to how well the job is done, and the form was flatly repudiated. By 1961 cost plus fixed fee contracts had risen to 38 percent of the total; by the end of 1963 they were down to 12 percent. There was a belief in Congress that incentive contracts were futile, a belief confirmed by a RAND study in 1966, but McNamara tried to overcome the problems by enlarging the possibilities for profit and loss in the contracts. Industry was still not convinced on incentive contracts, however, believing it was at the mercy of its subcontractors and of government negotiators who would still take the bureaucratic, cautious approach and set the contract profits as low as possible. McNamara also adopted an Air Force idea of the late fifties which tried to secure the most efficient combination of negotiated contracts and bidding; it was called "two-step procurement." In the first step, winners were selected in a design competition which disregarded price; the second step consisted of submission by the winners of sealed price bids. The 1957 decision to delay progress payments was reversed because this led to government allowance of interest as an expense, and McNamara believed this was more expensive than prompt payment; but he continued the efforts to remove the government from ownership of plant and equipment.

McNamara also tried the reverse of an Air Force experiment of the fifties. The Air Force was not favorably impressed with the paper proposals it had been getting, and it thought it might save money and time by eliminating the preliminary design stage in development. Contractors would be selected on the basis of past performance and present available capacity. But this either eliminated competition or shifted it to the prototype stage; either course was subject to criticism, and the Air Force dropped the idea. Because the paper stage is cheapest, McNamara chose to emphasize it. He sought to arrive at as great a level of definition as possible in the earliest design work. This effort ran counter to another McNamara desire: that of ending the cost overruns associated with the practice of "buying-in" to programs. To buy in was to submit deliberately low initial estimates in hopes of winning an award, and then recouping losses later in the production phase, called "getting well." These tactics were also aptly called "iceberg procurement." The trouble with the paper stage is that it is the level at which there must be the greatest vagueness and uncertainty; therefore it lends itself to double-talk and "brochuremanship": fancy briefings, brochures, pictures, and charts. The best bidder may not be apparent under such circumstances. In the F-111 design competition McNamara sent the designers "back to the drawing board" three times to get what he wanted; the proposals ran about 1,500 pages and cost Boeing, General Dynamics, and Grumman $25 million in the runoff period.[9] The peak of brochuremanship was probably reached with the C-5A; the three competitors submitted 35 *tons* of paper proposals, enough to have loaded fourteen DC-3's.[10]

The F-111 contract competition was chosen by McNamara for his second step: to assert civilian dominance over procurement. Before the F-111, the USAF's multilayered selection and review arrangement, capped by the Air Council, had controlled procurement. Civilian leaders had been loath to reverse all that military opinion; their reluctance appeared wise when the unintimidated McNamara upset the generals' preference for the Boeing proposal and thereby set off a congressional investigation. The F-111 case has received intensive study, and McNamara's judgment holds up fairly well; the military's decision was tinged with emotionalism.[11] McNamara's decision stuck after Congress had examined it, and he followed it up with a revision of procurement procedures which was designed to reduce the military's voice: he changed the service secretary's role from one of approval to one of decision.

After the F-111 decision, McNamara moved to his third step: to establish the new contract form, the Total Package Procurement Concept (TPPC), which he hoped would end buying-in, improve service specifications, cut costs, and raise industry profits. This system required contractors to bid in their original proposals for the entire development and production of an aircraft or missile. TPPC was called "womb to tomb." The first total package contract was for the C-5A; it was negotiated by the government and Lockheed at a time when the administration sought to fight a guns *and* butter war in Vietnam. Despite shortages of manpower, tools, plants, subcontractors, and suppliers, no restraint was put on the civilian economy. The inflation rate rose, but it had been set in the C-5A contract at the past peacetime level, so the estimates were low. But the objectives of TPPC foundered on more basic reasons: provision was made for price redetermination for the second production run, and consequently the contract as signed was only a variant of a cost-plus arrangement; fixed prices for critical items such as ground-support equipment were not set, allowing the possibility of transferring overruns on the aircraft to the equipment; and the worst problem of all was the belief that the C-5A could use existing technology. TPPC was intended only for projects using state-of-art development, and since Lockheed had easily extrapolated the 67,000-pound C-130 into the 132,000-pound C-141, it believed the process could be repeated up to the 320,000-pound C-5A. But as the British investigators of the Comet disasters said, "Extrapolation is the fertile parent of error." Lockheed found itself struggling with unexpected technological problems which were a product of the huge size of the C-5A. Finally, there was inadequate monitoring of progress, so that by the time gigantic overruns were apparent top Defense Department and Air Force management had to conceal the costs or admit mistakes. They attempted to conceal them.

A later TPPC contract was negotiated for the F-14, which Grumman believed would be almost a state-of-the-art airplane. But both C-5A and F-14 programs, together with the F-111, have been marked by exactly what McNamara sought to prevent: massive cost overruns. Robert Hotz of *Aviation Week* has suggested that McNamara's difficulties arose from

(From top to bottom) C-130 Hercules, C-141 StarLifter, and the outline of design L-500, which was to be the commercial version of the C-5A Galaxy and was to be the same size. The photo shows the step up in size from C-130 to C-5A. *Courtesy Lockheed Aircraft Corporation.*

the inflexibility of his contractual and managerial techniques.[12] A similar view was proposed by Gilbert W. Fitzhugh, chairman of the president's Blue Ribbon Defense Panel, who said that the total package problem was that the whole contract rested on a single decision made before the possibility of encountering "unk-unks."[13]

REACTION TO McNAMARA: 1968 ON

Faced with criticisms of the McNamara procurements because of cost overruns, the Nixon administration reacted to them individually while choosing a different procurement course. The total package contract was abandoned. The emphasis on incentive contracts was dropped. Their use in development contracts was probably ineffective and resulted in unnecessary costs. There was a return to cost reimbursement contracts for development and redetermination clauses in which periodic price reviews are called for. In the Laird Pentagon these were called "milestones." There was also a return to prototype testing—the "fly before you buy" concept—recommended by the RAND Corporation in 1963 after an analysis of the procurement record. The RAND report had examined sixteen developments, and the results appeared to endorse conclusively the use of prototypes. RAND found that design competition instead of prototypes would have resulted in building the mediocre B-45 instead of the excellent B-47, for example; and that by-passing a prototype test phase saved neither time nor money because of the cost of unexpected problems which crop up.[14] In 1970 the General Accounting Office (GAO) finished a study on Navy missile procurement and reached the same conclusion as the RAND study.[15] Since the GAO report makes no mention of the RAND paper, it apparently was an entirely independent effort and lends weight to "fly before you buy."

RETROACTIVE PRICING

While weighing the merits of prototype and test versus development-production is understandably useful, much of the emphasis on price formulas at contract time is incongruous because the government gave itself the power to reset prices after contract completion. There is a bureaucratic reason for fussing over contracts, however. If prices can be cut before or during a contract the service can use the funds elsewhere. When retroactive pricing is done, savings on lowered prices go to the treasury. The inconsistency was clearly seen by McNamara as an impediment to his hopes to cut costs through new procurement procedures.

The post–World War II vehicle for retroactively determining prices was the Renegotiation Act of 1948, which has been periodically renewed. The implementing board was given only a general formula, and has tried to produce reasonable or prudent findings. Although the opinion is denied by the board members, outside observers generally believe that return on net worth has weighed the most of all factors in its decisions. The industry has tried to get a higher return rate based on sales, an unrealistic desire because the income has been generated in large measure from government plant and equipment. The Stanford Research Institute and the GAO have recommended return be based principally on total physical assets or total capital investment.[16] The industry and McNamara were especially unhappy because many profits the Renegotiation Board tried to reclaim came from incentive contracts. In view of the problems of the incentive contract, the board has been realistic. Boeing fought hard to keep $5.8 million earned under incentive contracts in 1952, but the board contended that, contrary to gaining incentive profits through efficiency, Boeing had in fact been inefficient on the specific contracts.

It also noted that Boeing had a reputation with the Air Force as a high-cost producer. Boeing appealed, and the tax court found it to be efficient. Further appeals caused the Justice Department and the Supreme Court to review the case, and Boeing was then assessed more than the Renegotiation Board had originally sought. By 1965 the board had recovered a billion dollars in settlements, and only $120 million had been contested in the courts; and in most of these cases the board won.

The Renegotiation Board is the principal, but not the only, means the government has for retroactive pricing. From fiscal 1957 to 1964 the General Accounting Office claimed recovery of $109 million, mostly for erroneous cost data. By 1965 another pricing and profit problem existed for the aerospace companies. Profits on their government contracts were set as a percentage of the estimated cost. After World War II this percentage should have been, and was, lower than normal manufacturing rates as an adjustment for the large use of government instead of company owned plant and equipment. By 1965 the government share had declined, but the low profit percentages had not been corrected upward, largely because of the fear of bureaucrats who believed they would be criticized if they increased company profit payments above long-established levels.

The record of recoveries and of government price determination in general shows the desirability of retroactive price setting, for obviously some profits have been unearned. However, the government's inadequate consideration of profits based on private investment, and of the need for reinvestment in a capital-intensive business, for company initiated research funds, as well as for cash for costly contractual bidding which is not always reimbursed, has led to a situation in which profits, in general, have been lower than deserved; the history of failures in the industry supports such an assumption. Price determination for the big commercial market has been on a more economic basis.

VII

THE HEARTBREAK MARKET:
AIRLINERS

Since World War II the airliner market has exerted a considerable influence on the aerospace firms. Its end product is one that the firms are interested in and qualified to build; and it offers the promise of shelter from the downs of the military aircraft market, although the commercial business has not in fact proved countercyclical.

Its greatest appeal has been its potential for big sales and long, profitable production runs. Air transportation geography in the United States gives American manufacturers the advantage of a prosperous, large population with major urban centers scattered at great distances. This provides an economical basis for building many large airliners. The airline managers have usually been an optimistic group with regard to the growth of air transportation, and their attitude has been shared by the manufacturers. And results have often outrun optimistic forecasts: revenue passenger-miles, the best index of airline traffic in the period, have risen over 2400 percent since 1946 and virtually destroyed the once-dominant railroad and steamship passenger services. Yet the commercial market has been fraught with risk. Every single one of the successful types built has taken worrisome years to move into the black. The commercial airliner business has caused desperate crises twice for Douglas, General Dynamics, Lockheed, and Martin, and once for Fairchild and Northrop. Douglas' second time finished the company, although Douglas once dominated the commercial business more thoroughly than did Ford the auto industry, and in the early seventies Lockheed's fate was still unknown. Every single one of the companies studied has made at least one try for the commercial market. The aggregate failure costs would be large even without such enormous before-tax losses as General Dynamics' loss of more than $400 million on the 880/990 and Lockheed's $120 million loss on the Electra.[1] Dozens of types have been essayed and have died in various stages from desk-top designs to prototypes.

The reasons for difficulty have been manifold. Timing has been critical. The market has often been too small to support production of all the entries. There were twenty-seven designs offered in the immediate postwar years when the total number of airliners in American service was only about a thousand, and breakeven levels called for production of 200 to 350 aircraft. The state of airline finances has occasionally held back purchases. The airlines' management has sometimes misjudged the type of equipment needed even though the airlines have a basic advantage over the military in such decisions because commercial transportation is always "at war." Airline managers have ordered more aircraft than they finally purchased, and the manufacturers have misjudged both their immediate customers and the ultimate customer, the public. Sometimes inept production management has made things worse.

The difficulties listed above have both contributed to and have been aggravated by the cyclical purchase of airliners. The primary causes for the cycles have been technological advances, alternating exuberance and despair on the part of the airlines, and the economic basis of traffic. On the downside of the cycle, gluts on the used airliner market and financial problems have aggravated the gloom produced by operating results. Technological advances have produced aircraft with significantly lower operating costs and with markedly greater appeal to the passenger. Whenever this has happened, all airlines have been forced into large-scale re-equipping; if one airline alone had superior equipment it could achieve deep inroads into its competitors' business. One of Juan Trippe's coups was being the first to order *both* 707's and DC-8's, thus assuring Pan American Airways of *all* initial jetliner production. Increased traffic has caused too much buying in the euphoria of sudden prosperity and available funds. Although it was doubted for years, it is now generally accepted that the airline traffic demand is price-elastic. Efforts to capitalize on this by extravagantly promoting special fares may have contributed to the overoptimism on the upside of the cycle. Demand is also cyclical according to general business conditions. The result of all these forces has been crests in airliner buying and troughs of overcapacity which produced a great supply of seats in excess of the passenger demand.

OVEREXPANSION I: 1945–1946

When C. R. Smith, former major general and deputy commander of the 3,700-plane global Air Transport Command, returned to the presidency of American Airlines after the war, he voiced the exuberance of the times. In a speech to his executives he said: "Anybody who can't see the day when we will fly a thousand planes, damn well better get out right now."[2] Discounting the thousand planes as a figure of speech and the pep-talk exaggeration natural for such a situation, Smith still was grossly over-confident about the immediate future. Ten years later American had a fleet of 188 liners whose capacity was roughly equivalent to 500 of 1945's DC-3's.

Early traffic results in postwar 1945 and in 1946 seemed to confirm the rosy hopes, however, and there was an avalanche of orders for airliners. Revenue passenger miles doubled in one year, and transatlantic service began in earnest. In the summer of 1945 nineteen airlines ordered 409 transports of nine types and were talking about ordering another 566. Martin alone thought it would sell 700 of its 202 model twin-engine airliners. To supply this market the aircraft firms offered a wide variety of types with two, three, four, and six engines, from feeder airliners to land-based giants and flying boats. Everybody except Fairchild, Grumman, and North American was selling airliners.

Overoptimism was not the only reason for the aerospace companies' rush into airliners. With the progress in aeronautics it was expected that the old DC-3's would soon be made obsolete, a belief that was partly correct. Republic offered its Rainbow, hoping to capitalize on a wartime design. Douglas had a unique idea, contrarotating propellers behind the tail, among a variety of designs. Doubtless other companies besides Boeing and Martin and Convair took up commercial work partly as a means of keeping design and technical teams busy. If profits were not high, the ventures could still contribute to overhead costs while bridging the gap before anticipated new military work. Other factors contributing to the increase in airliner production were the cushion of tax law carry-back provisions, the gross miscalculation that development costs would run only about $3 to 5 million instead of the $40 million which was actually reached, and developmental momentum from the war. The companies were each aware of the proliferation of designs, and knew that few would succeed. Yet they pressed ahead. It seems evident that their situation fits the "prisoner's dilemma" of game theory, with the forced outcome of the choice to seek a contribution to overhead.[3] The bubble soon burst for the manufacturers when their big customer, the government, entered the used airplane market where bargain-basement asking prices were the rule. Four thousand C-47's, the military version of the DC-3, were dumped onto the market at around $60,000, and conversion costs were only $40,000 to $90,000. The total cost was thus about half the cost of a new Martin 202 or Convair 240, even though the new planes were grossly underpriced immediately after the war through miscalculation of development and production costs. In the spring of 1946, of 256 aircraft received by airlines, 146 were converted C-54's, the military version of the DC-4.

OVERCAPACITY I: 1947–1948

Directly behind the flood of used aircraft came airline problems. Revenue passenger-miles leveled off at around eight billion. Costs zoomed as the airlines had carelessly overextended themselves on equipment and personnel. The number of passenger seats doubled from 1945 to 1946, matching the increase in revenue passenger-miles. But in 1947, with the demand leveling off, the supply of passenger seats increased again about 50 percent. In 1948, with demand still stable, the seat capacity rose over 16 percent. The supply is understated because it rises faster than a physical count of the seats: the fact that the newer aircraft were faster gave their seats more "turnover." The bulk of airline operating costs are fixed, and with the supply of seats greatly in excess of demand and with other new high costs, industry losses mounted to $20 million in 1947. Fares were raised twice, for at this time air travel demand was believed to be inelastic, and some airlines sought help from the Reconstruction Finance Corporation. A retroactive subsidy payment of over a million dollars was rushed through to keep Trans World Airlines (TWA) from trusteeship.

The effect of this debacle on further purchasing was cancellation of $150 million in airliners ordered earlier, and as an additional blow export orders faded in 1947 because of the lack of dollars abroad. Not surprisingly, other government aid was sought and offered. In 1948 a bill passed the House of Representatives to provide government financing of civil transport development. Government monies mean government control, and when the aerospace industry learned that the government intended to restrict the number of firms involved to three, as well as to decide on the types made, design changes, and sales prices, the firms found the cure to be worse than the disease. The manufacturers fought the idea and it was defeated.

At the same time, a major change was in progress which had been interrupted by the war: the predominant airliner type was changing from two to four engines. The four-engine aircraft, with its greater speed, range, and capacity, was both cheaper to operate—unless it was a giant so large it could not be filled—and more appealing to passengers. It is cheaper to operate one aircraft with forty passengers than two planes with twenty passengers each. It was also important from a safety stand-point. Because of the wide gap in piston engine performance between the short-term and long-term power reliably produced, it is possible to take off with weights that cannot be sustained in cruise. The International Civil Aviation Conference in Chicago in 1945 recognized this potential hazard, and government rules setting demanding performance limits were established. These requirements added greatly to design problems, and therefore to costs, and were a spur to improvement. The indirect upshot was to force adoption of four-engine aircraft for many routes, for an engine failure is obviously less critical with four engines than with two. Thus, for operating and safety reasons the four-piston-engine airliner was a natural basic type for almost all commercial air transportation, and it represented the main market in the postwar years as conversion from twin-engine airliners took place.

EXPANSION: 1948–1955

The large four-engine airliner, with its then wide body, lent itself well to

It was the four-engine piston airliner which developed the mass market for air transportation, exemplified by the great Douglas DC-6. *Courtesy McDonnell Douglas Corporation.*

the desperate measure taken by Capital Airlines in 1948: the introduction of aircoach service. The idea had been pioneered by a nonscheduled airline, North American Airlines. Capital increased seating capacity per airliner by 50 percent and cut fares by one-third, so that, with the same number of transports, gross income would be equal. Their gains would have to come from attracting more customers, and Capital gambled on the possibility that air travel demand was elastic; their approach thus ran counter to the prevailing view, which relied on product differentiation in the form of services rather than competition with fares. Capital's experiment was opposed by other airlines, and it was permitted by the Civil Aeronautics Board (CAB) only with reluctance. United Airlines was bitterly opposed because its president, W. A. Patterson, believed strongly that demand was inelastic and that aircoach destroyed any hope for airline prosperity. United fought aircoach for years, and its final losing attack in 1952 was a charge that aircoach crowding was unsafe.

Aircoach proved hard to resist, as every additional passenger pays a fare which is almost totally a contribution to fixed costs. The concept was an instant success, but it grew slowly as the CAB gradually gave ground and airlines were forced into it by competition, for they long retained a belief in the inelasticity of demand. Its introduction coincided with a round of rail-fare increases so that railcoach tickets became more expensive than aircoach. The railroads, competitive until their fare increases and the introduction of aircoach, faded rapidly. In 1952 aircoach spread to transatlantic service, when Pan American introduced it despite reluctance on the part of the International Air Transport Association (IATA), and there was soon a decline in steamer traffic.

Aircoach, supplemented by other fare cuts, has changed air transport from a limited service to mass transportation. The airlines have come to accept the fact that they do deal with an elastic demand curve, although its shape has not been agreed upon. Some believe a cut of x percent in fares will generate a 2x percent increase in traffic. Following aircoach there have been credit systems and a flood of promotional fares: for youth, families, servicemen, wives—generally any group except businessmen, who have made up three-fourths of the customers.

Besides price competition, efforts at product differentiation have been intensive. The airlines have continuously sought to provide faster, more comfortable, and more attractive airliners, and this has enhanced aircraft sales. Aside from these marketing factors, the airlines in 1948 began to take internal measures to get their costs under control. Many executives had returned to the airlines in 1945 from service in the Army Air Forces' Air Transport Command and had retained a tendency to acquire staffs, facilities, and equipment without reference to cost. The natural trend in prosperity for business to add staff without emphasis on costs furthered the abuse; and another cause for overmanning was that the airlines at this time were recipients of government subsidy. In the shakeout of 1948–1949 United Airlines cut its staff by 20 percent without loss in efficiency. At the same time, the need for training on the postwar airliners fell off while the greater efficiencies of the newer transports were increasingly realized. With these measures the rest of the airline industry joined cost-conscious Eddie Rickenbacker's Eastern Air Lines to show profits in 1949. Eastern did not lose money any year. And as profitability returned so did airline credit revive, making purchase feasible.

Approaches taken by the different aerospace firms after World War II differed in method and in degree of success. After the war the Martin Company entered the commercial airline field for the first time. To assure success it took a market survey and sought advice from American Airlines, and it decided to get a head start on competition by by-passing the prototype stage and going directly into production. This tactic proved costly because of the changes that had to be made during production. Martin succeeded in 1947 in beating the twin-engine competition into deliveries, only to find that its product was inferior. Having followed indications of the survey and American's advice, it had an austere airliner which did not attract passengers. Worse, its operating costs were higher than the competition's. A company financial crisis followed, for there were no airline or military sales of consequence to sustain the firm. Successfully surmounting the crisis with government aid, Martin corrected its design

The airlines told Martin what they thought they wanted in an airliner, but when the 202 was built they found they had not known their own desires. *Courtesy Martin Marietta Corporation.*

errors and tried again; and it was into fabrication when the Korean War brought production dislocations and another financial crisis. The new management abandoned the commercial field to its rival, Convair, which by that time was well established as the leading manufacturer for twin-engine airliners.

Convair's path to this position was difficult. It had an advantage in design knowledge because of its wartime airline operation, Consairway. However, its first prototype, Model 110, did not sell. American Airlines suggested changes, which were adopted, although they were so extensive that the plane was renamed Model 240 and the 110's tooling was scrapped. Strikes and design changes raised costs, and Convair, like Martin, came close to bankruptcy. When the 240 did reach the market and airline expansion began at the end of the forties, it and its variations (340 and 440) proved to be the second most popular American piston twin-engine airliner built, with production totaling around 1,100.

Another company which put an airliner into serial production believed it had an advantage upon which it could capitalize. Boeing had been the first to produce a modern airliner, the 247, and the first in the U.S. to build a four-engine transport, the Stratoliner. Neither was successful, but after World War II Boeing believed it could translate its highly successful military B-29 and C-97 designs into an airliner. To help assure success, Pan American, an old collaborator, was made a virtual design partner. The military structure proved to be a handicap as well as an advantage, because extensive and costly changes were required for civil use and to meet the new civil regulations mentioned above; Boeing esti-

The only successful postwar piston two-engine airliner was the Convair 240 family. A 340 model is shown. *Courtesy General Dynamics Corporation.*

mated, however, that $25 million in development was saved by adapting the military designs. The company had set out to build an economic transport that would be popular with passengers. Popular it was, but not economic, and Boeing lost over $13 million on the Stratocruiser, having sold only 55 models.[4] This was a large but not crippling sum for a company whose sales averaged only $113 million from 1946 through 1949 when the Stratocruiser was developed and built.

The most successful airliner builder in terms of market penetration was Lockheed. Although Lockheed did not sell as many airliners as Douglas, it very much improved its market position over the thirties. Lockheed, an aggressive and daring competitor, took the risk of starting production of the civil version of its Constellation ("Connie") as soon as the war was over. It won a significant lead of eighteen months over Douglas and Boeing, gaining a secure foothold in the market of the forties and fifties. Its several versions of the Connie were developed in hot competition with Douglas, and they have proven to be among aviation's great designs.

Comparable, if not superior, to the Connies was the superb Douglas DC-4/DC-6/DC-7 family of airliners. Built in the Douglas tradition of low-cost operation for an airline, the DC-6 family continued Douglas' domination of the world's airlines in the fifties, while the revenue passenger-miles of U.S. airlines were increasing steadily at the growth market rate of around 14 percent a year.

The expansion of 1948 to 1955 was a gradual one. Because the large airlines were unenthusiastic about aircoach, its impact was underrated and delayed; for once, airline management lacked the overoptimism that has at other times led to buying too much too soon. During the Korean War, fabrication of airliners was held back for military production, an artificial restraint. There was also some uncertainty about the nature of the next "generation" of airliners: would they be piston or propjet conversions? These factors all produced an unusual period of prosperous airline expansion without the characteristic wave of enthusiastic buying followed by a glut of capacity.

THE FOREIGN CHALLENGE

The Douglas and Lockheed airliner domination might have been comfortable except for the jet engine and some determined competitors. During the Second World War, Britain decided to use its aeronautical leadership to create postwar global primacy in export aircraft. The key features of the program were government financial backing and the strategy of getting an early technological lead. The instrument was to be the revolutionary jump to jetliners and propjets.

Two of the British designs, the famous De Havilland Comet and the Vickers Viscount, achieved instant, startling success, verifying the soundness of the basic strategy. The Viscount even won a strong foothold in the American domestic market, and the Comet almost did. A total of 438 Viscounts were built.

The great expectations vanished almost as rapidly as they had seemed to be fulfilled. The Comet suffered a series of spectacular, devastating crashes. By the time the fault had been found in 1954, the Comet's lead had evaporated, its reputation had been tarnished, and its improved models faced stiff competitors in the Boeing and Douglas jetliners. Nor were the derivatives promoted as was Comet I. Although alternative propjet designs to the Viscount existed, there was no immediate back-up design for the Comet. Of necessity, the British pinned their hopes on the propjet Viscount, and the Viscount justified these hopes for awhile: its success probably contributed to Lockheed's decision to build a propjet instead of a jetliner. Its success also led the British to emphasize the propjet Britannia; but the Britannia competed when the jetliner was gaining passenger popularity, and only 80 were sold. Britain's share of the world aerospace market was 10.2 percent in 1964 and 14.5 percent in 1970.[5]

Hard on the heels of the British challenge came one from the Russians. A drive for export sales was made with their sleek Tu-104 jetliner, but negotiations broke down in 1958 with the first interested customers, Arabian airline firms, because the Russians refused to divulge performance data in advance of the sale. Hindsight indicates this was done because of poor performance and not the Russian penchant for secrecy. The Tu-104 proved very expensive to operate, in several ways, besides being a great fuel hog. After four years of regular service the Tu-104's averaged only 150 flying hours per month. Since the Tu-104 the Russians have attempted to export several airliner models to non-Communist countries with only minor success. Like the British, the Russians erred in emphasizing the propjet for awhile, and the Russian jetliners have simply not been as efficient as those of the West so far.

The French were the first to build an airliner using tail-mounted engines, a design which the American industry had long flirted with. The Caravelle pioneered the short-range jetliner when it went into service in 1959, and it was popular. France sold many for export, but production had not progressed far beyond the breakeven point when hot competition appeared from later American and British short-range jetliners. The famous Dutch Fokker company produced a high-wing propjet design, the F-27, which achieved some popularity but fell far short of Dutch ambitions for it as a DC-3 replacement. It was built by Fairchild in the United States, under license, beginning in 1957. But most Americans are of the opinion that the heavy weight penalty of longer landing gear and of structure to suspend the fuselage beneath the wing makes such an airliner unable to compete economically with a low-wing airliner; this factor is one reason that high-wing military transports have not been bought by U.S. airlines.

BOEING'S TRIUMPH: THE AMERICAN JETLINER

After much indecisiveness and many false starts the American aerospace manufacturers produced jetliners to meet the foreign competition. Despite the advantage of numerous jet bomber designs sponsored by the Air Force, and the profusion of postwar airliner designs, no jet development went beyond the paper stage for seven years, from 1945 to 1952. Americans did not realize the jetliner age was at hand. The airlines, which were struggling for most of these years and so lacked interest, money, and daring, gave the jetliner but a cursory glance because of the fuel-hungry jet engines of the period. During the fifties, when jets became available, the government thought the airlines were healthy enough to come off subsidy, a departure that caused some worry. Few persons except fighter pilots knew of the superiority of jet flight in human terms, and the jetliners' popularity was not anticipated. The hard-pressed aerospace manufacturers did not dare risk funds on as great an unknown as a jetliner. The airlines waited for the manufacturers to make a move, and the latter waited on the airlines. Yet there was continuous speculation, and design studies were made of jetliners when the industry emerged from the trough of 1947. Most planners believed that the first step should be to convert the DC-6's, Connies, and Convair 240's to propjet power, and a serious but aborted move in this direction was made by Convair with an Allison engine in 1950. The propjet, whether a conversion or a new design, was regarded as the natural and economic intermediate step to the jetliner, if not permanently better. As late as 1954 the initial jetliner market was believed to be only fifty aircraft. There was a significant exception to this line of thought, however: the brilliant Juan Trippe foresaw that the jet would be superior to the propjets, and he had already ordered Comets. It was Trippe's big jet order in 1955 for forty-five for Pan American alone, twenty 707's and twenty-five DC-8's, that truly opened the jet age in airliners. There had been enough interest in new designs before 1952 to

Unique among airliners is the General Dynamics 600. It alone is a conversion of a piston airliner to propjet power. *Courtesy General Dynamics Corporation.*

spur repeated efforts to get the government to pay for jetliner development; these calls were made vigorously after it became obvious that just talking was not an adequate response to the British challenge. The shock of finally recognizing the British lead caused an American reappraisal which was a small foretaste of the reaction to Sputnik.

Boeing was a leader in the attempt to obtain government financing. The company either accepted jet effectiveness intuitively, because of its experience with jet bombers, or was convinced by the Comet's performance. By 1954 Boeing knew the jet was superior, believing that a 707 would do three times as much work as a single piston DC-6 at only double the operating cost. Boeing underestimated: the jet would prove to do *five* times the work, not three. It had been generally expected that Lockheed would be the leader in jet transport development. Not only did Boeing score an upset, but Lockheed proved to be uncharacteristically timid, both in being late and in building a propjet. Boeing was the first American firm to move ahead into jetliners, and it forged one of the great business success stories. By 1972 Boeing had sold 2,300 jetliners for sales of about $20 billion; Douglas had sold 1,200; and Lockheed only 188 Electras.

Boeing's achievement was primarily a result of four factors. First, President William Allen's acumen provided the funds. Unable to get direct government financing, Allen created opportunities for Boeing which resulted in indirect government financing of much of the development and tooling costs. Thus he escaped the government controls which necessarily accompany direct government subsidy. Second, Boeing saw the technology far more accurately than the other firms, having studied large jet design in depth for years and having produced two superb bombers. Third, an aggressive sales campaign was undertaken. Fourth, Boeing's main competitors believed in another generation of piston liners and overrated the propjet. From being a three-time loser on airliners, Boeing became the jetliner champion.

With trepidation, Allen took the plunge on building his jet in early 1952. Having believed since 1948 that jet engines were feasible for airliners, he and his staff now thought the technology was ripe and the staff was straining to start. There was little prospect of shifting the whole financial risk to the government, after several unsuccessful attempts to do that had been made. But cash was flowing in with the Korean War boom in bombers. The stiff excess-profits tax, based on the lean 1946–1949 years, nearly eliminated profits; therefore monies could be spent on development instead of being paid in taxes, and the government indirectly would pay, not Boeing. The effective tax rate for Boeing was 82 percent, a figure which gave it an advantage in this means of financing over Lockheed, taxed at 48 percent, but not so much over Douglas at 68 percent. In 1962 the tax court ruled that Boeing was not entitled to divert tax money in this way, but by then Boeing could easily afford to pay the taxes.

Allen also anticipated the Air Force's desire for a jet tanker, and the 707 was designed to be compatible with both tanker and airliner requirements. The prototype was built so it could be a tanker, but when it was rolled out in 1954 it carried airliner-style paint. The Air Force was conducting a jet tanker design competition at this time and named Lockheed the winner over Boeing, Douglas, Convair, and Fairchild; but since Boeing had an acceptable prototype it got a production order in 1954, and ultimately built 564 KC-135's. Thus Boeing had a prototype and a production order in the same year that the Comet was permanently grounded. The timing meant that when production began on the tankers nearly all prototype and initial production problems were found and fixed at government expense. Finally, Allen persuaded Air Force Secre-

The master stroke: this is the Boeing prototype for the 707 jetliner and the KC-135 tanker at rollout on 14 May 1954. Notice the absence of windows and the implied airline markings. The paint scheme was brown and yellow. Symbolic of its grand achievement, this airplane was turned over to the Smithsonian Institution in 1972 as "one of the 12 most significant aircraft of all time." *Courtesy The Boeing Company.*

tary Harold Talbott in 1955 that production of the 707 and KC-135 on the same line would save money for the government as well as for Boeing; so the production tooling for the tanker was available for the liner. Lawyer Allen's series of financial maneuvers must be one of the shrewdest coups in business history. The importance to Boeing is shown by the fact that the company did not break even with these advantages until 1964, twelve and a half years after starting the jetliner. Additional costs were incurred, after initial development, by work on variant models which were necessary to remain in competition but which delayed reaching the break-even point. With overall financial success, however, Boeing could afford this product diversification; but other companies, Douglas for example, could not.

Despite Boeing's experience with jet bombers its progress in designing the 707 was not simple. One hundred and fifty designs on paper were made before the final one. Until 1950 the effort went into a false start. Boeing, like the other aerospace companies and despite its bomber experience, was a prisoner of the idea that the jetliner should be a direct outgrowth of the four-engine piston airliner design. Two very practical reasons for clinging to the old form was Boeing's desire to use the Stratocruiser assembly line and tools to save money, and also the strategy to produce a design useful for both tanker and transport. As work progressed and new engines were developed, the designs wavered back and forth between jet and propjet power. The first important model was even designed as a hybrid, with four piston and two jet engines, perhaps a parallel to the B-36 concept. Subsequent designs were propjet or jet. In 1950 a new direction was started which did not use Stratocruiser parts, and this approach became the 707, dominated by its B-47 and B-52 heritage. Design elements of the Stratocruiser fuselage were incorporated into the 707 as well, so that all three aircraft are its forebears.

Triumph in design was not enough. To be successful the 707 would have to be sold by a company traditionally weak in commercial transports and in competition with the long-time champion, Douglas. Boeing did succeed, even though after the achievement its salesmen were still regarded as amateurs alongside Douglas'. To counter Douglas' sales point of its long airliner experience, Boeing presented its record with big jets; to Douglas' claim that its later design could accommodate customer wishes, Boeing opposed a promise to deliver earlier and to alter the 707 to airline desires; and in fact the fuselage was widened by four inches at American Airlines' demand. To overcome inexperience of the sales staff, Allen sent his top executives out to sell. The number two man at Boeing, Wellwood Beall, an engineer who had a role in developing the 707, was sent with a team to sell in Europe; he held the authority to make decisions on the spot. Boeing devised a particular stratagem to sell to Britain's main airline, British Overseas Airways Corporation (BOAC); this was to sell first to Commonwealth countries, in the anticipation that there would then be less resentment to BOAC's purchase of an American jetliner. Transactions were made with Australia and India; then in England the Boeing men made their appointments through BOAC with government officials whose approval they needed. BOAC bought the 707. In their sales efforts, the Boeing men traveled more than Douglas', and it seems evident that Boeing's drive, ingenuity, flexibility, and hustle paid off.

While Boeing was conducting its design development in secrecy, its competitors were floundering with indecision and abortive efforts. Their success with piston airliners deceived both Lockheed and Douglas into overrating the future of the type, and made them chary of change. Lockheed mistakenly believed that by 1965 only 1 percent of airliners in service would be jets. Sales for piston airliners were high; a powerful piston compound engine became available, and with it both companies launched new stretched versions of their piston airliners. The new models sold well; for example, Douglas received 200 orders for piston liners in the first half of 1955. Their faith in propjet versions of their new airliners was misplaced: conversion failed because the airframes of the piston liners were designed for low speeds and proved unadaptable. Both companies, however, continued to believe that the propjet airliner had the best sales potential for the next decade. The highly successful Lockheed C-130 propjet military transport and Douglas' abortive C-132 propjet probably helped lead the companies along the false direction, and when Lockheed won the American Airlines design competition for a medium-range propjet airliner in 1954 the die was cast. Lockheed was committed to the Electra, being influenced by the fact that it had allowed both Boeing and Douglas to get ahead in time on jets. The Electra ultimately failed, not so much becamse of the series of disastrous crashes which resulted in a costly modification, but because the propjet could not compete with the jet. The Electra was the best, although not the only, proof that the airlines are not always the best judges of their equipment needs.

In addition to pursuing unsuccessful leads in design, Lockheed and Douglas had shrunk from taking the financial risk of starting development early; when they decided they had no choice but to go ahead, the risk had become greater because of Boeing's lead. Both delayed in hopes of getting the tanker contract, allowing themselves to be outmaneuvered by Boeing. Thus Lockheed's timely L-193 jet design of 1951, a swept-wing with the engines mounted at the tail, was allowed to die. In fairness

Lockheed won the American Airlines design competition for a propjet airliner, the Electra, which only demonstrated again that the airlines have not been the best judges of their needs. *Courtesy Lockheed Aircraft Corporation.*

92

to Douglas it must be recognized how large the financing problem was without the clever stratagem used by Boeing. When Douglas failed in 1966, its DC-8 development costs still had not been paid off. Douglas had a psychological reason to delay. The first two times that Boeing had taken a major step forward in airliner design, with Model 247 and the first Stratoliner, Douglas had followed with superior results, the DC-3 and the DC-4, which took advantage of the Boeing research and experience. Donald Douglas, Sr., said, "In our business, the race is not always to the swiftest nor the first to start," and "There may be some distinction in being the first to build a jet transport. It is our ambition at Douglas to build the best and most successful."[6] This time the strategy was a fatal mistake. Not only was Boeing ahead in time, but it had a design which Douglas was unable to improve upon significantly at first.

An even later entrant in the jetliner sweepstakes was General Dynamics, which hoped to continue to expand its commercial business. To avoid direct competition with the giants, Boeing and Douglas, General Dynamics elected to enter a new field, the medium-range jetliner, where no other company was involved except Lockheed with its Electra. The General Dynamics airplane, the 880, was well designed, but it foundered for several reasons. It was, like all Boeing's competition, late, a condition that was aggravated—perhaps decisively—by Howard Hughes' order. Hughes persuaded General Dynamics to accept a condition along with his purchase for TWA that no 880's would be sold to anyone else for a year, a condition which was intended to assure supply. The timing cost sales and it also prevented General Dynamics from sidestepping competi-

Douglas' bid for the jet age, the DC-8, was not superior in performance to the competitive Boeing entry. The resultant financial, managerial, and engineering strains seriously damaged Douglas. *Courtesy McDonnell Douglas Corporation.*

tion, for after Boeing completed its 707 it shrank the design, in 1957, to offer a medium-range airliner, the 720.[7] It was more economical for maintenance and supply reasons for an airline to have an all-Boeing or an all-Douglas fleet than to mix brands of aircraft or engines. General Dynamics found itself in further difficulty with the 880 because the capricious Howard Hughes vacillated and, in an internal TWA squabble, ordered his 880's, in various stages of completion, into storage. Finishing these aircraft, once they were half completed and off the assembly line, was very expensive. General Dynamics also suffered from a lack of cost control and supervision.

With the 880 in trouble, General Dynamics sought to recoup through technology instead of cutting its losses. In 1958 it designed the 990, a full-scale jetliner, hoping to compete with the 707 and DC-8 by using Whitcomb's area rule on an airliner for the first time. The new design was intended to give the 990 a significant speed advantage. The first model failed to reach the desired speed, and extensive modifications to reduce drag had to be made. When the 990 did achieve its design speed, it became apparent that it still lacked a competitive advantage: the margin in speed would have been decisive in the piston age but was relatively small compared to the 707 and DC-8, and the 990's range was also somewhat less than its competitors'. In addition, to get the desired speed General Dynamics reduced seating from six to five abreast, an arrangement which the airlines considered to be less advantageous. The 990 did not sell in any numbers: only 37 were built. It's timing was even worse than the 880's, coming out in 1961 during a period of overcapacity for the airlines. The 880/990 program was a financial disaster, losing over

An excellent but ill-fated design was the 880, which was General Dynamics' bid to maintain its short-range airliner market. *Courtesy General Dynamics Corporation.*

94

The double-or-nothing airliner. With 880 sales in difficulty General Dynamics sought an end-run through technology with the 990. This view shows the bulges on the trailing edges of the wings, which were an adaptation of Richard T. Whitcomb's area rule. *Courtesy General Dynamics Corporation.*

$400 million and bringing mighty General Dynamics to its knees. The company has since toyed with the idea of returning to commercial aviation with its own design but has not committed itself beyond studies.

The final entry in the first wave of jet-age airliners was Fairchild. This company sought to sidestep both competition and development costs by entering the short-range market as a licensee of the Dutch Fokker two-propjet F-27 Friendship. Fairchild hoped it would replace the DC-3, at last, so that total sales would be 1,000. A market survey in 1954 was favorable, but hopes to sidestep competition ran into trouble when General Dynamics produced a kit for easy and cheap conversion of its Convair 240 family to propjets.[8] A major problem was that Fairchild's market, the feeder airlines, lacked access to funds. By 1963, after six years of production, only 101 had been built. Fairchild had run into expensive problems —in adapting the airframe to its own production, with language, with Fokker's handcraft manufacturing methods, and with the metric system— and although Fairchild's difficulties were modest compared to those of Lockheed and General Dynamics, they caused a corporate crisis. From 1958 through 1960 Fairchild lost $29 million, before taxes, on sales of $347 million. Net worth fell from $37 to $16 million.

OVEREXPANSION II: 1956–1960

With the production restraints of the Korean War removed, the airlines embarked on a second airliner buying spree in the last half of the fifties which caused them to join the transport makers in travail. Passenger revenue-miles in the early and midfifties grew at a rapid rate. High earnings and the rapid depreciation allowances of the Korean War years provided purchasing funds. The last improvement on piston airliners became available and made up most of the buying wave of 1956 to 1958, as airlines were still skeptical of the jet. Just behind an order surge of $250 million for piston liners came the first wave of propjet and jetliner buying for delivery in 1959 to 1960, kicked off by a Pan American order in 1955 worth $269 million, the largest in airline history to that time. The airlines now had a situation which was very nearly double-equipping, a result of the error in timing the advent of the jet age. The over 850 transports which went to the American airlines in this buying orgy involved a capital investment, in flight equipment alone, of over $1.5 billion, almost 50 percent more than the original cost of the 1955 fleet. For the significance of the size of this sum it can be compared to trunk-line assets of $1.3 billion and net worth of $650 million. The role played by competitive pressure in buying the jets is implied in the lament of C. E. Woolman, the president of Delta Airlines: "We are buying airplanes that haven't been fully designed, with millions of dollars we don't have, and we are going to operate them off airports that are too small, in an air traffic control system that is too slow, and we must fill them with more passengers than we have ever carried before."[9]

At first the airlines worried about finding the funds for this growth, but long-term financing was readily found in banks and insurance companies. The financial community was impressed by the volume of traffic the airlines had reached, and accepted air transportation as being on a firm foundation. But *Fortune* magazine ran an article in 1956 expressing alarm at the buying binge, calling it a flight from reality.[10] C. R. Smith, the president of American Airlines whose overoptimism in 1946 is reported above, scoffed at the pessimism, saying demand would prove higher and supply lower, and that *Fortune* had failed to consider the retirement of older aircraft.[11]

OVERCAPACITY II: "THE PIT" (1957–1962)

It turned out that it was Smith who miscalculated, for the binge generated the hangover of another period of overcapacity, beginning almost as he wrote. The number of seats had tripled in a decade; as before, costs were allowed to rise outside the need for training expenditures for the new jetliners; the Civil Aeronautics Board, like the airlines, repeated the error of assuming permanent prosperity had arrived, and busily added carriers to routes; the used airliner market temporarily collapsed under the supply: nearly new DC-7's and Connies would not sell at any price in 1958, although the airlines were able to pass on some of this problem to the sales-hungry manufacturers by demanding trade-in discounts for piston airliners. The productivity and reliability of the jets greatly exceeded general expectations. A graphic example is the $5 million 707, which could carry as many transatlantic passengers in a year as the $30 million *Queen Mary*, and with about one-tenth of the fuel; and one 707 flew 250 million seat-miles per year compared to 50 million for a DC-6B.

With the long-range jets driving the pistons and propjets onto the medium- and short-range routes, the aerospace manufacturers turned their attention to the latter markets during this period of overcapacity. With the failure of the Lockheed Electra, the Convair 880, and the Fairchild F-27, the sole competitors at first were Boeing and Douglas. Boeing first shrank the 707 to a four-engine medium-range jet, the 720, in 1957. Soon thereafter it decided there was a market for another step-down in size, but this time the step was not so easy. Continuing downwards in scale while keeping four engines was uneconomic, but the use of two engines ran into the safety-reliability prejudice, backed by government regulations, held over from the less powerful and less reliable piston engine. Another prejudice long delayed another option, adaptation for three engines.[12] Boeing's consultations with the buyers were of little help: American Airlines believed twin engines was the answer; United and Continental wanted four engines; Eastern and TWA suggested three. Boeing finally shook itself free of the piston tradition and started in 1960 to design the three-jet 727, which may prove to be the most successful jetliner, and at that time the Federal Aviation Agency (FAA) began lifting some of the restrictions on jets that were derived from the piston era.

Boeing's decision to broaden its product line, although ultimately wise, meant development costs, and the 707 family continued in the red during the period of airline overcapacity. The abrupt twilight of the bomber ended its lucrative military-production days, and Boeing's finances were difficult. But if finances were strained for Boeing, they were critical for Douglas, which also believed there was a market for short-range jetliners. The disastrous decision to allow Boeing the jetliner lead meant many lost sales, and Douglas found itself in the familiar position of incurring heavier development costs than expected. Also, it moved down the DC-8 learning curve abnormally slowly and without benefit of the shrewd gambits that Allen had pulled off. Douglas, like Boeing, was

The Fokker and Ford trimotors won a major but very transitory place in airline history. The three-engine concept returned with the versatile and efficient Boeing 727, whose success encroaches on that of the past champion: the Douglas DC-3. *Courtesy The Boeing Company.*

also seeing its government business wither, removing a financial prop. Douglas tried a gambit of its own: it agreed with the French to build and sell the short-range Caravelle as a means of avoiding development costs. But Douglas found itself unable to sell the Caravelle, and it was forced to go ahead with designing its short-range two-jet DC-9.

OVEREXPANSION III: THE JETS TAKE OVER (1965–1968)

The DC-9 was ready when the next period of violent overexpansion began. By 1963 the American economy had turned upwards, and the continued growth of air traffic, as the jet showed its superiority, had caught up with the supply of seats. Piston airliners still made up 57 percent of all commercial transports but were relegated to the short-range routes; they had by then been amortized. With economical short-range jets available—the Douglas DC-9, the Boeing 727, and the later 737—the airlines undertook to go all-jet, exactly as Douglas and Boeing had hoped. This time there was a renewed British invasion with a similar short-range jet, the BAC-111, a successor to the Viscount. The BAC-111 even entered service months before the DC-9 in 1965, but the American airlines preferred the Boeing and Douglas products. On 1 January 1969 there were 543 727's, 266 DC-9's and 60 BAC-111's in service on U.S. airlines. A third contender in the short-range market was again Fairchild, offering an improved version of its highwing propjet, the FH-227. Airline preference was for the low-wing jet, however, and sales for the FH-227 were only 68 in the boom years of 1966 to 1968.

The popularity of the slick, comfortable small jets made them profitable, even when their trips were so short they started descent immediately after reaching cruise altitude.[13] In 1965 air travel demand took a sudden jump, and in 1967 100 billion passenger revenue-miles were flown, to be compared to less than 50 billion in 1962. In 1966 the U.S. airlines added as much seat capacity as they had possessed in 1950. They now had more jet transports than pistons, 1,378 to 873, and the pistons provided only 11 percent of the service. In 1967 the airlines accepted deliveries of 388 jetliners worth $2.1 billion, and had another $10.5 billion worth on order. In 1970 75 percent of U.S. domestic air travel was for less than 500 miles, and jets made up 57 percent of the liners serving this market.

Amidst the euphoria customary at such a time, the reequipping turned into another buying binge. Money was easily borrowed because of the profit record of the jets, and the jets themselves were producing a high cash flow. Besides making massive equipment purchases, the airlines behaved as they usually have in other such prosperous times, adding

Despite its virtues the short-range Fairchild FH-227 could not overcome the view by United States airlines that a high-wing design has too many disadvantages for an airliner. *Courtesy Fairchild Industries, Inc.*

new flights until empty seats were epidemic, hiring many persons, and granting huge wage increases. The Civil Aeronautics Board followed its customary pattern on the upside of the cycle with a flood of new route awards, crowned by more new ones in 1969 than in the previous thirty years combined.

By 1969 the inevitable crisis returned. Costs had begun to outrun revenues. Douglas had been swamped with orders for which it was totally unprepared and which generated capital problems similar to those of a new company expanding out of its beginner size. Giant though it was, Douglas failed in 1966 in the midst of the boom and was absorbed by McDonnell.

During the prosperous period, development was begun on two new types of airliner design. With improved thrust-to-weight ratios it was hoped that a giant airliner, or "airbus," with high performance and an expected one-third lower seat-mile cost, was practical. The new jumbos, designed with two or three engines, were aimed primarily at forcing the retirement of the more operationally expensive 707's and DC-8's. Design work on the C-5A strategic transport had assured the jet makers that giants were practical, and the three leading contenders for the C-5A contract now adapted their C-5A bids to commercial purposes. Boeing designed its 747, Lockheed its L-1011, and Douglas the DC-10.

This time Boeing was too early. In 1965 it adapted its C-5A design with the same engines, producing a heavy, four-engine model; and having made this investment Boeing was reluctant to build a new design when better engines were imminent. The new designs broke with the past sufficiently to give Lockheed a chance to regain a leading position in commercial aviation. It seized the opportunity aggressively but lost its time advantage in the crisis following the collapse of its engine supplier, Rolls Royce, in 1971. Douglas had delayed working on the new designs because of its financial problems; but after the merger, McDonnell's firm leadership and desire for commercial business finished the development of the DC-10. With Lockheed's lead lost, and because of the great similarity between the L-1011 and the DC-10, intense price competition resulted between Lockheed and Douglas; there was a series of price cuts between the two companies in 1968.

Meanwhile, Boeing was diverted by its concentration on the troubled technical development of the second new type of design, a supersonic transport (SST), under a government contract awarded in 1966. The SST was eventually canceled because it lacked an economic basis and was opposed by environmentalists. And the giant airliner undoubtedly contributed to the death of the SST, for it was cheaper and it offered possible solutions to some of the pollution and congestion problems arising in air travel. Boeing lost the time spent working on the SST, and the 747 went into service in 1969, just as the airlines entered another overcapacity crisis; the L-1011 and the DC-10 went into service in 1972, when conditions were still worse.

THE EXPORT MARKET

By the time of the giants, American dominance of the world airliner market had been retained; 70 percent of the free-world airliners were of U.S. manufacture, and about 90 percent of the jetliners. After 1948 dozens of new ones were exported each year, with over 400 delivered in the years 1966 to 1968. In the sixties their value, plus the lucrative parts sales, was in the hundreds of millions of dollars; it reached one billion in 1968 and one and one-half billion in 1970. There has also been a large business in used civil aircraft.

Exports of military aircraft, new and used, have also been a valuable market, despite some political restrictions such as denying sales to countries which our government thinks should buy butter and not guns. After the war military exports were primarily financial aid, but with the American balance-of-payments problem they have become a tool of fiscal as well as defense policy since 1963. The principal salesman has been the Department of Defense, a fact which may have inhibited rather than spurred sales. From 1949 to 1966 the U.S. government sold $16.1 billion

Long the backbone of the free world's air forces was the Lockheed F-104, a success in the export market. Shown is the Japanese version, the F-104J. Seven nations manufactured F-104's for use by fourteen countries. *Courtesy Lockheed Aircraft Corporation.*

worth of arms and gave away \$30.2 billion worth; the military aircraft share of arms sales was about one-third. Most of this business was not handled directly by private firms. The biggest single program was the building of F-104's for export and the licensing of their manufacture abroad: 600 were sold abroad, and 1,500 were built under license. Foreign aerospace products have been imported, but the balance has run heavily in the American favor.

FIGURE I

FACTORS EXPANDING OR REDUCING AIRFRAME INDUSTRY MARKETS

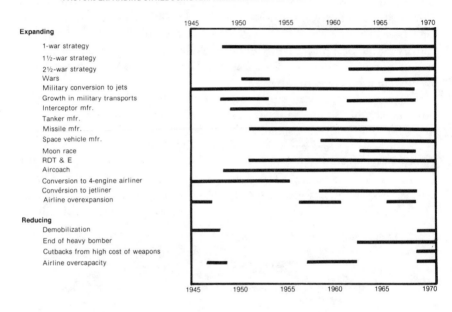

Source: Summary of text.

Figure I presents a chart which sums up the helpful or harmful effects of the political, economic, and technological events on the aerospace industry's markets, military and space as well as commercial.

VIII

DESIGN OR DIE:
THE SUPREME TECHNOLOGICAL INDUSTRY

From the beginning of the aerospace industry, a high quality of designs has been necessary for full success. This factor has not been sufficient of itself to assure basic corporate success, as the Douglas failure in 1966 showed, nor has lack of it inevitably led to failure. Fairchild has not had a winning major design of its own since the C-119, which ceased production in 1954. How far designs must be pushed to the edge of knowledge is illustrated by the unidentified airframe maker who told a reporter, "The art of aircraft building used to be defined as the art of building things that almost don't work."[1]

A high proportion of designs are begun with major conceptual flaws, and without final salable designs of its own a company is forced to become a subcontractor. Although this can be a profitable business, it makes the company dependent upon the designs and success of others, and such arrangements mean that the company must please two customers, government and the prime contractor, at the same time; they also shift competitive survival to the production area, where there is less opportunity for competitive advantage. All companies can engage in price competition, but product differentiation is less subject to instant competition, especially if it is based on superior technology. Since under the military procurement system design competition is usually by sole-source negotiation, winning the design competition is the most important business function. It is no coincidence that the major companies have generally been the great designers.

103

Besides being of high quality, winning designs have occasionally resulted from exceptional managerial foresight. Striking examples in which management accurately foresaw a need long before the customer, made extensive preparations, and thereby clinched an advantage include the KC-135/707, Atlas, Minuteman, and Mercury. The one notable breakdown of this advantage was with the F-111, where Boeing's lead in ideas was taken away by McNamara and given to General Dynamics to spur design competition. This factor is especially important when technology is advancing rapidly and there are several technical revolutions at once, as in the fifties.

Foresight, even at a less striking level, was more critical after World War II than before. In the thirties the starting point for design, the engine, required little choice of design or flexibility. Only piston engines were practical, in air- or liquid-cooled forms. Technical considerations made even this choice less important than one might think. The Navy and the airlines found distinct advantages to the air-cooled engine because it was lighter. In the United States, only land-based fighters used liquid-cooled engines, and this was because the smaller frontal area meant less total drag and therefore higher speeds. The requirement for propellers limited the possibilities for locating engines in the design. Subsonic flight permitted simple wing and tail designs.

ENGINE PROLIFERATION

The advent of jet propulsion greatly expanded design options and created much uncertainty in choosing the most suitable propulsion or power. At first the piston engine was still competitive, for although it was slightly less powerful it was economical. Its low fuel consumption appealed to the airlines and appeared to be necessary for the ranges the USAF wanted and the take-off and landing requirements of the Navy. A modification of the piston engine appeared in the late forties, the turbo-compound, which combined piston and jet by getting thrust from the piston's exhaust gases. Then there were the simple jet engine and the propjet engine, and the possibility of using both piston and jet engines together—operational aircraft which were such hybrids were the B-36, KB-50, FR, AJ, and P2V. Other possibilities which were not to prove useful were the ramjet and pulse jet engines. At one point in 1952, Douglas was working on airplanes using piston, jet, propjet, and rocket engines. Fewer than one-fourth of the aircraft developed between 1945 and 1958 were completed with the engine models originally planned for them.

The designer's dilemma in the circumstances is that often he does not deal with proven, or existing, engines. The justification for a new aircraft is improved performance, and this rests upon better, or future, engines. Thus the designer must select an engine from a shopping list of expectations, and in the immediate post–World War II period the designers found themselves spending as much time in analyzing possible engine-airframe combinations as they had formerly spent in the entire preliminary design of aircraft.

For the engines lacking propellers, the designers were faced with new questions of engine locations. Jets could be mounted inside the fuselage, alongside the fuselage, at the tail, inside the wings, under the wings, at the wing tips, or in pods. One of the long-time disadvantages of the twin-engine fighter, that of mounting the engines far from the longitudinal axis, no longer applied because the propeller was no longer required. Over the years, American designers have shown a preference for pod and tail mounts for large aircraft and for internal engine installation along the longitudinal axis for smaller aircraft.

At first the Air Force thought the jet was the engine of the future. The Navy believed in the propjet and pushed its development. The Navy thus continued its conservatism; it had kept biplanes as long as it could, then the piston engine, and finally the propeller. Each time one of these had to be abandoned, the difficulty of shipboard operations increased. Because of the success achieved by the Navy in propjet development, the Air Force wavered in its belief in the early fifties. But by the midfifties technology settled the issue for years to come. There were large increases in power in the jet engine and small ones in the piston, and the economical by-pass, or fan, jet engine became available; the piston engine was now hopelessly obsolete. The by-pass engine also struck at the main advantage of the propjet: economy. This, plus the inherent propjet disadvantages of propeller limitations and greater engine complexity, mostly in its cantankerous gearing, meant the propjet was badly outclassed. A contributory jet engine development of the time was thrust augmentation, or afterburning, which provided a great burst of power. Although it was limited to short periods because of its high fuel-consumption rate, afterburning eliminated the need for aircraft rocket engines to provide take-off boost, interceptor climb rates, and dash speeds.

By the late fifties the engine proliferation period was over. Since then the jet has reigned supreme as the engine for all but lighter aircraft. In this same period, missiles and space vehicles became important and their best engine is the rocket; only the unmanned aircraft-type guided missiles have not used rocket engines.

Of interest to design was the number of engines required. The growing power-to-weight ratio of the jet permitted a reduction in the number of engines at the same time that jet reliability improved the safety factor. From the six-engine B-47 and eight-engine B-52, design has gone to the three-engine L-1011 and DC-10. A reduction in the number of engines simplifies design in general, although two in wing pods and one in the tail may be more complex to design than four in wing pods. An important exception to this trend has been the increasing American use of two-engine fighters. This perverse development is a result of three conditions. First, the American fondness for gadgetry and desire for safety through multiple back-up systems adds weight; the resultant dinosaur needs power so badly that even the powerful modern jets must be mounted in pairs. Second, since the jet engine can be mounted in pairs alongside the horizontal axis, the performance penalty of a two-engine fighter is less conspicuous than in the piston age. Third, it has been argued that the two-engine fighter is safer, an argument which appeals to the top USAF leaders. These officers have been devoted to the big bomber, a multiengine aircraft in which engine redundancy does add to safety, and their flying careers largely embrace the era of the less re-liable piston engine. But the safety argument for a fighter is unacceptable. "Safe" for a wartime fighter means superior performance, and two engines are a handicap for that. Further, having two engines means more weight, a factor which decreases safety even in peacetime, and doubles the probability of failure of one engine as well as the volume of space vulnerable to battle damage. Finally, safety records do not support the intuitive view that two-engine fighters are safer, according to Lockheed, and the conclusion is substantiated by published Air Force figures for what appears to be fiscal year 1968. The service's twin-engine fighters had an accident rate which was 20 percent higher than that of its single-engine fighters.[2] Air Force official accident data must be used with caution, however, for some have been influenced by subjective and policy considerations.

TRANSONIC AND SUPERSONIC AIRFRAMES

While the jet expanded the engine options in the early postwar period, it also threw airframe design into turmoil because traditional structures were inadequate at the new high speeds. During World War II the Germans started work on solutions to the design problems of high-speed flight. Their principal answers were to sweep the wings and tail, or to use a delta (triangular-shaped) wing. The American aerospace industry and NASA have refined these successful ideas which have been used on most post–World War II transonic and supersonic aircraft. It should be noted that Americans succeeded in designing an efficient supersonic straight wing. The F-104 has one. In themselves these wing designs have not been enough for the demands of modern flight, however, and the area-rule and variable-sweep designs have also been used.

Aside from assuming the shapes necessary for high-speed flight, structures had to be changed to meet the resultant increased stresses. This problem has been met principally by heavier structures and new materials. The greater lift provided by higher speeds permitted shortening wing spans and deepening chords, making it easier to design strong structures. For the fastest aircraft, complex honeycomb-in-a-sandwich structures have been used for the greatest strength-to-weight relationship. These structural changes have had major impacts on development costs and production processes. Larger, higher-performance, and therefore more expensive test facilities had to be built. The easiest example to cite is the wind tunnels that had to be built to explore supersonic speeds. A comparison of the engineering man-hours taken to first flight for the

A General Dynamics FB-111A with wings fully swung for high-speed flight. *Courtesy General Dynamics Corporation.*

A General Dynamics FB-111A with its variable-sweep wings fully extended for slow-speed flight. *Courtesy General Dynamics Corporation.*

The best USAAF fighter to see action in World War II was the North American P-51. Designed in a crash effort, the first aircraft (not shown) had many minor engineering faults. *Courtesy Rockwell International Corporation.*

The first flight of the North American F-86D took place only nine years after that of the P-51. Yet the F-86D absorbed a horrendously greater amount of engineering time than did the P-51. *Courtesy Rockwell International Corporation.*

piston P-51 fighter and for the jet F-86D interceptor shows the trend in design. The figures appear in Table VIII-1, but they must be compared with caution. A fighter is a much simpler machine than an interceptor. The P-51 was designed in haste because the British order for it allowed only 120 days for construction of a prototype. The F-86D was designed at a more leisurely pace. Finally, the F-86D was probably subjected to the costly influences which are discussed below and in Chapter XI.

TABLE VIII-1
DESIGN AND ITS EFFECT ON ENGINEERING MAN-HOURS

Design Function	P-51	F-86D
Aerodynamics	600	75,520
Windtunnel	2,077	42,006
Stress	2,985	116,075
Detail design	34,963	640,381
Flight test	725	84,817
Research	0	66,512
Miscellaneous	530	109,681
Total hours	41,880	1,131,992
Number of drawings	1,100	6,572

Source: *Aviation Week,* 27 Aug. 1951, p. 23.

Before the problems of high-speed flight for aircraft were resolved, designers were called upon to develop ballistic missiles and space vehicles. For the most part these new airframes presented conditions that followed the same development trends as those of the progression to jet from piston aircraft, but they were another seven-league step.

THE ELECTRONIC AIRFRAME

Concurrent with the jet age, another technology experienced rapid growth and development: electronics. Possessing great usefulness to aerospace vehicles for communications, navigation, weapons control, and defense against ground-based electronics, electronic devices have multiplied. In the industry they are called avionics. Despite effective miniaturization, they represent much volume and weight in the aggregate, and by 1959 they made up 25 percent of the cost of an aircraft and 35 percent of a missile's. Therefore they present to the designers serious problems in accommodation inside an airframe which has become cramped for space and has desperate overweight tendencies. Like compulsive eaters, the customers find it hard to resist adding attractive items to their wants. In addition, the various avionics systems must be integrated with the airframe and with the vehicle's purpose, a major design problem in itself.

THE PROVING OF DESIGN

The problems of design do not end with the assembly of engine, airframe, and avionics into a prototype. A series of critical flight tests must follow, so that the design can be verified in its performance and in its basic safety. Lacking a small margin of performance will make a military aircraft or an airliner obsolete. An unsafe aircraft is unbearably expensive to the military, and is intolerable to the air traveler. Consequently, flight tests are exhaustive for military aircraft and for airliners; the latter's final governmental examination is called certification.

Introduction and modification of governmental requirements for airliners have not been simple, for the Civil Aeronautics Administration (CAA), predecessor of the Federal Aviation Agency, had difficulty with the technical details. The manufacturers objected to some of the new rules and expected to have them altered. Some went ahead with designs as they wanted to do them, and then failed to win their arguments. The Boeing Stratocruiser was a victim of this situation as well as of labor troubles; and its tests, certification, and modifications took seventeen months from 1948 to 1949: Boeing blamed the certification tests for much of the company's loss on the airliner. The airliners of this era had manufacturer's flight tests of 300 to 500 hours, and certification tests then brought the totals to 800 to 1,000 hours before carrying passengers. The costs ran up to $7,000 an hour. Despite this procedure airlines had fatal crashes, and the rules were tightened each time.

The Comet disasters of 1954 spurred an even more rigorous approach. The Comet affair was still fresh when the Lockheed Electra was put through intensive tests in 1957 and 1958, but even this did not prevent its structural disintegration while in service. Undoubtedly, the Comet also influenced the DC-8's extensive flight tests in 1958 and 1959, which lasted for 2,284 hours. The per hour cost now ranged up to $10,000, and flight tests for the 727 in 1962 and 1963, and for the 737 in 1967, cost $16 million for each. The 747 flight-test plan in 1969 called for 780 hours of manufacturer's tests and 490 hours of certification tests over 11 months, for a cost of $28 million. The tests on the DC-10 in 1970 cost $26,000 an hour. These costs are obviously a heavy and unavoidable burden in the design and manufacture of airliners. They also provide an insight into the procurement experiments examined in Chapter VI.

UNEVEN PROGRESS

Aerospace technology from 1945 to 1972 has been divided into different periods in several ways above, but another approach should be recognized. Frederic M. Scherer, of the University of Michigan, has divided the technology into three periods based upon its degree of difficulty.[3]

The first period, or generation, had rich possibilities which could be exploited easily, and shortcuts were feasible. This period produced jet bombers, surface-to-air missiles, submarine-launched missiles, satellites, and manned space flight. The second period developed the technologies which had been recognized in the first but had been known to be less easily brought into operation. The hardware in this class was miniaturized nuclear warheads, aircraft capable of Mach 2.2 speeds, more accurate and reliable missiles, and hardened missile silos. Now, Scherer sees a third generation where diminished returns have set in: to get a relatively small increment of improved weaponry, enormous effort must be expended. Scherer, therefore, sees aerospace technology as having advanced with decreasing rapidity since World War II, and as having arrived at a near-plateau. It can also be inferred that a curve of costs would be of an inverse shape for the period. The first revolt against the general progression took place during and after the Korean War.

Frustrated by lost victories and dead buddies in combat against the lightweight and nimble MiG-15, USAF fighter pilots mounted a campaign in the Korean War to trim the lard off their obese fighters, which they called "lead sleds." The effort coincided with concern in Congress over the steeply rising costs of aircraft and with worry over the high quality of the lightweight Russian fighters. The Air Force bowed to the drive, and the F-104 Starfighter was designed under Lockheed's Kelly Johnson to be the fighter pilot's dream airplane. Light, designed for easy production and therefore maintenance, and with superb performance, the Starfighter was an excellent fighter. It did not go all the way to lightness, for Johnson believed some of the stripping desired by the fighter pilots was not justified by the performance gained. But it reversed the trend of rising costs, for its price was half that of the contemporary heavy, sluggish F-100. By the time the F-104 was ready for production in 1956 the fighter pilot campaign had lost its momentum, war memories were fading rapidly, and only token amounts were bought by the USAF. Instead, the Air Council returned to buying expensive "fighters" that had bomber characteristics, such as the elephantine F-105, the "Thud." The F-104 was produced in quantity, but only for our allies.

A third group contributed to the general revolt of the early fifties against runaway weight and cost. These were designers, and their most outspoken member was E. H. Heinemann, chief engineer at Douglas' El Segundo plant. Heinemann's accomplishments included three excellent piston attack planes: the A-20, the A-26, and the A-1. Heinemann insisted that insufficient attention was paid to eliminating needless equipment, and that this was the main villain in the weight-cost spiral.[4] He contended that equipment added resulted in a multiplier effect of ten times in the gross weight, although other estimates ranged down to seven. Thus, an excess crew member, with man and his equipment weighing 200 pounds, meant aircraft gross weight would jump 2,000 pounds to accommodate him, because of necessary structural modifications and additions in fuel. Two thousand pounds adds a critical burden to fighters and attack aircraft as well as to design and production costs.

Heinemann got a chance to practice what he preached. In the Navy's jet reequipping program a replacement was sought for his A-1. An earlier attempt had been made with the propjet A2D, but its engine's technical problems were never mastered. Meeting Navy specifications for the new plane without weight-saving efforts meant an appalling weight of 45,000 pounds. But Heinemann produced a masterpiece, the 1954 A-4, which weighed less than 10,000 pounds empty and 17,000 pounds loaded. It had only one-third the number of structural parts of earlier Douglas attack designs. For example, a skin one-tenth of an inch thick was used

The fighter pilot's fighter plane: performance with simplicity. The Lockheed F-104 with Lockheed test pilot Tony LeVier. *Courtesy Lockheed Aircraft Corporation.*

An American classic, the McDonnell Douglas A-4 shows the virtues of simple design. *Courtesy McDonnell Douglas Corporation.*

at the cockpit, eliminating stiffeners and thereby reducing aircraft size, as well as greatly facilitating production. A favorite with the Navy, the A-4 has been called "Heinemann's Hot Rod." It was a workhorse aircraft in Vietnam and was still in production after nineteen years.

Heinemann may have proved his point but he, other engineers, the fighter pilots, and Congress did not arrest the cost spiral, for reasons that will be apparent in Chapter XI.

CAMPUS OR INDUSTRY?

Design can be said to have been a major growth section of the aerospace industry, if it is interpreted to include research, development, test, and evaluation (RDT&E). When newly created, the USAF, lacking an arsenal system, was forced to turn to industry for weapons R&D. Universities were far from being ignored, however, and they were soon devoting a heavy share of their capacity to defense research. The aerospace industry itself began faintly to resemble a research campus with shops attached. And this was a major development for that industry, which had previously relied for the most part on NACA. NACA itself switched from its quick-fix role in World War II when the reports on German aeronautical progress began to flow in. From then until Sputnik in 1957, NACA plunged into supersonic research. Notable was the development of the area-rule and variable-sweep wings. The advent of space flight meant a massive re-orientation by the reorganized agency, now NASA, into primarily space R&D.

But the postwar situation was concurrent R&D by both NACA/NASA and the aerospace industry. The industry's participation in research coincided with the great technological revolutions of the period after World War II, and that part of the aerospace business which does RDT&E for the Defense Department grew tenfold from $758 million in 1951 to almost $7.75 billion in 1967. One of the giant companies, North American, evolved so that its business was primarily in this area although its airplane production has continued, and there has been production of other hardware such as rocket engines and avionics. In 1961 North American had 22,000 scientists and engineers out of a workforce of 88,000 men. Since then, North American's proportion of scientists and engineers declined. In 1966, the last year before its merger, North American had 16,000 researchers out of a workforce of 92,000. An extreme indication of the role of R&D in design is the report that North American put *15 million* engineering man-hours into the XB-70, and this was only to first flight. Thousands of engineers have been used on some projects: 2,600 on the B-58, 2,500 on the C-141, and 3,600 on Minuteman.

ENGINEER PROLIFERATION

Over the years, as the aerospace companies recruited these armies of engineers, there were often cries of a "shortage," and much publicity has been given to such an idea. From an economic point of view, of course, there was no shortage; rather, there were fewer engineers who would work for the aerospace companies at the pay offered than the firms desired to have. During the "shortage" there was a steady stream of engineers' letters to the editor of *Aviation Week*—and there were too many for too long to be written by a few cranks—which asserted that engineers in the aerospace industry were underused and subjected to mismanagement by personnel officers and management. A study of 1956, repeated in 1959, appeared to confirm this.[5]

Besides the study and the persistent letter-writing, there are other indications that engineer requirements of the aerospace industry should have been lower. In 1971 A. Scheffer Lang of MIT said of the defense companies, "Their engineering approach relies heavily on dollar overkill as the way to solve problems."[6] Kelly Johnson of Lockheed had an ordinary engineering department of 5,000 men in 1956. He found that only 5 percent of their time was spent on making hardware.[7] The brilliant Floyd Odlum, former president of Convair, expressed disbelief in 1956 that any single airframe project using as many as 2,000 engineers could have satisfactory productivity.[8] These circumstances may go far to explain why roughly *half* of military and civil aircraft developed since 1945 have been disappointing performers. It is obviously a policy of expediency to accept mediocrity, but it is not in the long-run interest of a firm because its products may gradually acquire an unsavory reputation. Perhaps the general situation was best summed up in 1971 by Edward G. Uhl, president of Fairchild; "We have . . . gotten into the bad habit of heaping people onto projects without regard to the quality or performance of the people. The trap we've fallen into is to believe that a thousand incompetents properly organized can do the job of a few dozen outstanding, well-trained, experienced people."[9]

The most telling criticism of massed-manpower engineering practices is the record of the "Skunk Works." Starting with the XF-80, this technique has been used periodically by Lockheed's Kelly Johnson to produce the U-2, the JetStar business jet, and the A-11 (F-12). The XF-80, it will be recalled, used 23 engineers and was designed in 143 days; the U-2 also

115

The famous Lockheed U-2, another development triumph of the Skunk Works.
Courtesy Lockheed Aircraft Corporation.

used 23 engineers and took 80 days; the JetStar used 41 engineers and took 241 days; Johnson used 135 engineers to build the A-11, which was designed to go over Mach 3 at 20 miles high. This contrasts with the 3,500 engineers used to build North American's XB-70, which went Mach 3 at 15 miles high. Although it must be acknowledged that none of these aircraft are large, the XF-80, the U-2, and the A-11 all pushed beyond the state of the art, and the repeated success of the "Skunk Works" shows that effectiveness of the system is no fluke.

Even American airliner design practices must be suspect. Since the airlines have not accepted substandard equipment, have paid for enormous overruns, have been willing to wait, and have been most price-conscious, one would expect the use of engineers on airliner design to be economic. However, it must be acknowledged that airliner competition is between "equals" in one sense: none of the American companies are in a strictly civilian market. They are all veterans of the military aircraft business, and therefore they lack the skill of firms in the civilian market to hold down costs. One thousand engineers were used to design both the Electra and the 727, despite the circumstance that the 727 used as many existing 707 and 720 parts as possible. The 747 used 2,500 engineers, and the L-1011, 1,500. The Electra grossed 113,000 pounds; the 727, 170,000 pounds; the 747, 713,000 pounds; and the L-1011, 430,000

Design engineers at work at Lockheed. *Courtesy Lockheed Aircraft Corporation.*

pounds. Discounting the existence of some ability to transfer airliner costs to military contracts, called "migration," the record on airliners still contrasts sharply with the record of Lockheed's special unit. Perhaps a better comparison would be with the French Avions Marcel Dassault company, a shrewd and aggressive firm which produces top-notch designs at low prices. Its Mirage fighter was the basic equipment with which Israel smashed the Arab forces in the war of 1967. Dassault uses a Kelly Johnson style of development. To produce its Mirage IV, a 77,000-pound (gross weight) supersonic strategic bomber comparable to the F-111, Dassault used fewer than 85 engineers and draftsmen for development. From design approval to first flight took only eleven months. Producing such a bomber should be a problem of at least the same engineering magnitude as a jetliner. One can only conclude that ingrained traditional methods, including a carry-over from military contracts, account for the American use of masses of engineers, even on airliners.

IX

PRODUCTION: THE PAYOFF

If selling a design concept means survival in the aerospace industry, getting into production means profits. Research and development contains the uncertainties of advancing technology, especially with its "unk-unks." As successful design in the aerospace industry usually pushes the state of the art, technological unknowns dominate, and the knowns are subordinate. The relationship is reversed in production: despite some innovations, most techniques are familiar. Lockheed's colorful statement that the industry "attempts to mass produce undesigned articles" contains worthwhile insight but is an exaggeration.[1] Costs can be determined fairly early in the production process, and are thereafter highly predictable. This has remained true throughout the technological revolutions since World War II.

THE "TIN BENDERS"

In the all-metal piston-engine era, the aircraft industry called itself the "tin benders." This was a fairly descriptive term. To achieve lightness with strength, the skin of the aircraft was designed to be load-bearing, and the structure was called monocoque (single shell). With the low stresses of subsonic flight and the light weights imposed by the power levels of piston engines, the sheet metal used in the skin could be of thin gauges. The strength was increased by adding supporting structures within the skin. These consisted of strips of aluminum, frequently channeled for strength, and bulkheads, spars, and ribs. Fabrication was basically a sheet metal process, but machines were useful for cutting

119

stacks of sheet or for welding. The principal problem in assembly was to align the light, flexible material so it could be formed into the proper shape, and the alignment was accomplished by jigs and fixtures, large and small, which represented expensive and special tooling for each fundamental aircraft design. The final operation was installation of large quantities of complex, and often delicate, equipment into cramped quarters.

In the tin bending days, then, fabrication and assembly techniques for airplanes were decisively different from those for automobiles. The auto's use of heavier materials whose alignment was simpler and less critical meant that its tooling concentrated on fabrication rather than on assembly. The auto's installed equipment was simpler and more rugged, and it was mounted in comparative roominess. Aircraft quantities that could justify serial production and mechanized lines were seldom achieved after World War II, although aircraft production is high when it is in the thousands as compared to the auto's hundreds of thousands. Finally, technological advance in aircraft has been so rapid that design change is a way of life; in automobiles the technology has been so stable that design change has been artificially induced to spur sales.

It is clear, then, why the auto industry in World War II was more involved in aircraft engine manufacture than in airframe production, and why the auto industry found the transition to airframe production to be traumatic at times. The auto firms withdrew from aircraft manufacture at the end of World War II, and the last financial tie, General Motors' 25 percent ownership of North American, was severed in 1948.

Fortunately for the old-time aircraft makers, the withdrawal of the auto companies came just before changes which made the production processes of the two industries more alike.

THE MACHINE AGE

Transsonic and supersonic flight loads, together with the greater weights made possible by jet engine power, greatly increased the demands made on airframe structures. An obvious solution was to thicken structural members. Here is part of the reason for the weight spiral; payload goes up, so structure does as well in a multiplier effect, as Heinemann recognized.

The heavier structural parts reduced tin-bending and forced the use of machine techniques. The B-47, coming early in the jet age, was a fitting introduction to the new era in production. Designed with an unusual number of doors, access panels, and other breaks in the load-

Mass production of aircraft near the end of World War II is shown in this view of F-80 and P-38 assembly lines. A 558 m.p.h. aircraft, the F-80 could be built with piston-era techniques. *Courtesy Lockheed Aircraft Corporation.*

bearing skin, it required much thicker aluminum. For example, the B-47's wing skin was an unheard-of five-eighths of an inch thick at the wing root. To save weight the thickness was reduced outboard along the wing, because the stress loads decreased; at the tip the thickness was reduced to three-sixteenths. Large sheets of wing panels had therefore to be cut and tapered, and giant milling machines were required.

The other jets have used thicker structural members, although they have generally not been as heavy as the B-47's. Parts have become larger because aircraft are bigger and because joints have been eliminated as much as possible to save weight. A good description of many of these parts is "sculptured." As these aircraft came along, the aerospace industry has had to invest heavily in machine tools, including many special ones. This process began before the Korean War and has continued. On a dollar basis, machining is the dominant metal fabrication process now, although sheet-metal work is still done; on a structural weight basis, it was planned to machine 50 percent of the B-1.

Some parts do not lend themselves to chip-machining methods because of their strength, complexity, or delicacy. To meet this challenge, North American introduced chemical milling during the Second World War, and its use has grown. Besides being suitable for certain parts it has low labor and tooling costs, although it is a slow process.

THE AIR FORCE SPURS PRODUCTIVITY

Immediately after World War II the Air Force became convinced that some foreign developments could greatly improve aerospace production methods. The Germans had built some enormous presses of 30,000 tons for airframe production. These giants were built as substitutes for scarce rolling mills and not because they were a preferred method, but the Air Force believed they would be superior in the jet age by serially extruding large sections. This process could improve speed of assembly and strength for weight, because extrusion made it possible to include stiffeners with skin as a one-piece part rather than as an assembled unit. Before the program was completed, funds were cut back as it became apparent that World War II quantity production would never be repeated. Some presses had been built, however, and have been used since. They appear to have paid for themselves over the years, but the Air Force vision of stamping out thousands of planes from the presses has never been fulfilled.

Two other Air Force attempts to spur productivity were developed by Republic Aviation under contract. Republic was probably a good choice at the time. During World War II its president was a famous production specialist, Alfred J. Marchev, a man who held more than 500 patents for manufacturing processes. One of the projects was to improve optical alignment of the large tooling fixtures, a procedure which had been developed by the British. The British system was excellent in quality but difficult and clumsy to use. Republic achieved the Air Force's goal of making the system simpler.

The other project was adoption of a German jig system. Devised during the war, it consisted of a set of standardized jig parts that were cast and could be clamped together, forming a jig. As with a great erector set, there were virtually limitless possible combinations. The best utilization of the great variety required widespread use, and the German government had ordered industry-wide adoption. This "cast-clamp" system permitted jig construction in 40 percent of the time used by the Americans, easy alteration to accommodate design changes, and reuse of the fixture parts after a production run was completed. After a large initial investment, the cast-clamp system saved time and money. The system

122

was especially economical for prototype or short-run production. (By contrast, the American system was to laboriously weld a one-time jig. If the run was expected to be short, some money could be saved by making less durable, or "soft," tooling.)

The significance of a major improvement in jig-fixture tooling can be illustrated by the effort involved in a particular one-time weld system: by the time North American had produced 620 F-86's, 2,223,940 man-hours had been invested in tooling, topping the 2,088,160 engineering man-hours spent.[2] Tooling may well be the greatest single indirect production cost.

Republic and the Air Force offered the optical and cast-clamp systems to an industry conference in 1951. The industry accepted the optical system but rejected the cast-clamp. Opposition was ill-defined, being mostly satisfaction with the one-time weld method. And reinforcing the normal human resistance to change was the lack of incentive at that particular time to adopt the new system. Mobilization was under way, and costs were of little consequence to either the industry or the Air Force. Also, conversion would divert effort from the pressing need to increase production.

The cast-clamp tool system has not been proposed since 1951, and its rejection probably represents a major loss in production efficiency. The short-run production cost problem has risen in relative importance, and this is the condition for which cast-clamp was most useful. Strong recommendations for the system are the German success with it and its adoption after the war by Avions Marcel Dassault.

In 1952 the Air Force gave a contract to MIT to develop the numerical control of machine tools, and the first machine equipped with such controls went into use in 1956. The system proved to be a major improvement and soon produced 80 percent of all machined parts. It was highly suitable for aerospace work, which consisted of complex parts made in small lots, and it has been estimated that it has been four times as productive as nonnumerical control. It should be noted that major Air Force efforts to increase productivity ended in the middle fifties. This de-emphasis may have contributed to cost problems, which are discussed in Chapter XI.

HOT SANDWICHES

Beefing up the aluminum structures sufficed for the supersonic jets until speeds reached around Mach 2. At that speed, and faster, air friction builds up enough heat in the aircraft skin to destroy the strength of aluminum. Therefore, a need arose for heat-resistant and insulating structures. The first airframe in which this was a problem was the Mach 2 B-58 of the midfifties. The problem did not encompass the entire skin; an area of 1,000 square feet, 15 percent of the total, was affected, mostly around the engines. General Dynamics' solution was to use a stainless steel honeycomb-in-a-sandwich structure for the critical areas. Plastic sandwich structures and aluminum honeycomb had been used before this for a high strength-to-weight material, but they represented an enormous increase in production effort over the use of heavy sheet. The cost of the B-58's honeycomb ranged from $200 to $600 a square foot. For the Mach 3 XB-70 of the late fifties, the heat problem was not partial but total, requiring massive engineering and production efforts to solve. The honeycomb sandwich structure was basic to the expensive XB-70, amounting to 10,000 square feet, and it has been used frequently since in other aircraft.

Even before the heat problem, the industry was interested in titanium as a structural metal because its strength-to-weight ratio is superior to that of aluminum. But the costs of extraction and extreme difficulties in working the hard metal limited its use to a few hundred pounds per airframe. When the Mach 3 A-11 was designed in the early sixties a major effort was made to solve titanium's problems because the

Cruising at speeds in excess of Mach 3 and altitudes over 80,000 feet, the SR-71 (based on the A-11) demanded much in materials and production development. The Lockheed Skunk Works met the challenge. *Courtesy Lockheed Aircraft Corporation.*

metal is heat-resistant and therefore has ideal properties for the Mach 3 airframe. Working the metal was mastered, but it was not simple and its expensiveness remains. The A-11 was practically 100 percent titanium, and in this it is exceptional. The 1958 F-4 was 9 percent titanium by weight, or 1,300 pounds. By 1969 McDonnell had delivered 37,000 tons of titanium in its products since the 1954 F-101. For the F-15, the firm planned to use as much as 40 percent to 60 percent of the metal. This has its price. Titanium, steel, and other hard metals require high-power, high-torque, and low-speed machines. The harder metals require six times the cutting capacity for the same metal removal rate as on aluminum. For the F-15 the result was that 90 percent of the total machining hours were spent on those metals. The severity of the problem is further illustrated by the development of the B-1: originally planned with 45 percent of its structural weight in titanium, it eventually had only 20 percent; high costs required the change, and structural weight was increased by 4,000 pounds because of the substitution.

PRODUCTION TODAY

Aircraft with sustained high supersonic speeds have not been in great demand, so that most production aircraft technology remains fit for transsonic requirements. The result is that aircraft production today has three main characteristics. Initial fabrication is done largely with machine tools; component and final assembly techniques remain much as they were in the tin-bending days; and the trend to heavier and more complex aircraft has meant a return to more handcraft methods compared to World War II. A significant production problem contributing to higher costs and handcraft methods is the growing density of airframes as more and more equipment is sardined into the limited volume.

Handcrafting has become almost necessary. Production of giant aerospace products is far removed from a Detroit assembly line. Final assembly of the 747, in fact, is strikingly like shipbuilding. It is done in the world's largest enclosed space, containing 160 million cubic feet. One assembly bay is 1,100 by 300 by 75 feet. That aerospace manufacturing has characteristics similar to shipbuilding techniques is demonstrated by Lockheed and General Dynamics, which do both, and by the Defense Department's attempt in 1965 to turn over some shipbuilding to the aerospace companies in an effort to improve shipbuilding production methods.

It is natural that larger and costlier units will result in fewer units made. From 1956 to 1965 the average annual production of fixed-wing military aircraft was 1,800. In the early seventies it had fallen to around

Assembly of the largest of the Boeing family of airliners, the 747, for which a special mammoth building had to be built. *Courtesy The Boeing Company.*

500. Yet the dollar value of the production was roughly the same, unadjusted for inflation. Figure II shows no strong trend to fewer types of airframes produced, although the number of aircraft types was down by one-third. Production runs of popular models continued to be long: by the early seventies over 2,700 of the 1954 A-4's had been built, and over 500 F-111's, 1,200 C-130's, 4,200 F-4's, and 1,900 T-38/F-5's.

Missile production shows evolutionary development from aircraft: the materials used and the production methods are similar to those for supersonic planes. Atlas is a good example. Its main skin, made of stainless steel sheet, served both as structure and as fuel tank, as do those of other missiles and some modern aircraft. For example, in airliners the fuel tank has disappeared, and the wing structure serves this function after application of an internal sealant. The Atlas skin was thin to save weight and was reinforced by internal tank pressures so that it has been aptly described as a "steel balloon." Titan was closer to earlier aircraft techniques. The first-stage airframe was welded of extruded, integrally stiffened aluminum alloy which had been machined and then chemically milled. Its thickness was about one-sixteenth of an inch. The second stage used unstiffened sheet. Since the airframe was cylindrical, large form presses or drop hammers were not needed and conventional sheet metal machines could be used. Some missiles have used sheet steel 30 feet long, 10 feet wide, and .060 to .125 inches thick. Lightness, strength, and reliability are requirements, as they are in aircraft, and handcraft methods remain in evidence even in the smaller missiles, which are built

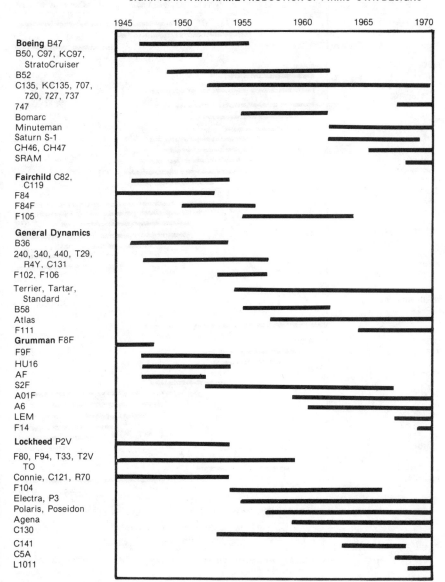

FIGURE II
SIGNIFICANT AIRFRAME PRODUCTION OF FIRMS' OWN DESIGNS

FIGURE II [continued]

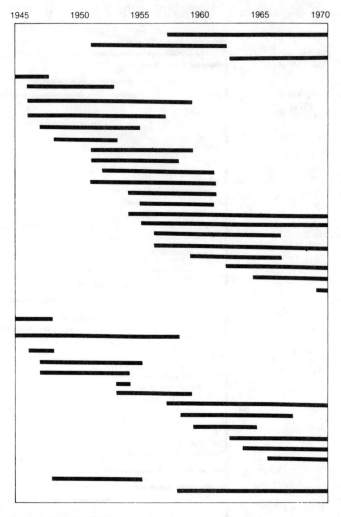

Sources: **Aviation Week,**

F.G. Swanborough, **United States Military Aircraft Since 1909** (London: Putnam, 1963).

Ray Wagner, **American Combat Planes** (Garden City, New York: Doubleday, 1968). Revised edition.

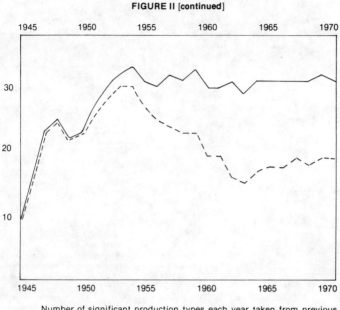

FIGURE II [continued]

_____ Number of significant production types each year taken from previous two pages.

------ Number which are aircraft.

by the hundreds. The missile has a simpler airframe structure than an aircraft, with far fewer parts. Production of smaller missiles looks like a cross between airframe and auto manufacture.

Space vehicles are a further extension of the aircraft-to-missile evolution. The smaller space vehicles use the larger missile engines as boosters. Construction of large boosters is like airframe manufacture. The spaceships are extensions of the high-speed aircraft systems which reached the edge of space, although the requirement for reliability is higher and handcraft and clean methods are emphasized.

Probably the greatest difference in production methods of aircraft and of missiles and spacecraft is in plant. Aircraft have called for large open-bay buildings, of which the 747 assembly building and Willow Run are extreme examples, because of their structures which extend far into each dimension. Aircraft plants are adaptable to serial manufacture of other large structures; the same facilities have been used for manufacture of both aircraft and autos, sometimes concurrently, at Willow Run and other locations. Missiles and spaceships do not need vast open bays, except for the huge Saturn. Like many missiles and boosters, Saturn was

129

Assembly of Martin Marietta Titans showing the cleanliness of the process. *Courtesy Martin Marietta Corporation.*

assembled in vertical position because its light structure was designed to carry the vertical loads of upright launch. So the Saturn assembly building, containing 130 million cubic feet, is somewhat like an aircraft assembly bay stood on end. Missile and space vehicle requirements demand precision and cleanliness. Consequently, they are built in sterile, air-conditioned plants which are much smaller than aircraft plants and which resemble laboratories more than factories.

This change in plant type has had a major effect on the aerospace industry. Adapting the open bays was more expensive and less satisfactory than building afresh. The need for new plants to accommodate the new product lines came in the late fifties and early sixties, at a time when the government was seeking to divest itself of the plants and equipment it had financed in World War II and the Korean War. The result has been that the aerospace industry has had to engage in a massive capital formation while already possessing facilities that are underused. The growth of the RDT&E business described in Chapter VIII has required a similar expansion of fixed assets to provide office, laboratory, and range-type installations. Boeing's investment in *net* plant and equipment grew

Production of the McDonnell Mercury spaceship contrasted with more traditional methods for manufacturing aircraft, which required new laboratory-like plant in the aerospace industry in the sixties. *Courtesy McDonnell Douglas Corporation.*

twelvefold from $52 million in 1956 to $628 million in 1968, while net worth rose fivefold from $152 to $810 million. Company and leased floor space grew fourfold from 6.5 million square feet to 28.8 million, while government-owned plant increased only 11 percent from 9.4 million square feet to 10.7. These figures reflect the shift in Boeing's government work from aircraft to missile and space, and the large need for company-financed new plant.

SUBCONTRACTING

All large producing companies are faced with make or buy decisions, but such questions in the aerospace industry are in many ways very different from those of mostly civilian firms. Ideally, the decision should be economic, based on incremental, or marginal or net-effects, costs. In the aerospace industry political factors have usually dominated, and economic considerations have been oriented more toward survival than profits.

In the aerospace industry extensive subcontracting in its modern

131

form began during World War II, when it reached 50 percent of airframe sales, including suppliers. When the war was over, subcontracting virtually died out. The industry generally believed all subcontracting was more costly than in-house production, because of start-up costs, a belief which was probably accurate during that period of idle capacity. Besides, in-house production permitted more effective control and planning, as well as more rapid changes. Most important, in-house production reduced dependence on the vagaries of other companies. Failure of others to deliver parts contributed greatly to Douglas' collapse in 1966.

When the Korean War began, subcontracting on a large scale was revived. Government pressure, in the form of a quota or withholding financing for facilities, was used to encourage subcontracting. The government's desires were based on social objectives: to give work to areas with a labor surplus and to favor small businesses. The military had their own reason for subcontracting: to disperse industry as part of passive air defense measures.

The permanently expanded nature of the industry after the Korean War resulted in a continuation of subcontracting at the 30 percent to 40 percent level of production. Government pressures continued, but, more importantly, there was a shift in attitude by the aerospace industry. The new era was introduced with extensive subcontracting of the Electra by Lockheed.

The significant nature of subcontracting in recent years has been its large-scale use between the main aerospace companies themselves. Aerospace firms have always preferred their own kind as subcontractors, a natural choice. The auto industry has always been objected to, allegedly because of a "know-it-all" attitude on the part of the auto managers, and an expensive tendency to use too many tools. Probably more important, the auto industry is unaccustomed to the level of reliability required in airframes; and it is a potential competitor. Beyond this, the decline in the number of types of aircraft in production has forced some companies to end or greatly reduce their manufacture of aircraft and to become large-scale subcontractors. This has been the case with Fairchild, General Dynamics, Martin, and Northrop. For the aerospace prime contractor these arrangements have been desirable in an underwriting sense. The system enables the principal designer company to share engineering, production and financial resources, and risks. Subcontracting also converts some of the designer company's costs from fixed to variable, and it can reduce the impact of a slowdown in business. These factors are especially important in surviving the business risks of the present jetliner business.

X

DIVERSIFICATION:
THE HEDGE FOR SURVIVAL

THE NEED TO DIVERSIFY

For the best chance to continue in business an aerospace company must not only design and produce, it must have shelter against government contract termination. Unlike civil business, which usually slides into recession, the airframe company faces instant, often unexpected, and near-total collapse of sales when the government cancels a program. Though the companies are adequately reimbursed in a cancellation for work in progress and other costs associated with the specific program, the large overhead costs, including maintenance of the vital design teams, go on after contract termination. Without other business to support these costs, the firm is soon in financial trouble or loses too many men.

"Other business" can be subcontracting, but this provides only temporary shelter and puts a company's future partly in the hands of others. "Other business," therefore, is better if it is permanent and fully under the company's control. Obviously, it is even better if it is not subject to government contract stretchouts, cutbacks, or cancellations. A wave of reductions, like those in 1957 and in the latter sixties, in which several orders are canceled in succession, can be fatal, even if a single one is not. Consequently, the aerospace companies have tried since World War II to diversify, seeking protection against failure to get or keep government business.

There are some parallels in the auto industry. Lawrence J. White has found that the few survivors in that business are the ones who successfully established multiple model lines.[1] This has enabled them to survive bad judgment in a particular model. Because of the long development time in autos—three years—recovery from an error in any one line is delayed so long that financial and morale crises can set in. These crises do not become disasters when concurrent successful lines provide cash and confidence. The Edsel is a case in point, as is Kaiser's compact car, the Henry J.

Where cash and confidence are lacking, survival obviously is the goal of a company. In normal business, profits are regarded as the basic incentive. There is reason to believe that profit maximization does not perform this role in the aerospace industry; that survival is the permanent driving force. The use of an elite group of engineers to work from contract bid to bid, and not from the beginning on to the final design and production phases, illustrates the emphasis. The record of the aerospace companies on cost control indicates less concern for profits than for survival or sales. The investment structure of the aerospace companies does not put heavy pressure on management to provide more profits. The personal remuneration and personal power of the managers has been tied more closely to the sales than to the profit level. J. L. Atwood, onetime chief executive for North American Aviation, said reputation was the motivation for management.[2] Finally and most important, the government as customer, with its retroactive pricing, limits profits; consequently, emphasis on them is somewhat fruitless. David S. Lewis, when he was president of McDonnell, said: "In this industry, disaster *always* seems just over the horizon."[3]

It is natural, then, that diversification, which is even more important to survival than design competence, has received great, though uneven, emphasis. The possibilities of diversification have been to (1) diversify within the aerospace industry by making aircraft plus missiles or space vehicles or all three; (2) enlarge interests within the broader defense industry, in shipbuilding, for example; (3) acquire more variety in aircraft by building commercial or general airplanes; (4) expand into technologies in which the aerospace industry science and engineering provide an initial competence, such as basic research or avionics, or engines; (5) develop fields related to airframe production process, such as aluminum boats; and (6) acquire totally unrelated endeavors to obtain stable sales or, preferably, those countercyclical to the aerospace business.

These are all reasonable approaches, and all have been tried with varying degrees of vigor and success. When the efforts have been very successful they have often been counterproductive because the original

134

business has gone into sharp decline, leaving the company undiversified again.

RECONVERSION DESPERATION AND IMPROVISATION

As a hedge against the expected great decline in government business after World War II, there was a wave of diversification attempts. In this period the methods ran the gamut of possibilities. Nearly all the companies sought to get a foothold in the airliner business, a form of diversification which has been ever popular since, but from this great field of early entrants only three were to make money with piston-era airliners: Douglas, Lockheed, and Convair.

Besides commercial aircraft there was widespread entry into the general aviation market. Convair, Fairchild, Grumman, Lockheed, North American, and Republic seriously studied or entered the field. The general airplane market boomed in 1946 and collapsed the next year. Soon after, all the great aerospace companies had cut their losses and withdrawn from this market and have not reentered it on a large scale.

North American tried to diversify into fields related to its production processes. President E. H. Kindelberger liked to relate that the company examined the Sears, Roebuck and Montgomery Ward catalogs to find products it could make. After a selection was made, it was analyzed for cost. North American found its production costs would run 30 percent higher than retail prices and the whole idea was abandoned.[4]

Despite the other aerospace companies' lack of civil marketing skills and organization, they tried a wide variety of retail and industrial products. Some were internally developed. Others were acquisitions which appear, for the most part, to have been haphazard or opportunistic purchases. Curtiss-Wright entered into photographic equipment, metals, and clutch businesses and made a small profit. Convair, Douglas, and McDonnell explored the prefabricated house business but did not enter. McDonnell was the only company which did not diversify. Douglas and Boeing limited their diversification to a return to commercial airliners. Convair made kitchen ranges and freezers, transit buses, and auto and marine engines besides its light plane, a flying auto. These investments grew to $19 million out of Convair's total assets of $81 million, but the firm's losses were large. Republic built engines. Fairchild made radio cabinets, small boats, auto trailers, and four-wheel velocipedes for a toy company. The results were unsatisfactory. Grumman made aluminum canoes, fiberglass boats, and truck bodies; Lockheed kept ownership of the Pacific Finance Corp., a consumer finance company, and did well;

Martin went into plastics, photo emulsion, and light panels used as structural material; Northrop made a motor scooter, light metal goods, and small engines, but its losses on these ventures ran to more than a million dollars, a heavy figure for a company whose sales were under $30 million a year.

These miscellaneous diversification ventures into the private market by the aerospace companies, used to selling only to the government or the airlines, resulted in a dreary record. Because they were, first of all, aircraft companies, they probably neglected their less glamorous sideline operations where different production and sales techniques had to be acquired. Even in a sellers' market, when businessmen could sell almost anything they made to satisfy the pent-up demand from the war, the aerospace manufacturers managed to lose money. Most of the ventures had been abandoned by 1948, ending a unique period in the aerospace industry. Never again would it try to enter such varied fields as it did in the immediate postwar years.

Two companies did find a new road to the future by diversifying in this period. Convair, as already noted, started the ICBM Atlas, which was to lead the company to the missiles and space fields. North American believed that there was a future in missiles and established corporate units for avionics and rocket engines. North American's later successful leadership in these fields, and its related R&D work, ultimately transformed the company basically from an aircraft to an R&D one.

With the resurgence of military aircraft business and airline expansion, the fears over survival were temporarily allayed, and the aerospace industry's only important diversification was again the airliner. Boeing and Martin lost large sums on their attempts to get pieces of the business, and the limited extent to which the diversification succeeded even for the successful airliner builders can be seen in Lockheed's record: from 1948, when government business turned upwards, through 1955, when new markets were opening and jetliner competition began, Lockheed averaged a little over 80 percent government business. In the diversification efforts since then, aerospace companies have consistently had a goal of no more than 50 percent government business. The constancy of this very round figure over many years and from several companies indicates it is a purely intuitive figure. The long record of crisis and failure in the aerospace industry since World War II suggests that 50 percent government business is probably too high for a reasonable level of risk.

THE SECOND WAVE OF DIVERSIFICATION

The fifties saw a new form of diversification within government business.

136

The first was the absorption of Convair by General Dynamics in 1953. The resultant conglomerate's principal products were military and commercial aircraft, missiles, ships, electronics, and R&D. In 1955 97 percent of its sales were to the government, but its participation in five product lines for two government markets represents the greatest degree of diversification up to that time. Yet General Dynamics did not believe this was adequate security, and its desire for diversification was a strong contributing factor in its entrance into the jetliner race. For General Dynamics this was an effort to at least retain, and it was hoped to expand, its market penetration in commercial airliners; its objective in the late fifties was nongovernment sales at the rate of 50 percent. To attain this level the company went outside its established fields of high technology and merged with Material Service Corporation, whose business was construction and construction materials. The construction products thereafter provided roughly a quarter of General Dynamics' sales.

Under Robert E. Gross, Lockheed undertook a diversification program for rapid growth as well as security, and the result was a company much like General Dynamics. Lockheed bought out a shipbuilder, hoping to get construction work which it believed would be countercyclical to the aerospace business; it won the major Polaris missile contract; and it started electronics and rocket-engine endeavors.

The Martin Company evolved in a similar manner. Despite strenuous efforts it was forced out of the commercial aircraft market. It repeatedly lost bids to build military aircraft, and that business shrank.[5] With the end of flying-boat production in 1959, Martin was, except as a subcontractor or rebuilder, out of the airplane business. While it was struggling with its dying airplane business, opportunities in missiles opened. For ailing Martin there was little choice; it secured a contract for the back-up liquid-fueled ICBM, the Titan, and entered vigorously into the missiles and R&D fields. In 1961 it followed General Dynamics' example and acquired American Marietta Company, a construction and construction materials firm. The new organization was called Martin Marietta. Martin thus joined the aerospace companies which have become diversified into the nonairplane parts of the industry, maintaining a substantial nongovernment line.

North American, as noted, entered into the missile and R&D fields immediately after World War II, and as these lines expanded in the fifties North American prospered and grew. But it exhibited the self-defeating aspects of diversification: as the new fields expanded, North American's aircraft production withered away. With the end of F-100 production, the manufacture of major combat airplanes stopped. North

137

The Martin Marietta B-57 is distinguished as Martin's last major aircraft production effort and as the only important foreign design adapted for American military use after the Second World War. *Courtesy Martin Marietta Corporation.*

American won only bids to develop the hapless XB-70, the prototype of which was finished in 1962, and the aborted XF-108, sacrificed by the Air Council in 1959 in an effort to save the XB-70. Thus, after North American's successful penetration of new markets, it found itself practically without the old, at least for well over a decade.

North American's unwilling withdrawal from the military aircraft market after years as a major company in the business was paralleled by Boeing and Douglas. Boeing's triumphant conquest of the commercial airliner business occurred at the same time that its decline in military aircraft sales began. Boeing had specialized in the big bomber and was unable to win contracts with other types of aircraft when the Air Force was forced to stop buying big bombers in 1962. The company had gotten into missiles early with its unmanned airplane, Bomarc, and it was able to stay in missiles by winning development of the Minuteman. Boeing's government business remained high until it finished its production contracts on the B-52 and KC-135. Similarly, Douglas' losses of military aircraft business coincided with the beginnings of the jetliner age. Its government business was 82 percent of sales in 1954 but only 53 percent by the end of the fifties, despite a good start in the missile business.

Douglas deliberately passed up one diversification field, avionics, believing it would be better off staying with its specialty, airframe design and production, and getting its avionics from suppliers. Other aerospace firms took different courses. Avionics is a more critical part of missiles than of aircraft. A natural result was that, when missiles began to boom, avionics companies like Hughes and Raytheon bid to be prime airframe contractors. Most existing airframe firms believed that to be able to compete with these entrants into the industry they had to enter the electronics business. It was not a radical step, since by 1954 18 percent of airframe company engineers were doing avionics work. Most airframe firms did enter competition for both government and nongovernment electronics business, even though they were ordered to stop in 1955 by the Air Force under a vague threat of unnamed reprisals.

Northrop was one such company. Although its F-89 interceptor had a long production run, it was not highly regarded by the Air Force. Its unmanned aircraft was the hapless Snark. Northrop turned to the light weight fighter field in 1954, producing on its own initiative what was to become the F-5. Along with all other lightweight designs the F-5 was disliked by the USAF, but it achieved success in foreign sales and saw some use in the Vietnam War. A version of this aircraft became the popular Air Force T-38 trainer, but trainers rate low as military aircraft. Northrop got a new president in 1959, Thomas V. Jones, who believed Northrop must cease its reliance on the aircraft field, in which its success was not clear-cut. The aircraft line was retained, but Jones, an engineer, took Northrop further into specialty technology fields, into avionics R&D. Northrop has done well since. Its F-5 and T-38 were better received than the F-89 and the Snark, and its diversification has ended its dependence on government business, which was at about 50 percent of sales in the early seventies.

In the fifties Grumman lost its position as the premier maker of Navy fighters, as McDonnell and Vought produced superior designs. Whereas Northrop tried to become a lightweight specialist, Grumman sought to carve a secure niche by building unusual workhorse aircraft: anti-submarine, aircraft carrier transport, and amphibian airplanes. Grumman never gave up on the naval fighter, however, and its F-14 was an important aircraft in the seventies.

The missile boom of the fifties led to a wide variety of types, with a cost range lower than aircraft, a situation that facilitated the entrance of nonairframe companies into the field. And since missiles were a follow-on technology to aircraft all the airframe firms except Republic participated in this initial boom. By the beginning of the sixties, the second wave of diversification in the aerospace industry had resulted in a pattern.

Figure III is rough and it is not quantified, but it does illustrate two points. The technological revolutions of the fifties had provided a natural encouragement to diversify, yet some firms attempted to go on beyond the new technological openings. The process was spurred by the wave of cancellations of defense programs in the summer of 1957 which had sent a chill through the industry. Also, it can be seen that the extent of diversification varied widely within the industry at that time.

THE RECURRENT EFFORTS

Since the wave of diversification which took place in the fifties, efforts to broaden product lines have continued on a sporadic basis. The status of the space program as a major contributor to diversification was established in the sixties with the race to the moon. All the aerospace firms were interested in NASA contracts, but the big winners were North American with the Apollo project, McDonnell with Mercury and Gemini, Grumman with the Lunar Module, and Boeing, Douglas, and North

FIGURE III
PATTERN OF DIVERSIFICATION, EARLY SIXTIES

Company	Military Aircraft	Missiles (large only)	R&D	Electronics	Shipbuilding	Commercial Aircraft	Construction
Boeing	X	X				X	
Douglas	X	X				X	
Fairchild		†				X	
General Dynamics	X	X	X	X	X	X	X
Grumman	X						
Lockheed	X	X	X	X	X	X	
Martin		X	X	X			X
McDonnell	X						
North American	X	X	X	X			
Northrop	X	‡	X	X			
Republic	X						

† Fairchild's missile contracts had been canceled by the sixties.
‡ Northrop abandoned large missiles as a prime after Snark.

140

American with Saturn stages. The builders of liquid-fueled boosters, all of them except Agena being former ballistic missiles, gave business to Douglas with Thor, General Dynamics with Atlas, Lockheed with Agena, and Martin with Titan.

A special effort to get into space was made by two companies that had not been aggressive in diversifying before, Republic and Douglas. These companies recognized belatedly that failure to broadly diversify had been a mistake for them in their particular industry position, and they now invested capital in facilities to enter the space field. For Republic it was to no avail. With the termination of its F-105 contract in 1964, Republic was badly hurt. It was bought out by Fairchild in 1965, who wanted Republic for its engineering staff and production facilities. Fairchild also made other moves to diversify, including acquisition of a helicopter company, Hiller.

Despite Douglas' late efforts to diversify, it became more specialized in the sixties. Its military aircraft line shrank to its classic design, the A-4, and loss of military aircraft production was a heavy blow to profits. Two main attempts to sustain or improve its government business were Skybolt and the Manned Orbiting Laboratory (MOL), but Skybolt was canceled in 1962 and the MOL in 1969. The military business stayed at a low level: in 1966, of Douglas' sales, only 22 percent was to the government and only a third of that was for aircraft. When Douglas' commercial airliner business skyrocketed in 1966, causing cash problems, the level of government sales was of little help. Thus a lack of sufficient diversification contributed to Douglas' failure and absorption by McDonnell. More diversified General Dynamics survived its 880/990 crisis, which was about the same size as Douglas' 1966 DC-9 crisis; and Lockheed, also broadly diversified, surmounted its smaller Electra crisis.

Lack of diversification contributed to Douglas' failure, and this weakness dominated its successor's plans. McDonnell had sought diversification since the forties. It had built a succession of fighters for the Navy, but James S. McDonnell, or "Mr. Mac," McDonnell's chief executive, felt insecure in having only that business. His first move was to attempt to sell to the Air Force. Two 1948 attempts, the XF-85 and XF-88, were not bought. The Air Force wanted the XF-88, but the Navy said it needed McDonnell's full productive capacity. The XF-88 was upgraded to the F-101 of 1954, and this was bought by the Air Force, as was the later F-4. McDonnell's next efforts were civil. It offered a jetliner design and brought to the prototype stage a business airplane. Both attempts failed. At about the same time, McDonnell entered the missile field, and, from the beginning of the space efforts, James S. Mc-

Donnell saw the desirability of manned space flight. The company began early work on a spaceship, and when NASA asked for bids McDonnell had gone furthest in design and won the competition for Mercury. Still concerned over diversification, Mr. McDonnell bought up Douglas shares in 1963 hoping to enter the commercial airliner field through merger. Douglas repulsed his efforts at this time, but when Douglas collapsed in 1966 McDonnell tried again and succeeded against the other bidders by offering the largest sum at the earliest time. With the acquisition McDonnell restored in one company the balance of government and commercial business that Douglas had lost in the fifties.

The leading jetliner builder, Boeing, has continued its efforts to find more of the same kind of balance. Unable to win military aircraft contracts in the sixties, Boeing sought to regain a place in the business by acquiring Vertol, a helicopter manufacturer. This has been successful, but the business is slight by comparison with Boeing's former military aircraft business. Boeing continued in the missile business with Minuteman and the Short Range Attack Missile (SRAM), and the space business with its Saturn first-stage booster. Yet the share of Boeing's sales which were government business continued to decline, from 100 percent in the early fifties to around 20 percent in the early seventies. Renewed efforts were made to find new directions, and by 1971 Boeing had considered 160 proposals for possible new products or services. Among them were police radio scramblers, desalting of water, community developments, computer services, and construction.

In contrast Lockheed has been highly successful in winning government business but has never resigned itself to having lost out in airliners. In the decade of the sixties Lockheed hoped to recoup by winning Air Force transport contracts and selling civil variants to the airlines, another example of the continuing attempts by aerospace companies to shift airliner development costs to the government. Lockheed won both the C-141 and the C-5A competitions. These, with the C-130, have given Lockheed the kind of dominance on military transports once held by Boeing in bombers. But as a means to an end this accomplishment has been a total failure. The airlines have shown little serious interest in the high-wing Air Force transports, believing that the military virtues of nose and tail loading, high-wing structure, and short field performance result in an uneconomic burden for airline operation. To reenter the airliner field, Lockheed has been forced to take its C-5A data and design the L-1011. This persistent effort to reestablish itself in commercial airlines represented nearly its entire diversification effort in the sixties. As can be seen by Figure III, Lockheed was relatively well diversified by 1961,

Lockheed's bid to diversify and reestablish itself in the airliner market was made with the efficient L-1011 TriStar. *Courtesy Lockheed Aircraft Corporation.*

when Robert E. Gross, its long-time leader, died. With his death, the diversification drive ended. His successor, brother Courtland, believed an aerospace company was ill-suited for nondefense work because of its emphasis on science and reliability. He also believed that diversification could not contribute to the support of idle defense facilities. In the fifties and sixties Lockheed was highly successful in winning government projects and completing them, and the management probably began to feel secure. Unfortunately, one diversification effort, shipbuilding, had become a cripple. Almost $16 million was lost on this operation in 1966. A disastrous series of setbacks carrying into the seventies—early termination of the C-5A production, cancellation of the Army Cheyenne helicopter, shipbuilding losses, and the Rolls-Royce receivership which delayed the engines for the L-1011—brought Lockheed to its knees. The management had probably believed the odds were unlikely for such simultaneous disasters, and the circumstances demonstrate that diversification is only a partial answer to survival for the aerospace industry.

That diversification can even be a handicap is shown by General Dynamics' major troubles with the Quincy shipyard in the sixties, although the company's surmounting of the crisis was undoubtedly helped by the healthy parts of the conglomerate. By 1970 shipbuilding writeoffs had totaled $237 million. General Dynamics has not sought further diversification in the decade except through cautious feelers to the airlines about paper proposals on airliners. Its caution is understandable because of the loss on its 880/990 program.

With the decline of its nonaircraft lines, mostly with the end of Apollo, Grumman was, against its will, specializing again in military aircraft. Its diversification into an air cushion vehicle, prefabricated housing, pleasure boats, aluminum truck bodies, and business jets had not provided an adequate replacement for defense business in the early seventies. Unable or unwilling to cut the overhead from the other programs, Grumman tried to transfer their costs to the F-14 project, precipitating a crisis with its traditional customer, the Navy. The desperate Grumman illustrates again the weakness of the company with only one major product.

Martin, which diversified out of aircraft, sought at intervals in the sixties to sell new airplane designs of its own. Unable to do so, it remained in the early seventies much as it was a decade earlier.

North American also tried to diversify by regaining some aircraft business. It produced trainers (T-2) and an attack plane (OV-10), and it won the B-1 competition. It also made cautious overtures for airliner business, for the perennial attempt at a DC-3 replacement, without success. Concerned about North American's near total dependence on the government for sales, its top executive, J. L. Atwood, hoped for a merger with a civilian market company in the years after 1959. Atwood was nervous despite North American's outstanding successes in getting contracts in the space program and R&D, which gave it sales of over $2 billion from 1964 on. That Atwood was well-justified was shown in 1967. The investigation of the fatal Apollo ground fire led to highly critical attacks on North American, by NASA, for a lack of technical and managerial competence. These attacks seriously impaired North American's reputation with business and government. This blow came as North American merged with Rockwell Standard, and the merger probably came just in time to save North American. A downturn began in 1967, and Apollo started to close down in 1969. Until the B-1 award of 1970 and the space shuttle in 1972, the North American part of the new company had a grim outlook.

North American had not married in haste, and it had chosen a company which had large automobile interests. Thus North American Rockwell is the first of its kind in recent years: a company interested in both aerospace and autos. The aerospace and auto industries can be complementary and somewhat countercyclical to each other, and each possesses know-how and attitudes of use to the other. Aerospace companies have been more aggressive in technological advancement, and the auto companies have been more cost and marketing conscious. Atwood's merger achievement may prove to be one of the best business decisions ever made in the aerospace industry.

THE FALSE HOPE

In 1965, amidst the enthusiasm for the "great society," an idea was broached for another new market for the aerospace industry. This was to apply its analytical skills to the solution of social problems: of how best to transport people, end crime, provide welfare, and so forth. This would be, of course, a new government market, but not necessarily the federal government. The first contracts were from the state of California. But the idea soon faded away, for the contracts were for small sums and the aerospace firms' products proved disappointing. A. Scheffer Lang, head of the transportation division of MIT's civil engineering department, complained that the aerospace industry's solutions were more research, more analysis, and more management, an approach based on the lavish use of funds. He said that in a transportation study North American "demonstrated very clearly that they didn't understand the problems. Technology per se is the easiest part. They couldn't get their heads around to understanding the situation within which one has to market."[6]

WHY NOT MERGER?

Conspicuously absent from the record are mergers between aerospace companies other than absorption of a failing company, like Republic or Douglas. This appears to be curious, considering the troubles the companies have had during the periods of large overcapacity following World War II and the Vietnam War. In Britain the government encouraged merger as a solution to aerospace industry overcapacity. Why, then, has merger between ambitious or distressed, but not desperate, American aerospace firms been conspicuously absent?

The lack has not been for a complete absence of proposals, some of which have been referred to above. In 1945 Curtiss-Wright tried to merge with Lockheed, but negotiations broke down over Curtiss-Wright's complicated capital structure. In the spring of 1946 Lockheed and Convair considered a merger, so as to have one company offering a full spectrum of airliner types; the proposal was shaky because of an unsteady securities market and Convair's alarm over a grounding of the

Connie, but the merger was actually called off because the attorney general objected on antitrust grounds. In 1948 weak Convair approached both North American and Northrop and was rebuffed. In November 1948 Curtiss-Wright approached Boeing, declaring that its management needed strengthening; but Boeing's president said Boeing could not afford to dilute its management, and he also declared that mixing the airframe and engine businesses was undesirable.

Three years passed before there was renewed merger interest. Again the proponent was Convair, seeking to assure continued possession of large plant space after B-36 production ended. Convair's president approached Kaiser-Frazer because it owned Willow Run and other airframe facilities. Also, Kaiser's losses provided tax credits, the company had a reputation for engineering skills, and Odlum saw an advantage to joining the aircraft and auto businesses in one company. The prospects changed with creation of the excess profits tax, for then profits were higher without merger.

It was eleven years before there was another attempt. This time McDonnell quietly bought up shares in Douglas so as to join its own government business with Douglas' commercial production. The Douglases, father and son, rejected the proposal, however, and were able to block it. They gave these reasons: separately the companies would do more business; consolidation would produce no economies; Douglas' customers would be driven off by a merger with McDonnell; and there would be no gains in diversification.[7] These rationalizations are difficult to accept at face value, and they have been proved wrong by the eventual absorption of Douglas by McDonnell.

In all these negotiations there was no overt involvement by the government, except in the one case where the attorney general intervened. The government role is difficult to assess because it was often indirect. When Stuart Symington was secretary of the Air Force, from 1947 to 1950, he and high-ranking officers in the USAF took the position that there were more firms than necessary in the aerospace industry; they suggested that mergers should be effected. This line of reasoning was again presented in 1970 and 1973 by Deputy Defense Secretary David Packard, who also specifically suggested that Lockheed merge to solve its problems.

There is no evidence that this gratuitous managerial advice has ever been taken seriously by the aerospace companies. What is surprising is that the antitrust laws are not emphasized by Defense Department officials, for the Justice Department has shown an aversion to aerospace mergers. Besides the interposition by the attorney general in the 1946

Lockheed-Convair proposals, Justice Department approval of the North American–Rockwell merger came only after Rockwell agreed to divest itself of its jet general aviation business because North American had a competing line. McDonnell was allowed to absorb Douglas because it lacked commercial business and Douglas had few government sales. The dominant governmental attitude is to oppose mergers, in contrast to the British position.

As for business reasons, the strongest influence against mergers has probably been the widespread presence until recently of founders as company leaders within the aerospace industry. Such men would have a natural reluctance to put an end to their creations.

XI

COSTS: INTO THE STRATOSPHERE

Costs have risen so high and so fast that they constitute in themselves a threat to the future of the areospace industry. If it has not yet priced itself out of the market, it may be close to doing so. The prices of aircraft had roughly *quadrupled each decade* by the early seventies. A similar increase in the productivity of airliners, measured in terms of seat-miles, had taken place since the advent of the jet engine. Figure IV gives a graphic comparison of the rise in airliner prices, seat-mile productivity, and the consumer price index. Although it is more difficult to measure military aircraft productivity, it may be found to have risen comparably if all types are considered as a unit.

Another way to look at the cost picture is to analyze the price rise of a single type. When McNamara studied the costs-benefits of reviving production of the piston A-1 for the Vietnam War, he was shocked at the cost. With no need for development, production of 300 A-1's was estimated to cost $800,000 apiece. They had cost $175,000 to $200,000 apiece in the late forties. The price of the A-1 had thus quadrupled in less than two decades; McNamara decided the plane was not "cost-effective." Over the same period of time, the average hourly earnings in aircraft and parts plants, including overtime, only doubled. The price of an F-4 more than doubled between 1963 and 1970 during a modest increase in weight in the Air Force version. This cost rise took place in spite of the learning curve on a lengthy production run.

Allowing for some increase in manufacturing productivity, something, then, has caused costs to more than double over what one would expect in the production phase alone.

149

FIGURE IV

COMPARISON OF GROWTH IN AIRLINER PRICES, PRODUCTIVITY, &
THE CONSUMER PRICE INDEX

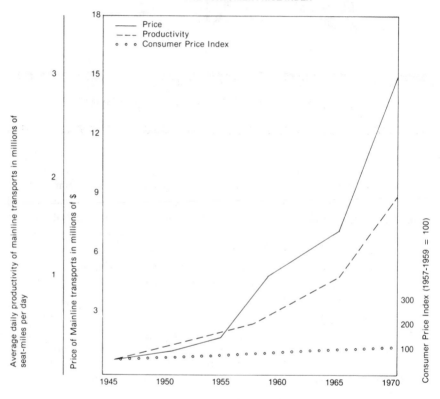

*1970 point estimated on productivity.

Sources:

Airliner prices from **Aviation Week** and **Wall Street Journal**.

Airliner productivity from **Aviation Week**, Jul. 11, 1966, p. 109.

Consumer Price Index from **Economic Almanac, 1967-1968 Business
Factbook** (New York: Macmillan, 1967) and **The World Almanac and Book of
Facts** (New York: Newspaper Enterprise Assn., 1973).

In the Vietnam War the low cost-effectiveness of the Douglas A-1 meant the end of the piston combat aircraft. *Courtesy McDonnell Douglas Corporation.*

The broadest influence must be the society of which the industry is a part. Ours is a society which has kept its love of gadgets, but which has become disenchanted with technology, production, and the work ethic. It has become a service rather than a production society. In the latter half of the sixties the productivity of Europe rose 40 to 50 percent, that of Japan 90 percent, and that of the United States only 10 percent. And for the United States this was down by half from the two previous decades.

THE CUSTOMER AS THE CULPRIT

It is clear that sharply rising costs are characteristic of all federal government programs and not just aerospace. In recent years the costs of tanks have risen at the same rate as aerospace costs. Shipbuilding has suffered large cost overruns. The carrier *Nimitz's* costs had risen from an original estimate of $544 million to $647 million, and the *Eisenhower's* from $519 million to $691 million as of 1973. The problem is not even limited to defense projects, for other government agencies have run up similar skyrocketing costs. The interstate highway system was planned to cost $37.6 billion but the 1973 estimate was $69.9 billion. The Secaucus, N.J.,

The huge increase in productivity which the jet engine gives over the piston is graphically shown by these airliner interior views. At the top is a Lockheed Super Constellation and below is a Lockheed TriStar. *Courtesy Lockheed Aircraft Corporation.*

bulk mail distributing plant was supposed to cost $9 million but the final bill was $60 million. The Kennedy Center for the Performing Arts rose from $31 million to $72 million. The Washington, D.C., subway's estimate had risen from $2.5 billion to $3 billion by 1973.

Within the government, Congress has both economized and helped costs rise. Often Congress has been aggressive in trying to hold profits down, undertaking many effective investigations such as the one of Kaiser-Frazer in 1953; it has attempted to police procurement, it has used the GAO to make analyses, and it has scrutinized appropriations. The results of these efforts have been that Congress is the most effective government agency in holding down costs, despite the fact that it has also done much to increase them. Congress has been generous to defense, often appropriating more than was requested by the civilian leaders in the Defense Department. Perhaps the strongest expression of this attitude was given in 1972 by the influential F. Edward Hebert, chairman of the House Armed Services Committee. He said, "In war they don't pay off for second place. There's one bet and you've got to have the winner. I intend to build the strongest military we can get. Money's no question." Besides this attitude, there is politics. It cannot be attributed as a factor in any one contract, but its influence is apparent in the aggregate. Defense contracts are concentrated in areas represented by influential congressmen, and Congress strongly intervenes to promote social programs which may have long-run economic benefits, but not necessarily short-run ones. These social objectives include racial considerations and favoritism for small business and labor surplus areas. Defense contracts came to dominate the pork barrel over patronage and public works. In 1971 when the Pentagon tried to reduce contract costs by simplifying specifications for a project, it still produced a twenty-five–page document; two pages listed the design specifications and twenty-three listed the social and political requirements imposed by Congress.[1] It is probably impossible to measure the cumulative effect on costs over decades of these policies.

The executive branch of the government has more direct controls over costs and therefore bears heavy responsibility for them. Yet, from the early days of the cold war to 1970, the Bureau of the Budget, one of the principal governmental watchdogs, left the Defense Department alone.

The above are monitoring organizations for the most part; the Pentagon is the action agency and is therefore best placed to avoid costs. Its overall failure to do so is conspicuous. The French, Swedes, English, and Russians, all were producing aircraft for a fraction of American costs in the early seventies. Perhaps the main reason for the Pentagon's failure lay in its nature as a bloated and musclebound bureaucracy. In the early seventies it contained enough personnel for a World War II army corps. And to compound the problem, the services had more generals and admirals than in World War II. The Pentagon is a good example of Parkinson's Law. Since 1947 power has been increasingly centralized in the Pentagon, and within it in the Office of the Secretary of Defense. The evidence points to increasing paralysis as a result. In the early seventies even routine contract matters might call for *fifty* written concurrences. When Deputy Defense Secretary David Packard left the Pentagon he said, "There are a great many people in the department and . . . it just takes a long time to get anything done, even some of the most simple recommendations." Earlier he had told Congress that he would like to "give the contractor a contract without all of this damn red tape."²

The musclebound condition of the Pentagon has been enough to cause procurement inefficiency, but attitudes might prevent adequate cost controls even in a streamlined organization. Among the legions of bureaucrats, there has been only a handful of production experts, the group which is naturally cost-conscious. The only military officer famous for doing something about costs has been the maverick Vice Admiral Hyman Rickover, who was kept on active duty only by the will of Congress. The most famous civil-servant advocates of the belief that procurement costs could and should have been reduced, the Air Force's Deputy for Management Systems A. E. Fitzgerald and Navy Director of Procurement Control and Clearance Gordon Rule, obviously were regarded as troublemakers; the euphemism "not a team player" was used by top management about Fitzgerald.³ To be an empire builder, a spender, has been to be honored and promoted. To be sharp on costs has been to be ostracized. One reason for this has been a prevalent view that performance and time are of overriding concern and cost is not. Another reason was a belief that spending, in itself, was in the national interest. One Air Force officer, Major General "Zeke" Zoeckler, even said in the late sixties, "Inefficiency is national policy."⁴ This is consistent with the most common problem-solving approach in the services, where it has been believed that almost all difficulties can be removed with the application of masses of money and men, the counterpart to the engineers' solution of "more technology." The problems of Rickover, Fitzgerald, and Rule illustrate that service attitudes have fostered sycophantism and repressed unpopular judgments. Holding to unfashionable beliefs can jeopardize an officer's career.

Service practices which have impaired effective decision-making, and which have therefore meant higher costs, have been caused by working conditions. An efficient procurement job has been impossible because personnel have rotated too frequently. The problem has been compounded by the service belief that a senior officer is so competent that he can do any kind of job well, an opinion not substantiated by results, and by the illusion that to be assigned to a position confers competence upon the officeholder. An officer assigned to a position outside his competence is derisively called "the instant expert." Finally, there has been so much busy work that decision makers have found it difficult to devote the proper amount of time to their problems. This was even codified in the idea that a manager should spend only 15 percent of his time in being creative.

The centralization and the mass approach to problem solving led the Pentagon to impose its style of management upon the aerospace companies. The Pentagon and its procurement satellites became, in fact, the managers in detail of the aerospace companies. The process began with a cost contract that required monitoring of a company to protect the government from overpayments. Bureaucrats were therefore in a position to expand their power and, quite naturally, did so. Too, bureaucrats have sought to protect themselves from review agencies by expanding controls. The aerospace companies acquiesced bit by bit, each time to get a new contract for which they were hungry. Another form of pressure to conform was put on North American. Air Force Major General Samuel C. Phillips, director of the NASA Apollo program in 1965, studied North American's management, and the general thrust of his conclusions was that the firm's management concepts should be similar to the Air Force's. He did not say "Air Force" but merely described his own views.[5] His report surfaced during the Apollo fire investigation in 1967; it probably damaged North American's reputation and may have caused the imposition of additional bureaucratic systems on the company.

The general result has been that the aerospace companies came to be run by a huge government bureaucracy, in which many individuals could obstruct action by their nonagreement. By 1971 defense procurement was regulated by over 14,000 documents. And not only was there the defense bureaucracy, but also there were the necessary counterparts within the aerospace company to serve the government officials. Professor Frederic M. Scherer said this has made the firms "arteriosclerotic."[6] Reporting is naturally immense under such circumstances: Kelly Johnson said, "Every project we have ends up with tons and tons of needless paperwork";[7] Martin had to send biweekly reports on 2,500 items on Titan III; 23 percent of the A-7's cost was attributed to paperwork. Costs also rise as engineering problems are solved by mass attack. The

Air Force's reaction to problems on the Titan in 1960 was that the difficulty was caused by too few bosses.[8] Similarly, when Skybolt had troubles the Air Force asserted that the problem was that the project needed 67 percent more engineers. The attitude has been a reflex in the Air Force.

The centralization which has proved to be an organizational problem has been compounded by a fashion in decision-making. In the services the old custom of briefing has been abused. Briefings are a most useful and efficient means for communicating simple or background information. Like the TV news, briefings are part showmanship and are particularly suitable for gimmickry. They are routinely used as propaganda and almost always present a Pollyanna approach to matters. Briefings have proved so popular that they have nearly driven the staff study, which is intended to be a thorough, objective, documented paper, out of use. They have come to be a major basis for decisions for the centralized top managers. In the important F-111 selection decision, most of the top military officers involved did not even glance at the written report furnished them; they made their decision solely on a briefing of a few minutes which emphasized Boeing's optimistic hopes of reaching certain performance levels, and which omitted the criticism contained in the written report.[9]

A related form of deception which protects waste has been concealment of the extent of financial errors or overruns; success in this tactic naturally obstructs efficiency. Another Pentagon process has been to use historical cost data to determine present costs. Fitzgerald has accurately described this as having a ratchet effect ensuring rising costs. Thus if one uses historical costs without analysis, every case of waste becomes incorporated in later estimates, so that costs have only one direction: up. Some of the waste has been provided by the annual rush in June to ensure that the whole budget was spent and no monies were saved.

Yet another difficulty in the Pentagon system is related to "buying-in." There are advantages to a service in "buying-in" on a program, whereby costs are understated in order to get a program started. Once money is spent, there is natural reluctance, even in Congress, to cut losses on sunk costs. Starting several programs in which the costs are relatively small at the beginning provides leverage to expand service budgets later, when sunk costs exist and the projects have advanced to more expensive stages. Somewhat related to this is the personal investment in a program which results from choosing a leader for it who has a chance for promotion. His opportunity is therefore directly dependent on the success of the program, a good policy for most tasks but not necessarily where it might be to the nation's benefit to drop the project. An officer in this circumstance normally will be a partisan for the program at all costs, in every sense of the word, instead of the objective manager he should be. This practice alone may be the major reason that the Air Force has developed a reputation for keeping unpromising projects alive far too long.

Another personal influence in the equation has been the relation between military officers in procurement positions and the aerospace firms. Many procurement officers have retired from the service and then gone to work for an aerospace company. This raises serious cost implications: how well does the officer protect the government's interests when dealing with a potential future employer? How much influence does the ex-officer exert on friends and acquaintances still in the service? Vincent Davis' study, *The Admirals' Lobby*, concludes that the ex-Navy officers' influence has been nil.[10] Other evidence may be found in the cases of two former Air Force officers who became company presidents. One was General Oliver P. Echols, who had an undistinguished career with Northrop from 1949 to 1954; the company was in relative decline under him. The other was General Joseph T. McNarney, once commander of the Air Materiel Command when it was the USAF's procurement organization. He was hired as president of Convair, ostensibly to give General Dynamics the ability to think ahead of the Defense Department. However, McNarney was given "credit" for doing most of the selling on Atlas, the B-58, and the F-102, so persuasion may have been his principal function.[11] He gave an inept defense before Congress in 1956 of the practice of a military procurement officer's becoming an executive of an aerospace company; it is probably a fitting commentary on the practice. Part of the exchange went as follows:

> MR. [Congressman F. EDWARD] HEBERT: . . . Your [McNARNEY'S] previous defense . . . of the B-36 and your consistent appearance in the front ranks of those advocating or recommending the continuation of the controversial B-36 contract with Consolidated has nothing to do with your almost immediate employment by the Consolidated Co.?
>
> MR. McNARNEY: That is correct sir.
>
> MR. HEBERT: Did you at any time ever consider that perhaps such a connection, an almost immediate connection, might make you suspect?
>
> MR. McNARNEY: No, I never considered that. I felt that my reputation in the services was such that a thing like that would never be charged against me.

And later:

> MR. HEBERT: We are getting nowhere fast. But I think your replies will indicate exactly what you have said. And I can understand now, General, how you saw nothing wrong or did not think anybody else would see anything wrong in your taking employment with a company like Consolidated in view of the previous happenings in connection with the B-36. Such naivete is refreshing, but I don't think practical.[12]

Some U.S. government practices have been even more directly connected to aerospace costs. It has already been said that aircraft selection has been made in the Air Force by a group interested principally in the big bomber. That such a limited view was a handicap in choosing fighters, attack aircraft, or transports should be apparent; the advanced technology of planes demands expert knowledge because of the degree of specialization in the types. One need only review the difficulties that airline experts have had in ordering the less complicated airliners to see that selection of fighters by bomber pilots was a gross error.

Related to the basic big bomber bias was the casual attitude toward weight, which is expensive, and the desire to add every gadget known to a military aircraft to increase its "performance," while neglecting the importance of weight as a factor in how well a plane flies. Perfection has been sought without regard for the high cost of attaining that final 5, or even only 1, percent increment. In the late fifties Northrop asserted that going for the final 5 percent would *double* development costs, and it designed its successful F-5 without that last 5 percent.[13] Perhaps the clearest example of the Air Force's attitude on weight is the B-66, which was originally designed for the Navy's carriers as the A-3. The Air Force liked it and ordered its own version. Since the structural requirements for a land-based aircraft are less than for a carrier-based one, the B-66 should have been lighter than the A-3. But after the Air Force had insisted on weight-producing additions, the B-66 ended up much heavier, slower, and costlier than the A-3. This implies that the Navy is free from the gadget and weight complex, but reference to the isolated case of the A-4 and general aircraft development indicates that the Navy has the same bias but to a lesser degree.

That gadget and weight increases raise costs greatly has been of little concern to the military, who for decades have been concerned with attaining the last ounce of operational ability at the earliest time. This has a rational basis, for a slender margin of equipment performance can be the source of victory. But that costly high quality can be overemphasized

158

has so far not been accepted, nor has the fact that high costs may limit the quantities that can be bought to inadequate levels. As indicator of a lack of concern for costs is use of letter contracts, because they have the fewest controls. They originated as a means to expedite production regardless of cost during the panic days of June 1940. Because they can be useful in saving small amounts of time, they are still of potential value. But in 1968, a time of wartime equilibrium, they were used 1,500 times for contracts totaling $7 billion. This is not use but abuse.

The airlines have had the restraints of the profit system, yet they have contributed to the costs of airliners in their insistence upon product differentiation. Some of this is probably unavoidable, but it appears to have been carried too far. Boeing estimated that nearly one-third of its loss on the Stratocruiser was due to catering to the individuality of airline desires. The cost for individual interiors alone on the Stratocruiser was $8 million. For the 737 Boeing offered 100 standard options. The 727 had 6,000 customer-peculiar parts. For its entire commercial transport line there were 21 models with 9 lengths, 10 wing styles, and 21 different engines, for a total of 113 customer varieties or possible combinations.

THE COMPANIES AS THE CULPRIT

There is no doubt that the aerospace companies themselves have contributed to the escalation of costs. With all the billions of dollars of government business, there were no company crises because of cost overruns until 1969. It is obvious that government business insured the companies against losses on any single contract. Gordon Rule said, "No matter how poor the quality, how late the product and how high the cost, they [industry] know nothing will happen to them [because of] representatives of the government who today are condoning and acquiescing in the failure of industry to perform as they should."[14] There can be little doubt that, over the years, such a situation will lead to complacency, a callous disregard of costs, and gross inefficiency. And the problem is not excess profits but excess waste. That such a situation has existed is confirmed by the contract struggles that have come in rapid succession since North American's in 1967.

After the fatal Apollo capsule fire of 1967, North American was accused of gross inefficiencies and padding payrolls; the management of the space division was sacked. The Lockheed C-5A scandal appeared to reveal gross inefficiencies there as well, and there was a minor shakeup in Lockheed's staff. Both Lockheed, with its C-5A and Cheyenne contract losses, and Grumman, with its F-14, have obviously been shocked to be held to contracts in this new era of antimilitarism; and there is a basis for saying that the government even broke the original contracts. There is no doubt they have been treated roughly as compared to the manner to which they had become accustomed, and Lockheed was forced to take a $200 million loss despite the redetermination clause of the C-5A contract. The shock must have been all the greater to the companies because, by comparison with earlier programs in the industry that averaged 220 percent overruns, the C-5A and F-14 have been conservative in their overruns. A perusal of programs from Apollo to the F-14, therefore, reveals inefficiencies by both government and management, resulting in excessive costs.

Better evidence has come from the upheavals of the failed companies and those in recent crises, beginning with Republic in 1965. After Fairchild had taken over, it found Republic's overhead to be excessive. McDonnell has had the reputation of being the most efficient producer in the industry. Within six months of its takeover of Douglas in 1967, deep cuts had been made in the latter's engineering and indirect staff despite the need to expand jetliner output. David S. Lewis, a production man, was put in charge of the Douglas operation, and changes were made in top and middle management. From January to August 1968, 10,000 man-hours were pared from DC-9 production, and the number of men on final assembly was cut from 2,400 to 1,600. Some of this reduction was made possible by growing worker experience and not just improved management. Earlier, the inefficient practice of work done late and away from the proper production station had been followed by over 200 manufacturing personnel.

In 1971 Lewis took over General Dynamics in the wake of its shipbuilding and Datagraphix woes. He found a lack of control over procurement and inventories. And this is what he said about his Pomona Division, which was manufacturing the Standard missile: "The production line looked like a supermarket with pieces scattered here and there. There was no flow . . . ."[15]

Similar actions were being taken at North American. As its business slid after the Apollo disaster, Chairman Willard F. Rockwell, Jr., sent in some men from the automobile industry to do something about costs at North American. They were Robert Anderson, with twenty years at Chrysler, and Wallace W. Booth, with twenty years at Ford. Other auto men were hired to work at lower levels. The auto men were surprised at the laxness towards costs they found. The company had been centralized but responsibilities were vague. Controls were inadequate and cost estimating was so casual that programs worth millions of dollars had

160

been started without consideration for returns. The space division, for example, had launched one program for which no market was known. The auto men had cut the overhead from 1,100 men to 600 by 1972, and had slashed inventories, receivables, and plant by $200 million. McKinsey and Company, management consultants, were brought in to improve the avionics business. McKinsey found it to be top heavy. Seven subdivisions were cut to two, and a campus-like manufacturing plant was put up for sale. The North American experience well illustrates the utility to the aerospace business of an alliance with the auto industry.

When Boeing's sales dived, going into the seventies, it cut itself so much that the company believed it had carried through the deepest and most successful retrenchment in business history. In the process it learned that it had been carrying much fat and could produce aircraft with many fewer workers than believed previously. Delivery time on 727's and 737's was slashed from seventeen to eleven months, reducing inventories. Engines had been held for four months, and this time was reduced to two to four weeks. John E. Steiner, vice president and general manager of the 707/727/737 division, said, "You may ask why the hell didn't we do that earlier, and the answer is I don't know. *We never had to.* We could have done better" (emphasis added).[16] An analysis of production workers found that they were at their work place only 26 percent of the time because of associated activities such as obtaining approvals. Work and layout changes raised the percentage to 70. These experiences are not unusual for companies cutting back in a recession and discovering accumulated fat, but they seem excessive in the aerospace industry.

A major share of the rise in costs in companies must be assigned to the expanding share of overhead expenses. Much attention has been given to the industry's increasing technology and to the resultant increase in scientists and engineers compared to production men. From 1955 to 1961 there was a 113 percent increase in scientists and engineers. But in the same period overhead personnel rose by 163 percent. Finally, in their periods of rapid expansion, the aerospace companies have probably promoted many men beyond their capabilities.

The rank and file personnel of the aerospace companies have not been as productive as possible. Foremen overmanned their shops in the industry because they were more subject to criticism over missed deadlines than over escalating costs. Overmanning hurts morale and has a spiraling effect on inefficiency. Yet aerospace management has lacked diligence in facing up to the workers over work standards and other cost matters. Morale has probably fallen progressively as the intermittent layoff and rehire cycle has gone on and on. In 1966 one of Douglas' major problems was hiring skilled workers, and the inefficiency of the inexperienced workers who were hired, and their training costs, added greatly to Douglas' desperate financial condition. Five years later, in the midst of a recession which had hit the aerospace industry and Southern California particularly hard, Lockheed found it to be most difficult to hire even a modest number of workers. The problem has been a continuing one since World War II, but Lockheed's experience indicates that it may be getting worse. The cumulative numbers of "fed-up" workers who will not tolerate the risk of another layoff must represent hidden, but very real, costs for the aerospace companies. The problem will affect even those who are not laid off, for they cannot be sure of their jobs. The human response, according to William McDonald Wallace, a management economist consultant, is makework; and he asserts that the white-collar workers in the aerospace industry have been an example of a makework group.[17]

COMMON EXPLANATIONS

Those who would be blamed for the above causes of excessive costs have other explanations. The most frequent assertion is that inflation has driven costs up. There is no arguing with that, but if aircraft costs have gone up sixteen times in two decades, the inflation argument falls flat, as is shown in Figure IV. It does not even hold up for the A-1 case discussed above, where costs went up over fourfold in less than two decades. Inflation is a factor, but it explains only a small fraction of the problem.

The rapid growth of technology is given as another reason. By this is meant the proliferation of gadgets, primarily electronic. Their impact, as discussed above, is not only in their own cost but in what they do to the rest of the airframe in adding structure, and in the fact that they make the airframe much more dense, increasing production costs. This argument has validity as well, but its problem as an explanation lies not only in its inapplicability to the A-1 case but also in its assumption that there is justification for the gadget proliferation. Many gadgets, this author strongly believes, are superfluous "gold plating." The firms themselves bear some responsibility for gadget proliferation: there is a saying in the industry that an elephant is a mouse designed and produced under a cost plus fixed fee contract to military specifications. Some arguments in favor of keeping the gadgets sound desperate. An Air Force colonel, H. J. Sands of the Air Research and Development Command, alleged in 1952 that the gadgets were necessary because inexperienced pilots could not fly simple aircraft.[18] Undoubtedly, some of the gadgets are necessary, some are useful, but some have a marginal return which is less than their marginal cost. The growth of technology is, therefore, a valid partial cause but is not as important as claimed.

In some specific contracts change orders have been advanced as the reasons for cost overruns. Yet change orders have always been a fact of life in the aircraft industry. This argument assumes that change orders always increase costs; but *some*, at least, must represent better methods and therefore act to reduce expenses. Also, the basic problem with assessing the impact of change orders goes deeper. The services have used change orders as a device to bail out contractors who have incurred more costs than officially forecast. The excess costs have been loaded onto the next change order in these cases. The process is called "contract nourishment," and the practice makes change orders indeterminant as an impact on costs. Further, there remains the suspicion that the only basic reason for some changes has been to serve as a vehicle for contract nourishment. For example, in 1954 it was estimated that only 10 to 15 percent of design changes were mandatory. In 1968 alone the Pentagon issued 12,563 change notices costing $2.6 billion, and these orders were not nickel and dime matters. There were 3,000 change orders for the C-5A. In contrast the excellent T-38 had less than 60 engineering changes before entering service in 1961, and the successful C-141 project had only 25 design changes over a roughly comparable two and a half years. It seems likely that far too many change orders represent poor initial engineering, the addition of frills, the failure of the customer to adequately anticipate his wants, contract nourishment, or a combination. These are hardly causes for unavoidable rises.

Labor trouble and subcontractor inefficiencies have also been blamed. These factors add to costs, but there has been no indication that they have been other than of minor impact.

The Pentagon has blamed stretch-outs for cost rises. This is valid, when it occurs, for the stretch-out increases the share of cost going to overhead. Another excuse has been to say there was overoptimism early in the program, or an honest mistake. But, because of "buying-in" practices, brochuremanship, and the Pollyanna nature of the briefing system, the overoptimism must also be regarded as a culpable failing and not always an honest mistake.

One of the most valid alleged causes of excessive costs is the stop-and-go nature of some programs. Perhaps the most expensive example of this was the B-58, which suffered from a struggle in the Air Force between the big bomber generals and others who wanted the particular performance the relatively small bomber could give. Obviously, this problem is generated entirely by the government. Also, as the B-58 example shows, it is nothing new, and there has not been any noticeable recent increase in indecisiveness. Stop-and-go is sometimes a valid cause of increased cost, but not of the excessively rising rate.

Related to stop-and-go as a cause for higher costs are the shorter production runs of today. Some airframes continue to be built in long production runs, but most do not. Short runs means production takes place entirely in the most expensive beginning stages.

Fitzgerald reports that the Pentagon acted defensively to set up a group which tried to find that the sharply rising costs were a result of "Inexorable Economic Process." They failed.[19] Critics from outside the government and industry have often blamed at least part of the high costs on "duplication." By this is meant competitive, parallel development or production of the same type of weapon because separate services exist. What appears to be true is not so in this case. In the case of novel designs, deliberate parallel efforts at the beginning and cheapest stages of development improve estimates and provide the best chance of determining the ultimately optimum project. Frequently, the initial ideas are so dissimilar that it is reasonable to assume that some will not even be practical, but sometimes this cannot be determined at an early stage. Thus, conducting projects in parallel, to a point, is a major cost reduction device rather than a waste.[20]

POSSIBLE CONTROL CASES

The most conclusive evidence that the high cost of the American aerospace industry is not justifiable can be deduced from some comparisons. First, there is the record of the "Skunk Works," already described. Then there are the aircraft of France, Sweden, England, and Russia, also already mentioned. These aircraft are simpler than America's "gold-plated" planes, and the mass approach is not used in their design or production. These countries use one-half to one-tenth the personnel employed in the United States for development, and the government teams that monitor project progress in those countries have been usually about one-fifth as large as ours. These elements are part of the Pentagon bureaucracy discussed above and in connection with the Agena D below.

There may be no airframe firm superior to the exemplary Avions Marcel Dassault. Its work force has run between 3,000 and 8,000, a contrast to Boeing's 58,000 in 1972 after its cutbacks, and McDonnell's 86,700 in 1972. In the quarter-century since World War II this meager—by American standards—work force has produced 200 flying prototypes and 3,000 production aircraft of different designs, from fighters to supersonic strategic bombers. The production figures must take into consideration that Dassault subcontracts extensively. All designs have been technologically advanced. The excellent Mirage III was produced by only 25 engineers, 50 draftsmen, and 100 craftsmen in less than 13 months from contract to first flight. The Mirage IIIC variant cost only a little over $1 million. The Mirage G was developed to first flight in 16 months at a total cost of only $35 million. Evidently, Dassault's engineers do not spend their time designing brochures instead of airframes. It is significant that Dassault, too, thinks U.S. designs are "gold plated."[21] The Russians use design teams like Dassault's.

Perhaps the best control case is the General Dynamics prototype, the 1965 Charger, built to compete with North American's OV-10. The Charger was built with company funds, and the OV-10 was a regular government program. The performance of the two aircraft differed little, but the development of the Charger cost only one-fifth that of the OV-10. The Defense Department bought the OV-10 because of the time and money sunk into it.

There was one isolated development designed to test the drawbacks of our heavy-handed bureaucracy. This was the 1961 development of Lockheed's Agena D space vehicle. The Agena D team was physically isolated for the development. Only six Air Force representatives were allowed into the work area, and they had highly unusual powers of decision in the Air Force areas of interest, including funds. The Lockheed counterparts were given direct access to their top management. Deliberately eliminated were the customary technical directive meetings, visits by groups, and the job of keeping persons informed who had little relation to the development. Detailed reports were not made. Although the project required a "modest" advance in technology, it used one-fourth of the engineers originally proposed, and was completed in half the scheduled time and at half the estimated cost. Despite the achievement, the method was not repeated. The Air Force maintained the success was due to a lack of change orders. As shown by the "contract nourishment" practice, the absence or presence of change orders means nothing in terms of the necessity for technical change. The Air Force judgment, therefore, although it cannot be disproven, seems inadequate.

Most of the above material concerns developmental costs, but there is one good comparison on production. It is old, but it is such an extreme case it probably still has validity. During the Korean War, the F-84F proved difficult for both Republic and General Motors to get into production. But by its last assembly run, General Motors had drastically reduced production time and costs, producing high profits. Most of its

General Dynamics' Charger. The development of this aircraft as a company project cost one-fifth that of the competitive North American OV-10 built under government contract. Aircraft performance was similar. *Courtesy General Dynamics Corporation.*

savings came from cutting production time and, therefore, overhead costs. Its learning curve was steeper than customary in manufacturing airframes. As a final achievement, General Motors' F-84F's were superior in quality to those of Republic, the originator. This achievement by General Motors was a repeat of its performance in World War II. In December 1941 Republic's plant at Evansville began production on P-47's. One month later General Motors began on F4F's and TBF's in two different plants. It took Republic 24 months to produce its one thousandth aircraft at Evansville; General Motors took 21 months to reach its thousandth F4F, and 23 for the thousandth TBF. Since Republic had a high reputation for efficient airframe production in the war, the results may indicate superior management attitudes and methods in the auto industry. It appears that the aerospace firms are not doing as well as they could in reducing or holding down production costs.

In 1965 Professor Herman O. Steckler claimed that defense contractors had about 25 percent more costs because of an absence of adequate competition. Many estimates were made later. Fitzgerald thought it was 50 percent. Air Force Colonel A. W. Buesking, who had extensive experience in military procurement, told Congress he believed that costs were 30 percent to 50 percent excessive. Professor Frederic M. Scherer estimated 50 percent in 1972. Pierre Sprey, manager of the Systems Division of Enviro Control, Inc., told the Senate in 1972 that our fighters should cost half the price then current. Robert Perry of RAND told the Senate that the U.S. could reduce development costs by 25 percent to 50 percent. Leonard Sullivan, principal deputy director of Defense Research and Engineering, estimated 35 percent in 1973.[22]

All in all, there seems to be no doubt that American practices have resulted in excessive costs through overmanagement and overmanning, caused by a wasteful government bureaucracy and acquiesced in by company managements.

XII

FINANCE AND MANAGEMENT

Rising aerospace product costs partly mirror a sharp growth in corporate investment in plant and work in progress in the latter half of the period from 1945 to 1972. The change was so great and so portentous that the financial story of the aerospace industry falls into two distinct periods.

THE GOVERNMENT AS CAPITALIST

In the expansion for World War II the aircraft industry was reluctant to finance the vast new plant and equipment needed, out of fear that over-expansion would result in an impossible burden of overcapacity when peace returned. Because private sources of funds were controlled by the same attitudes, they were not available for financing the tremendous war-time expansion. Internal sources of cash were inadequate. The answer was for the government to take most of the financial risks, and it did. First it was the British and French governments, anxious for American aircraft. Later the American government, as well as some private financing, provided funds for the industry. In the Korean War the federal government repeated its role as capitalist. Some of the World War II facilities had been sold, and new equipment was needed for the change to jet airframe production with its greater use of machines. But in this later war the companies took on a greater share of the burden because of increased optimism about postwar business. The wartime investments in the aircraft industry are shown in Table XII-1.

In the two wars privately furnished plant and equipment were only 22 percent of the total. Investment on work in progress also had to be

TABLE XII-1
WORLD WAR II AND KOREAN WAR INVESTMENT
IN AIRCRAFT INDUSTRY PLANT AND EQUIPMENT

Source of Funds	Plant ($\times$ 000,000)	Plant and Equipment ($\times$ 000,000)	Equipment ($\times$ 000,000)
World War II			
British and French		$123	
U.S. Government	$1,344		$2,130
Private	212		208
Korean War			
U.S. Government	280		2,044
Private	805		399

large, and this, too, was financed by the government in the form of "progress payments," at the rate of 90 percent.

With the coming of peace in 1945 and 1953, it was proved that the practice had helped reduce overexpansion and postwar crisis in the aerospace industry. In the peacetime years before 1957 facilities were not stable: some government plants were sold, and much equipment was stored, but progress payments continued. In 1956, at the end of this period with the government as willing capitalist, ownership of aerospace plant and equipment stood as follows: government ownership amounted to $800 million undepreciated; private, to $200 million depreciated. The source of private capital was nearly all retained earnings. It is difficult to compare undepreciated with depreciated quantities, and another basis is floor space: Boeing, Martin, North American, Northrop, and Republic occupied 16.6 million square feet of government-owned plant and also 18.9 million feet which they owned. The government's total share of the capitalization is probably larger after consideration of progress payments.

In 1957 a watershed in federal government financial policy was reached, and since then the government has tried to disengage from furnishing plant and tooling but to avoid a radical or abrupt termination of existing arrangements; it has continued, for example, to finance the extensive and expensive one-time tooling of special jigs and fixtures for a particular contract. Also in 1957, progress payments were cut back and were made less promptly.[1]

For years the policy change was not too painful, for the fifties were a prosperous period for the aerospace industry, and the existence of a large and apparently permanent military establishment made private sources more willing to grant credit to the defense businesses. The aerospace firms increased their private long-term indebtedness by roughly $2 billion from the late fifties to early seventies. The significance of this sum and the change may be seen in the fact that, at the end of 1956, the industry's long-term debt was on the order of $200 million. Thus the increase has been tenfold.

Some figures on investment in aerospace plant and equipment in the sixties appear in Table XII-2. It should be noted that the last of the seven years listed were war years, and that space sales were on the rise for three of the years. These were years in which government investment would have been high under its pre-1957 policy of preventing overcapacity. Countervailing factors in the figures were the sharp rise in jetliner sales and a four-year dip in missile sales, factors that would tend to reduce the government's share. In 1972 Barry J. Shillito, assistant secretary of the Department of Defense for Installations and Logistics, reported that government-owned plants had been reduced from 288 in 1954 to 189. He also said that reducing the amount of government-owned equipment had been held up by the Vietnam War because potential contractors had balked at accepting government business which would displace stable and profitable commercial business, unless the contracts were made more acceptable by government provision of equipment. The government had nevertheless been able to reduce its inventory of equipment by 25 percent in 1970 and 1971.[2] Since 1960 the government has not replaced machines as they wear out. In 1967 85 percent of the profile milling machines, a major airframe tool, were bought privately.[3] And although government facilities are still being used, such as the Boeing plant at Wichita, the value of the aging government facilities is low and still shrinking.

TABLE XII-2
INVESTMENT IN AEROSPACE INDUSTRY
PLANT AND EQUIPMENT, 1964–1970

Year	Government Financed ($\times$ 000,000)	Privately Financed ($\times$ 000,000)
1964	$26	$420
1965	39	460
1966	39	920
1967	67	930
1968	19	860
1969	5	830
1970	10	550
Total	205	4,970

171

It should be noted that the government withdrew from financing the industry in the middle of the technological revolutions of the advent of missiles, space, and the R&D business. As these events resulted in a demand for new and different facilities, the government withdrawal took place just when major capital investment was needed. Furthermore, because company profits on defense business were set at a percentage of contract value, profits were appropriately corrected downward when government investment was high. But after the change in investment policy in 1957 they were not readjusted upward, probably from inertia and from bureaucrats' fear of criticism should they increase company profits. The result was a squeeze on profits, making them less and less a source of funds for capital expenditures.

The policy of reducing and delaying progress payments has been modified at different times since 1957. By early 1971 the private investment in working capital exceeded the share provided by the government's progress payments, although at this time the payments by the Defense Department were running at the rate of $10 billion annually, which was up from $4 billion in 1964. Deputy Defense Secretary David Packard was dissatisfied with the level, and in November a new procurement regulation was issued which was intended to reduce the payments. The rule required a prime contractor to pay his subcontractors before he could collect his payments from the government for work done, and the frequency of payment was reduced from weekly to biweekly. The percentage to be paid was unchanged: 80 percent on fixed price and 100 percent on cost contracts. The Defense Department estimated that this would reduce government financing of working capital by $700 million.[4] The growing level of airliner business has also increased the proportion of private and airline-company financing. The airlines, too, make "progress payments" on their orders: normally 25 percent of the price has been paid upon order and the rest on delivery.

THE SHIN STUDY

In 1969 Tai Saeng Shin finished his economic analysis of the finances of the airframe industry.[5] Since he mostly used Boeing, Douglas, Grumman, Lockheed, Martin, McDonnell, North American, Northrop, and Republic, his findings are useful to this study. His approach was historical, and he applied the conventional economic and business tests, mostly for the period 1939 to 1963. Shin found that the finances of the aircraft industry were highly abnormal because of the large government investments in fixed assets and working capital. After a review of the nature of the industry, Shin concluded that "business risk to the aerospace industry has been substantial," and that "earnings of the aerospace industry have been inadequate relative to the level of risk and uncertainty in conducting aerospace business." He noted that the industry has relied upon short-term debt to avoid financial problems which might come during periods of little military spending, but that this relatively secure system of the past had given way to a new period of greater danger because of in-creased capital expenditures based on long-term debt. With this high financial risk, he warned, "the aerospace companies violated a basic principle of sound corporate financing by super-imposing a high financial risk upon high business risk."[6]

William L. Baldwin came to similar conclusions:

> . . . The thin equity structures of the aircraft firms . . . as well as the rise in fixed charges which these firms have assumed in recent years, suggest that the financing of the group is becoming less rather than more appropriate to the industry whose very survival is subject to risk. The significance of this deterioration in protection for creditors and owners is heightened by the low rate of return on total assets employed in defense production and by the growing necessity for private financing of these assets.[7]

THE NEW FINANCING: COALITIONS

One response to governmental withdrawal from financing has been to form temporary alliances between firms. These industrial consortia have been called coalitions. Similar to mergers, the coalition can also be re-garded as an advanced form of natural evolution of subcontracting. Subcontracting, once avoided by the aerospace companies, was ultimately accepted; and recently it has been desired as protection from financial risk.[8]

The first significant coalition was General Dynamics and Grumman for the F-111. Others have been McDonnell and General Dynamics for the DC-10; Lockheed and General Dynamics for the C-5A; and Boeing, Northrop, and Fairchild for the 747. For the 747, 70 percent of the weight and 50 percent of the effort was spread among 1,500 major and 15,000 secondary suppliers, whose share of the program was $600 million out of over $1.6 billion.[9]

The coalition system saved Lockheed from bankruptcy in 1971 in-directly, in the following manner: Lockheed's coalition partners had $350 million at stake on the L-1011. The airlines could also be called coalition members, having paid $240 million to Lockheed in advance.

173

TWA, in financial difficulties in 1971, had over $101 million invested in the L-1011, and it was believed that if Lockheed went under, TWA would soon follow. In fact there could well be an epidemic of failures. This the government found unacceptable; fear of a domino effect led to the granting of government guaranteed loans to save Lockheed.

The coalition system, along with diversification, should prove to be an aid to survival, by adding financial reserves to the aerospace industry.

PROFITS AND RISK

In Chapter VI it was shown that there is disagreement on whether the industry's profits have been high or low, depending on whether they are measured on net worth or sales.

A principal critic of aerospace industry profits was Professor Murray L. Weidenbaum of Washington University, St. Louis, whose findings were given to Congress in 1968.[10] Weidenbaum selected certain years to demonstrate that profits were too high: he used 1952 to 1955, and then he skipped to 1962 to 1965. This is a curious choice. He included three war years out of the eight used, a hardly representative selection, and he completely avoided the difficult years of contract cancellations and the introduction of the jetliners. In 1971 the GAO reported to Congress on defense industry profits, having measured profits for 1966 to 1969 on several bases: sales, total capital invested, and equity capital invested.[11] The results showed higher profits than in commercial business, but Karl G. Harr, Jr., president of the Aerospace Industries Association, criticized the report, claiming an overemphasis on investment.[12] J. M. Lyle, president of the National Security Industry Association, also criticized the report for failing to recognize the industry's high business risk, and stated that the profits were considered before the government's retroactive pricing procedures had been used.[13] This author would criticize the years used in the report. A period of four years was too short, and they were mostly years of wartime equilibrium and a short, untypical period of peak sales. The view that profits have been low has been advanced by the Logistics Management Institute (LMI), a nonprofit "think tank" whose contractual relationship with the Defense Department has led to suspicions of partiality. The LMI study concluded that profits were not only low from 1958 to 1967 but were declining.[14] They gave as the reason that favorable profits in the fifties attracted entrants to the industry, causing overcapacity in the sixties. In 1972 Professor Frederic M. Scherer presented the same conclusions to the Senate.[15]

Business risk concerns the potential of a setback in profits, and in

1968 Gordon R. Conrad and Irving H. Plotkin tried to find a quantitative basis for evaluating this potential.[16] They used the idea that variation in profits was a measure of business risk, and that a high dispersion of earnings was equated to high risk. They examined fifty-nine industries and found that some, such as aerospace, publishing, pharmaceuticals, and automobiles, were at the top of their list for rate of return and risk. Aerospace ranked seventh. This suggests that aerospace and autos, although they might be a desirable combination in other ways, could well be unfavorable partners because of the business cycle. By contrast, the cement industry was thirty-ninth on the list, confirming General Dynamics' and Martin's good judgment in diversifying into it.

There is, then, no agreement on profit levels, but there is agreement on the existence of high risks in the aerospace business. Successful mastery of aerospace company finances and business risk requires skilled management.

CAPTAINS OF INDUSTRY

It has not been uncommon to think that the era of the captain of industry in the United States flourished in the nineteenth century and was replaced in the twentieth by the organization man. Yet the aerospace industry came of age in World War II under its original entrepreneurs, and some of them were young enough at war's end to continue to guide their firms and their industry to the number one position in size in the country. The teasing question arises: can any patterns be found in this all-important area of management? Recognizing the variety that characterizes human nature, and the historian's lack of access to much pertinent information, we should nevertheless make an attempt to speculate.

There is no doubt that the most successful enterprise in the industry since the war, McDonnell, was firmly led by its engineer-entrepreneur, James S. McDonnell, who was young in 1945. But another Scottish engineer-entrepreneur, Donald Douglas, who played a role in running his firm until the end despite "retiring" in 1957, saw his company go from leadership of the industry to collapse. Sherman Fairchild, more of an industrial generalist than an aerospace specialist, chose to leave the immediate direction of his aerospace company to others. Fairchild's role was to step in when the company's situation was deteriorating. The firm's survival may well be due to his ability to detect trouble early, although his company did not fulfill his hopes in terms of growth. Grumman is a special case. Although the founder, engineer LeRoy Grumman, became relatively inactive early in the period of this study, the company has since

175

been led by similar men. A closely knit association of fliers from the twenties, the management of Grumman has aptly been called inbred. Long a favorite with the Navy, Grumman's designs were called stodgy when conversion to the jet age began, and McDonnell took over Grumman's leadership in naval fighters. An attempt by Grumman to recoup with the F-14 led to a major crisis. Under founder Robert E. Gross, a business generalist, the modern Lockheed company flourished, living up to its motto, "Look to Lockheed for Leadership." When Gross died in 1961 the company was taken over by his brother, Courtland, also a business generalist but less aggressive. After Courtland came a team leadership by Daniel J. Haughton and A. Carl Kotchian. It is too early to know top management's role in Lockheed's recent years but, superficially at least, it appears that Lockheed has not been the same company since Robert Gross died. The Martin firm was still led at the end of World War II by its mechanic-entrepreneur Glenn E. Martin. He did not remain in active leadership after the company's Korean War crisis, when he was accused of contributing to the firm's problems. James H. Kindelberger, the partly trained engineer who was the entrepreneur of North American, guided the company until the end of the fifties and steered it in its conversion from aircraft to R&D. The firm was a notable success. Kindelberger was followed by a long-time associate, engineer J. L. Atwood. It was under Atwood that North American had its greatest difficulties since the forties. Yet Atwood may have accomplished more than Kindelberger, for he believed diversification was necessary and it was he who achieved the merger with Rockwell. For a few years after World War II John Northrop, a mechanic, led his company. The leadership was not spectacular, and Professor John B. Rae says Northrop was a genius of design but not of management.[17]

Thus, eight of the twelve aerospace companies studied were led by their founders for many years after 1945 and with varying results. The same variation characterized those eight when they were in the hands of successors and the four whose founders were already out of the picture in 1945. Boeing, the second most successful company since World War II, was led by a man who was well removed from the founder: lawyer William Allen. Republic was led from the late forties by another man far removed from the company founder; this was generalist Mundy Peale. Under Peale, Republic steadily lost ground relative to others in the industry and finally reached a dead end. Curtiss-Wright was in the hands of successors and faded early. General Dynamics, or Convair, had only one strong leader in the aerospace business until the present David Lewis, who is production oriented, and about whom it is too early to speculate.

176

That one outstanding man was financier Floyd Odlum, whose intention was only to rehabilitate the company and then step out, an intention which he carried out. A hypothesis has been advanced that General Dynamics has lacked adequate leadership through the top ranks because of the haste with which the company was assembled, that it never achieved the smooth efficiency of an established management. Martin was managed most of the time after 1945 by George Bunker, an engineer, who built a giant of a firm from the shambles he took over in 1951. In 1959 Northrop picked a winner in young engineer Thomas V. Jones, who altered the firm's direction and made it strong and successful for the first time.

Are there any patterns in the above? Some cautious hypotheses do present themselves. The entrepreneur-founders did exceptionally well until they became old. Then some stumbled. Perhaps they lost the ability to keep pace with the galloping technological, social, political, and economic changes. There is no pattern in founder versus successor as a guide to successful management; strong founders did not necessarily leave behind leadership vacuums when they retired. Generally, long tenure has been associated with successful management. Has dangerous complacency tended to set in after long production runs? The experiences of Grumman and Republic would indicate it does. Or perhaps they indicate that fliers do not make good businessmen when the competition gets stiff. During a period in American history when company leadership was mostly in the hands of financiers and market men, the most successful management in the aerospace industry—the supreme technological business—has been by engineers. Noticeably lacking have been production men, perhaps a dangerous flaw for an industry whose future is threatened by its nearly out-of-control costs.

XIII

The circumstances surrounding entry of new firms into the aerospace industry provide valuable insights into the nature of the industry. What are the incentives to enter? The classical economic reason would be that profits are high and therefore attractive. A possible variation on this would be the motive to escape partly or wholly from dependence on the commercial market so as to have assured, if lower, profits. Entry could be a means to acquire technological skills at government expense, or to exploit knowledge already gained by a firm, or to bring ideas to fruition. Firms might enter to diversify so as to expand or to gain countercyclical insurance. Finally, entry could be attempted in order to use a firm's excess capacity.

BARRIERS TO ENTRY

The value of such advantages must be large enough to make up for the cost of breaching the barriers to entry. Discussion here will be limited to entry into prime contractor status, which is critically different in composition and scale from entry at the subcontractor level. To become a prime contractor, a firm must convince a government agency that it has the best proposal among several offered. This means winning against companies with which the agency is familiar and which have demonstrated capability. The nature of this problem is best shown by the struggle by Boeing to overcome Douglas' reputation in airliners, and on an everyday basis by customer acceptance of brand names. If Boeing had this trouble with businessmen, it can be imagined how difficult it is to be in the same

179

position with a government agency. The bureaucrats must be assured that the facilities are of adequate size, the technical and managerial staff large and skilled, and the financial resources ample. It must be acknowledged that bureaucrats run personal risks by accepting a new firm over an experienced one. If the contract runs into difficulty criticism will be certain and, since time is critical in defense projects, there will be added reproaches on this score.

Some chance to by-pass competition is available through one of the exceptions to advertised bids which Congress has allowed. Negotiated contracts are permitted by these exceptions, and they form a large share of business done, especially with primes. There are seventeen exceptions: (1) a national emergency; (2) public exigency that will not allow delay; (3) purchases for less than $2,500; (4) procurement of personal or professional services; (5) the services of educational institutions; (6) purchases made outside the U.S.; (7) procurement of medicines or medical supplies; (8) supplies bought for authorized resale; (9) subsistence supply purchases; (10) supplies and services for which it is impractical to secure competition by formal advertising; (11) research, developmental or experimental work; (12) classified purchases; (13) purchase of technical equipment which requires standardization; (14) technical or specialized supplies requiring substantial initial investment or extended period of preparation for manufacture; (15) negotiation which follows advertising; (16) purchases in the interest of national defense or industrial mobilization; and (17) exceptions otherwise authorized, such as for Congress' politico-social objectives. The tenth exception is the one most often used.

The bureaucratic concern over facilities and finances is easiest to overcome because the government can still perform the role of capitalist, providing plant, equipment, and working capital if it appears desirable. There is the further assurance of the cost reimbursable contract. Herman O. Stekler estimated that if the government no longer furnished facilities, the minimum cost to build the necessary facilities to enter the space field alone was $12 million in 1965 dollars. This estimate was based upon Grumman's experience in diversifying into the space field.[1]

Whether such facilities are provided or not, they are useless without advanced technical skills, and these have been the basic key to entry into the aerospace industry. A firm must gain technical ability and then prepare proposals. Boeing spent three years acquiring the competence needed to develop the Saturn 5 first stage. Grumman spent $2 million for its research and proposals besides the sum it invested in facilities. And the money a company like Grumman must spend is probably less than for an outsider to the industry.

A more definitive assessment of the degree to which technical skill is a barrier has been given in a paper by Dennis C. Mueller and John E. Tilton.[2] They have broken the product cycle into four stages: innovation, imitation, technological competition, and standardization. Innovation involves a new product. Imitation comes after successful introduction, when the technical obstacles and market reaction can be estimated with a high degree of certainty. Technological competition follows the major advances, and only minor improvements can be made. Standardization arrives when technological progress is slow and production methods are standardized. Mueller and Tilton found entry into the innovation and imitation stages to be easy but the move into the technological competition stage to be difficult. This is a more detailed conclusion but basically the same one drawn by Peck and Scherer in 1962.[3] The reason for the difficulty is that in this stage the resources and specialization needed can be provided most easily by the larger and established companies. In the standardization period, technical skills are of little importance and the question of entry shifts almost entirely to the market, which has become so exploited that marginal profits are low.

The aerospace industry probably passed through the innovation stage for military jets in the late forties, and for jetliners, missiles, space, and R&D in the early and middle fifties. The imitation phase probably covered about another five years in each case, and the industry has since been in the technological competition stage. If Mueller and Tilton are correct, the best time for entry attempts would have been before the early sixties. Their thesis that a small firm can enter would seem justified on the basis of the success of small operations such as Dassault and Lockheed's "Skunk Works," although these have not exactly been entrants into the U.S. aerospace industry.

The most striking entry success has been McDonnell, the youngest of the giants. From sales of $7 million in 1946 it grew to a peak of nearly $3.7 billion in 1968. The company was started in 1939, but in its early years it was a subcontractor. It became a prime contractor in the last years of World War II, when it undertook the development of the FH Phantom 1, the Navy's first jet fighter. Thus McDonnell entered during the innovation stage for jet aircraft, and it may be significant that the most successful aerospace firm has been in the industry only since the advent of the jet.

An unsuccessful entrant in the late forties was Chase Aircraft, which had an excellent piston-engine tactical transport design, the C-123, of which over 300 were built. It has seen long service including use in the Vietnam War. But it was not Chase which got the production run in 1954; it was Fairchild. Chase tried to enter during the most difficult time for a small company, at the period of technological competition in the fading piston-engine technology. Still, the fact that the company's design was a success under the circumstances suggests that entry, and by a small firm, is possible.

An interesting case in entry was that of General Dynamics when it acquired Convair in 1954 in order to diversify. It was unusual because the smaller company absorbed the larger one. In the last year of independence, General Dynamics' sales were $206 million, while Convair's were $371 million. General Dynamics before the acquisition had consisted primarily of the former Electric Boat firm.

CHALLENGE FROM THE AUTOMOBILE INDUSTRY

The above entries neither threatened nor gave concern to the aerospace industry. But any move from the rich and efficient auto industry might have given the existing aerospace firms pause, especially because of the

The C-123 was unique as the only significant postwar aircraft designed by a small firm. It was developed by Chase Aircraft and produced by Fairchild. *Courtesy Fairchild Industries, Inc.*

production revolution of transition from tin bending to machining. The General Motors achievement in producing the F-84F illustrates how formidable the auto industry could have been as a competitor.

The first serious move was made during the panic mobilization days of December 1950. At 10 A.M. on 5 December the Reconstruction Finance Corporation gave ailing Kaiser-Frazer a $25 million loan and told it to get a defense contract. At 2 P.M. Air Force Lieutenant General K. B. Wolfe informed Fairchild, by telephone, that Henry and Edgar Kaiser would be at the Fairchild plant at 10 A.M. the next day to get engineering and technical data so as to manufacture C-119's. Kaiser's role was confirmed by the Air Force on 15 December even though the company's contract proposals had not yet been received by the airmen. To understand these unusual procedures, which appear on the surface to be hastily conceived decisions and to illustrate a cavalier attitude towards Fairchild, we must put them into context. In December 1950 it was feared that World War III might be imminent and that aircraft production should be increased as much and as quickly as possible. Consideration had already been given to reopening a plant for the planned expansion of C-119 production. Kaiser had experience with aircraft manufacturing as a World War II subcontractor; it had excellent plant capacity available in the giant airplane factory at Willow Run; and it already held study contracts for building bombers. Thus the transaction made some sense in the light of the situation at the time, although there is no doubt that Fairchild was treated inconsiderately. The arrangements appeared so ill considered at the time that the trade magazine *Aviation Week* warned that the contract should be closely monitored, saying Fairchild could build better C-119's sooner, and forecasting that Kaiser would be a high-cost producer. The following May, Kaiser, still with an ailing auto business, bought into Chase Aircraft with the intention of remaining in the aerospace business with Chase's C-123. In June 1953 a congressional investigation was started because Kaiser's production was lagging and its C-119's were costing $1,339,000 as compared to Fairchild's $265,000. In the investigation an Air Force report which was highly critical of Kaiser's efficiency was produced, and Air Force Deputy Chief of Staff for Materiel Lieutenant General Orval R. Cook, admitted that "the Air Force is disappointed . . . in the performance of the Kaiser-Frazer operation."[4] Henry Kaiser gave a spirited and able defense of his company's record, partly by drawing parallels with Ford's experience at Willow Run in World War II, but during the investigation the Air Force terminated its agreements with Kaiser for both C-119's and C-123's. The press asserted that the Air Force had ended the contracts because Congress had aired a wasteful situation; the Air Force denied this contention but offered no other explanation. With termination the investigation ceased, and so, too, did Kaiser's ill-starred attempt to enter the aerospace industry. Fairchild was given the C-123 contract.

The next auto firm to become interested was powerful Chrysler, at a time when the Army was competing with the Air Force for the control of long-range missiles. The Army by-passed the Air Force's allies in the interservice rivalry, the aerospace companies, and asked only the big three automakers to bid on its Redstone-Jupiter missile. A $750 million contract was negotiated with Chrysler. Thus entry was made during the innovative stage in missiles, but it was only partial. Although the auto firm participated in the development of Jupiter from the beginning, the arrangement was basically for Army arsenal development and Chrysler production. The auto company thereby failed to acquire all the technical skills involved in being a prime in the aerospace industry, but it did make a discovery ominous to that industry: Chrysler's production skills carried over easily from autos to missile airframes. The firm's experience led it to bid for a major role in missiles and space in 1959 while the fields were still in the innovative stages. Chrysler believed it had three advantages: (1) it had by then gained more experience with large missiles than many aerospace companies; (2) it had a close relationship with the German missile and space scientists of the Army's Ballistic Missile Agency, formed during the Redstone and Jupiter missile projects; and (3) it thought its reliability performance was superior to other automakers. It formed a Defense Products Group of a hundred men, most of whom were engineers. A basic flaw in these plans was that no avionics ability was built up, the same mistake Douglas made, and Chrysler was forced into coalition bidding. Further, there may have been managerial weaknesses. Instead of conducting negotiations directly with the Army, the firm found itself in competitive bidding. It lost in its efforts to get the Polaris and Minuteman projects, and its only success thereafter was to win the Saturn 1 booster contract in 1961, over companies which included Avco, Boeing, Ford, Lockheed, and Vought.

The presence of Ford in the Saturn 1 competition shows interest by the second of the big three of the auto industry; and the third, General Motors, made a determined effort to win the 1958 Minuteman competition. This was the contract ultimately received by Boeing, which had anticipated the call for bids and had made extensive preparations.

These attempts by the powerful and able auto companies to enter the aerospace industry might have turned out differently and resulted in a reduced share of the market by the companies who had long been in the

184

field. That the auto firms did not enter was a combination of inefficiency or bad luck for Kaiser, concentration on production instead of systems engineering by Chrysler, and Boeing's foresight in the case of General Motors. Also, the older aerospace companies benefited by their established relations with the Air Force when the Army lost the long-range ballistic missiles mission and was no longer in the market. Each service tends to do business with firms it has grown accustomed to. Without this odd combination of events the auto makers might today have a large role in the aerospace industry, for they tried to enter it at the innovative stage.

Rockwell, a diversified company with a major interest in the auto industry, entered the aerospace business in an apparently classical way, through merger with North American, as already described. But Rockwell's interest was less to invade the aerospace industry than it was to strengthen its existing lines. It hoped the marriage of North American's technological innovations with Rockwell's marketing skills would generate new commercial goods and services. Therefore Rockwell's action is something less than customary entry.

CHALLENGE FROM THE AVIONICS INDUSTRY

Formidable as would be any challenge from the automobile companies, the most effective threat was in fact from the electronics industry. The opportunity came with the innovation stage of missiles because that type of airframe is dominated by its avionics components. In addition, the smaller missiles can be considered as a twilight zone between armament and aerospace vehicles, as they are not clearly one or the other. They will be treated as airframes in this study because the aerospace industry viewed them as such.

It was fairly easy for the avionics companies to enter because they had already held subsystem contracts. Early entrants were Hughes with its Falcon and Philco with its Sidewinder and later Shillelagh. By the sixties there were also Raytheon with Sparrow and Hawk, Western Electric with the Nike family, Bendix with Talos, and Sperry with Sergeant. These were established and able companies.

Only when the avionics companies had established their foothold did the giant aerospace companies take alarm. Their answer was to counterattack, to enter the avionics field. As early as 1954 the aerospace industry had 6,200 electrical and electronic engineers, and 45 percent were working on guided missile R&D. The early avionics capability arose from the need to integrate electronic equipment into the airframe and from the initial lack of components available from electronics firms. But by 1954 Convair foresaw that an avionics capability would become a prerequisite to getting contracts as a prime, and moves were made by Convair and North American, Boeing, Northrop, and Martin to produce avionics themselves. It was at this point that the Air Force intervened to protect the electronics manufacturers by threatening retaliation against aerospace firms which produced avionics goods. The threat inhibited but did not prevent the development. Five years later the aerospace firms had over four times as many electrical and electronic engineers: 27,800. The value of avionics they manufactured was about $900 million annually, of which about $130 million represented sales to other companies.

The avionics firms, then, have firmly established themselves as airframe manufacturers, *but only of the smaller missiles.* The giant aerospace manufacturers make the larger missiles and some of the smaller ones. Perhaps it could be said that it was the aerospace firms which entered the munitions business. But it should be noted that, to a degree, the division of the missile business is logical. The avionics firms have been limited to the small missiles in which the airframes are relatively less significant, and the large aerospace companies mostly build the large missiles in which the airframes are far more important.

In general the entry attempts were all made in the initial stages of technology, identified as the easiest time for entry by Mueller and Tilton, yet that entry has been difficult at best. Also, the fact that the attempts are concentrated in the fifties tends to confirm the Logistics Management Institute's and Scherer's belief that the decade was profitable and that low profits and overcapacity appeared in the sixties. An economist would expect entrants during an industry's period of high profitability and an absence of them during a period of low profitability. The reverse pattern should occur with exits from the industry.

186

XIV

EXIT FROM THE AEROSPACE INDUSTRY

The expectation of economists that profitable periods would see entry into an industry and unprofitable ones would result in exits is roughly borne out with the aerospace companies. As shown in the last chapter, attempts at entry occurred mostly in the aerospace prosperity of the fifties. Curtiss-Wright left the industry at the end of the profitless forties, and Republic and Douglas collapsed in the troubled sixties and were absorbed by Fairchild and McDonnell. However, as will be seen, corporate crisis has been almost continuous among the aerospace firms since World War II, so these three exits could well have been coincidental in their timing.

BARRIERS TO EXIT

Of the exits, none were voluntary and two represented company failures. There must, then, be powerful barriers to exit. They are believed to be the highly specialized engineering and production technology of the industry. High quality and precision in construction do not fit civil needs for the most part, and they conflict with commercial demands for low cost. Finally, aerospace marketing skills are suited to sell to government agencies and not to business or consumers. The diversification struggles related in Chapter X covered the problems of exit except for corporate failure, the most common form of leaving the aerospace industry. Although it did not fail, Curtiss-Wright has never been the same since its exit from the business.

FADING AWAY: CURTISS-WRIGHT

Curtiss prepared for the post–World War II period by amassing large liquid reserves. In common with many able persons, its president, Guy Vaughn, expected the usual postwar depression. The company proceeded very cautiously with new designs, conserving its liquidity as much as it could. Curtiss failed to sell any of its postwar designs to the military, and its hopes for Commando airliner business faded when the AAF dumped its C-46's onto the used airplane market, where they flew on and on. None of its proposed new designs appealed to the airlines.

For a while the firm limped along on airframe subcontracting and modification work. Its engineer group declined in quality, and there were organizational convulsions. After the second one, Roy T. Hurley became president. A production expert from Ford, he had little use for a large design staff, and the engineering group was reduced to cut expenses. This was the execution order for Curtiss-Wright's airframe business, which was officially abandoned in 1950.

After leaving airframes Curtiss continued its policy of holding down engineering efforts on its remaining aircraft engine business. This enterprise, too, faded away. The company became an aerospace industry subcontractor, retaining some special fields such as instrumentation and the Wankel engine.

During and after Curtiss-Wright's decline and departure, other firms narrowly escaped exit through failure.

THE NARROW ESCAPES: MARTIN

Despite aggressive design and development, the Martin company achieved production for only small numbers of flying boats, all based on World War II types. Its postwar models appear to have been well done, but were narrowly bettered by other designs, military and commercial.

From 1947 to 1949 Martin was in crisis. The founder, Glenn Martin, stepped up to the position of chairman of the board; a new president, C. C. Pearson, was hired; and other management changes were made. The airliner projects, which had been draining cash, were shelved. Unable to get private credit, the company obtained a Reconstruction Finance Corporation loan of $28 million, which brought it through.

The firm made progress towards renewed financial health. Martin modified its airliner to make it more competitive. A conservative approach was followed to get business before committing funds, but the company still got into trouble with a combination of bad timing and managerial errors. It was committed to airliner production on fixed-price contracts when the Korean War inflation hit. At the same time military work increased. The expansion got out of control, and Martin's narrowly sufficient finances could not stand the strain.

In 1949 Martin had made the blunder of taking sides with the Navy in the B-36 controversy, an error which nearly ruined it in the new crisis, as relations with the Air Force were strained. A tactless error had been made earlier, during World War II, which may have been a factor as well. The Martin B-26 gained an unfavorable reputation with many pilots and had a high accident rate, earning the popular "record" of "a plane a day in Tampa Bay." At one of Senator Harry Truman's hearings in midwar, Glenn Martin made the mistake of telling the senator that the company refused to modify the plane. Truman said he would see that the plane was not bought. It was modified, but undoubtedly some ill will remained.[1]

Now, in 1951, Martin appealed for government aid again. V-loans were obtained but not enough. RFC financing was the last resort, but the head of that agency was now Stuart Symington, who had been secretary of the Air Force at the time of the B-36 controversy. Symington denied Martin a loan, expressing his belief that the industry had too many firms in it. He also said Glenn Martin was senile and a bad risk. As it turned out, Martin got the loan because President Harry Truman overrode Symington, but a condition imposed by the lenders was the complete dismissal of Glenn Martin. George M. Bunker was brought in as president, serving from 1952 to 1972, and under him Martin diversified and did well. One potential corporate crisis loomed when Titan was in trouble: at the time, the Martin launch pad at Canaveral was called "The Inferiority Complex." George Bunker took over personal direction of the program, and as he made only some minor organizational changes it was probably his presence which restored efficiency.

THE LONG STRUGGLE: FAIRCHILD AND NORTHROP

Fairchild has not been so close to exit through failure as Martin, but it has had severe crises. When the Air Force abruptly gave the large-scale C-119 contract to Kaiser-Frazer it treated Fairchild shabbily. Fairchild employees resented it, of course, and there have been claims that some of them took reprisals by working carelessly on assistance for Kaiser. This probably accounts for the ill will between Fairchild and the Air Force in the fifties, and, in turn, was probably reflected in the firm's difficulty in selling to the airmen. It has been asserted that the cool relations account for the fact that the F-27 was not adopted as a military

189

transport. Fairchild tried repeatedly to secure a follow-on transport of its own design to the C-82 and C-119 tradition, which had been a break-through in military transport design. All it could get was production of the Chase-designed C-123, and the C-130 gave to Lockheed the domi-nance in tactical transports once held by Fairchild. Following the end of C-119 and C-123 production, Fairchild came closest to success with the F-27 airliner and the Goose guided missile. When the F-27 did not sell and the Goose was canceled, Fairchild began a two-year crisis in 1958. A new president was named at that time, but he failed to improve things, and in 1960 Sherman Fairchild again took over temporarily. In 1961 Edward G. Uhl, an engineer, was named head. The actions he took included the sacking of executives, a cost reduction campaign, and a

As the first important transport for forward areas to embody design features desired by the military, the piston engine C-119 gave Fairchild the promise of a secure market niche. Trouble with the Air Force over the Kaiser-Frazer contract for building C-119's and the advent of the excellent propjet C-130 gave Lockheed this market.
Courtesy Fairchild Industries, Inc.

switch from product diversification to technical diversification. Uhl asserted that the basic problem was a weak engineering staff, and Republic was acquired to help strengthen Fairchild in this area.[2] By 1966 Fairchild was strong enough to bid for the Douglas Company. Sales trebled and earnings doubled, although there was a heavy loss in 1968 as Fairchild's 228 jetliner follow-on to the F-27 was written off with a loss of over $30 million. Uhl has sought mostly missile and space work but is still interested in aircraft, and in 1973 Fairchild won the A-X attack plane competition with its A-10.

Northrop's problems have been similar to Fairchild's. Its first post-war crisis came in 1947, when its proposed airliner did not sell; and the Air Force canceled its flying-wing bombers in 1949, probably because of the technical success of the longer-ranged B-36. An RFC loan kept Northrop going until its F-89 was accepted for production, but when the F-89 and Snark were terminated, Northrop was at another critical juncture. It diversified and finally prospered in the sixties.

The repeated near-exits by failure of Fairchild and Northrop represent points of progressive deterioration of their status in the industry. From full competitors of the larger giants, they have been forced to diversification and to peripheral status in order to survive among the design giants of the aerospace industry.

THREE-TIME LOSER: GENERAL DYNAMICS

Convair got into trouble in 1947 and nearly exited through failure in the same way as Martin. Convair lacked military production and airliner sales, and development costs on the commercial transport were high. Into this crisis stepped Floyd Odlum, who acquired a controlling interest. He had acted before to revive faltering firms, but what he found after acquisition was a sicker company than he had expected. Convair's cost management had been ineffective and losses were greater than Odlum had believed. Production of the Convair 240 was grossly inefficient, with a costly habit of continuing an incomplete aircraft down the assembly line to be finished later, which often meant teardown to install missing parts. Odlum raised cash by a stock sale and by borrowing from banks. He also tried to gain financial strength through merger with North American and then Northrop. Management was overhauled, production improved, and cost controls instituted. Yet the only thing that saved Convair was purchase of the B-36 by the Air Force.

Incredibly, when General Dynamics got into trouble with its 880/990, two of the 1947 mistakes were repeated: one was the lack of cost control and the other was running incomplete aircraft off the assembly line. This company crisis was studied in some depth by Richard Austin Smith.[3] But he has not noted a peculiar state of mind that existed at the time: early in the 880/990 program, a General Dynamics spokesman said that there was only room for two manufacturers of jetliners, but he failed to give a rationale for the company's late start against the competition of Boeing and Douglas under such circumstances.[4] It appears that General Dynamics knew better but went ahead regardless. Recovery from the 880/990 crisis was long and difficult; the heavy losses severely taxed the company even though it was by then a giant conglomerate. Probably, it was saved only by the cash flow from its large government contracts and from its cement business.

General Dynamics' third major difficulty arose from shipbuilding losses, $119 million from the Quincy shipyards, which had been acquired for the company by Roger Lewis. Again there had been inadequate control of costs. Perhaps more disturbing, General Dynamics had developed a great advance in business equipment, called Datagraphix, but had bungled the commercial opportunity it presented. This marketing blunder is an excellent example of one of the difficulties aerospace firms encounter in exiting to commercial business.

SUDDEN DEATH: REPUBLIC AND DOUGLAS

Republic's crisis broke suddenly with contract termination of the F-105, but it had long been brewing. Republic had staked its future on gaining the F-111 contract, and when it lost that competition it was left with nothing immediately to follow the F-105. The company had been unable to break out of its one-product status, partly because its overhead costs made it uncompetitive. Republic's demise, then, is not in any way peculiar to its being in the aerospace industry.

Douglas' corporate death also has aspects characteristic of general business situations. Because of its former dominant position in airliners, Douglas had once been the soundest aerospace maker. Its peak in sales was reached in 1958. Thereafter came the crisis over development costs of the DC-8, near-complete collapse of Douglas' government business, and the final catastrophe of 1966. What happened?

Corporate crisis arises from a complex of long-developing causes, according to the reasonable observation of Richard Austin Smith in his book *Corporations in Crisis*. Therefore the selection of any point in time to begin the story of Douglas' collapse is arbitrary. Yet the circumstances of the DC-8 decision, already related, indicate that the early fifties was the time when important events took place which bear on the ultimate crisis of 1966. The DC-8 was given the final go-ahead in 1955. The lag behind Boeing, the inability of Douglas to improve on the 707, and the problem of financing the DC-8 all created large and continuing problems. The early and middle fifties also were the period of the fateful decision by Donald Douglas, Sr., not to enter into avionics. The step was belatedly taken in 1961.

In 1957, in midstream on the DC-8 project when Douglas engineers were taxed harder than on any previous design, aging Donald, Sr., attempted to turn the company over to his forty-year-old son, Donald, Jr. The senior Douglas had been an autocrat whose rules were so detailed that they included restrictions on coffee-drinking by company scientists and engineers. His top managerial group had consisted of a relatively stable group of around ten vice presidents. When control was turned over, the older Douglas kept veto power, and he soon returned to work full time because of unexpected new company difficulties which arose.

The younger Douglas was also an autocrat, but he was less cost-conscious than his father. His principal preparation for the top job had been the position of vice president for military sales from 1950 to 1957, and there was widespread resentment over his accession, which he never overcame. Morale declined and stayed low enough to be apparent to outsiders.

In 1959 Douglas' net losses, before taxes, of over $68 million were incurred because of development and production costs on the DC-8, which was not moving down the learning curve as rapidly as expected. Plans for the DC-9 were shelved and company salaries cut. Key engineers for both government and civil business departed in 1960. The final results for 1960 were another disaster with a loss before taxes of over $40 million. Douglas' main hope for future government business, Skybolt, was lagging behind schedule, and two project managers for it were fired within a year's time. A complete managerial overhaul was undertaken in 1961; by the next year a total of fourteen former top executives had left the company since 1958 in firings, resignations, and retirements. A. V. Leslie, a financial expert, was brought into the company as vice president for finance, but he was never made privy to key company finances, right up to the 1966 collapse.

Skybolt was canceled in 1963 after five straight test failures, and the major contracts left were for Heinemann's perennial A-4, Genie, the Saturn third stage, Sparrow, and Thor. The same year Douglas took the hazardous step of going ahead with the DC-9, although it did not have orders in hand. For financing, Douglas entered into cost-sharing with its

DC-9 subcontractors. By the end of 1965 Douglas had lost many bid competitions on government jobs. The company's overall record in the preceding decade is shown in Table XIV-1.

Dividends were skipped for four years. Then suddenly the business outlook brightened. The DC-9 received its certificate in November 1965, and airliner sales zoomed. Douglas began to look for engineers and workers, and employment doubled in 1965 to almost 30,000 and then grew to about 35,000 by October 1966. This was achieved by accepting low-quality workers, as employees who had been let go in previous cutbacks

Sudden demand for the Douglas DC-9 led to the production and financial crisis which proved to be fatal for the company. The DC-9 had been designed to create the short-range jetliner market segment. *Courtesy McDonnell Douglas Corporation.*

TABLE XIV-1
SALES AND PROFITS FOR DOUGLAS, 1956–1965

Fiscal Year	Sales (× 000,000)	Profit (Loss) Before Taxes (× 000,000)
1956	$1,075	$72
1957	1,093	66
1958	1,210	38
1959	887	(68)
1960	1,175	(40)
1961	795	12
1962	757	20
1963	702	24
1964	654	26
1965	775	25

refused to return. Problems resulted, including expensive training and a high turnover. The firm had expected to hire 25,000 in order to increase its work force by a net 20,000, but found that a tight labor market forced it to hire 31,000 instead. Shortages and delays in the arrival of purchased components added to difficulties created by the need to spread middle management thin to help subcontractors with their many problems. Critics asserted that Douglas' policies had created an array of DC-9 subcontractors with low capability, and that the capital-poor company had been forced to impose such business terms that only firms desperate for sales had come in on the DC-9 program.

The delays were partly a result of the Vietnam War. Douglas' principal business and interest was in commercial aircraft, and this had a lower priority in the industry than military production. A major problem was late delivery of engines. As early as the spring of 1966, Douglas was two and a half months late on the delivery of DC-9's. In October twenty airplanes were late, and the company was falling further behind. Production was complicated by variations in designs: from one basic DC-8, the firm jumped to three stretched DC-8 and three basic DC-9 models, plus cargo versions of each. Airliner interiors offered 800 items with choices in color and finish. This excessive variety had been promised in an effort to bolster sales in the period before the boom began. Another difficulty was that Douglas clung to a single assembly line for too long, and its changeover to three lines caused more disruption than it would have if it had been done earlier. The production problems were aggravated by a a lack of information and control, despite a mushrooming growth in paperwork in the production departments. In August 1966 management consultants were hired to develop controls and to help on cost determination, and later it was found that DC-8 and DC-9 production costs had jumped 48 percent by June 1966.

All the problems outlined above strained Douglas' finances, which had never been strong since the DC-8 development. An indication of the cash demands was the growth in inventory from $368 million in late 1965 to $719 million a year later. Douglas was also forced to support its subcontractors financially. When Menasco Manufacturing had trouble delivering landing gears, Douglas set up a second supplier, Nordskog, at the expense of $500,000 in tooling and materials. It assumed obligations worth $35 million for De Havilland of Canada in return for tooling, inventories, and the lease of a plant. In the push for airliner sales Douglas had granted overly generous financing terms. In June 1966, Douglas first sought additional financing with a $75 million debenture issue. The size of the issue shows that Douglas did not realize the extent of the company's problems. There could be no doubt by August. A pretax loss of $33 million was reported for the previous quarter. In November the company sought to borrow $100 million from eight banks, and an application was made for government guarantee on $75 million of it which was eligible for a V-loan. The government granted the guarantee, but the banks had lost confidence in the Douglases. Douglas engaged investment bankers to help, but the company's reputation was now too low to raise equity funds. The bankers believed Douglas needed $400 million more for eighteen months, and that a merger was the only solution, a merger with a company with the managerial depth to take over Douglas at all levels. The companies interested in merger were General Dynamics, North American, McDonnell, Martin, Fairchild, and Signal Oil and Gas. Lockheed and Chrysler rejected overtures. All of the candidates but McDonnell and Signal were eliminated because they were unable or unwilling to put up the funds required. Signal lacked the management resources needed. So it was McDonnell that took over, and Douglas, once the leading aerospace company and the dominant airliner manufacturer, exited from the industry through failure.

TOTAL PACKAGE FAILURE: LOCKHEED

Lockheed's first major crisis was brought about by the Electra's failure in 1960. The problem never became as severe as Douglas' because Lockheed's government business remained high. Exit from the industry was only a remote possibility. But Lockheed's second crisis was unique and spectacular. First, it represents the nightmare of diversification, simultaneous disaster in different fields: military aircraft, commercial transports, and shipbuilding. Second, it represents the failure of the Total Package Procurement Concept, in which Lockheed had most of the contracts. Third, the bankruptcy of a coalition company, Rolls Royce, precipitated a domino effect on Lockheed. Fourth, the affair was a general surprise.

Until the C-5A scandal Lockheed was considered to have outstandingly imaginative and competent management. Among those who were highly impressed was the McNamara group. In the fifties and early sixties Lockheed had produced some exceptional airframes: the F-104, U-2, A-11, P-3, C-130, C-141, as well as the Polaris missile and Agena Space vehicle. Suddenly, with the next wave of designs, the C-5A, Cheyenne, and L-1011, nearly everything seemed to go wrong. Technical problems in the C-5A and Cheyenne were never overcome. Managerial inefficiencies surfaced with the C-5A, and prompt corrective action was taken. Despite the presence of cost experts, cost nearly got out of hand: some top executive turnover resulted, as well as giant transfusions of cash, including the $250 million government loan guarantee. What had happened to cause the dramatic reversal in performance? It can be only speculation, but excessive overconfidence in its ability to solve technical problems could have resulted from Lockheed's spectacular earlier successes. Also, management may have become overextended as the company grew from about 75,000 employees in 1964, early in the C-5A program, to over 97,000 in the problem year of 1969. Too, the rapid growth in net facilities, which trebled in the same period from $115 to $338 million, may reflect government-inspired overexpansion with resultant inefficiencies. Such overcapacity would make any cutback problems more severe than normal. What Lockheed cannot be faulted for is the circumstance that it held several huge contracts at an unfortunate time: when government willingness to underwrite unexpected costs was greatly reduced.

TALE OF THE TOMCAT: GRUMMAN

Grumman may also have been a victim of the same overconfidence and of the Total Package Procurement Concept when the costs of its F-14 Tomcat outran Navy willingness to pay, precipitating a company crisis. When the Navy version of the F-111 was canceled, Grumman won the contract for its replacement, the F-14 Tomcat. But other business dwindled, and when the Navy refused to pay for the cost overruns of the F-14 and technical problems arose, Grumman entered a crisis. As with Douglas and Lockheed, the government felt compelled to render financial assistance. By 1973 Grumman and the Navy concluded an "advance payment pool agreement" wherein the company could draw on Navy funds for the F-14 and ten other projects. This is the first time advance payments had been given to a top contractor. Grumman paid 6⅞ percent interest on these monies, and the Navy instituted common lender controls: restrictions on dividends, property disposition rules, and limits on the salaries of key officials. At the end of 1973 the Navy loans totaled $54 million, and the advance payment device had forestalled collapse.

Grumman's is the most recent incident in a long series of aerospace firm crises since World War II. These crises are summed up in Figure V. Two significant facts emerge. First, in only six out of twenty-eight years since World War II was no giant aerospace company in trouble. This is a dismal record. Second, the leading precipitating factors in the crises were failure to get government business, and the unevenness of the demand for airliners.

FIGURE V
AIRFRAME COMPANY CRISES

Company	Years of Crisis	Airliner Expenses	Contract Termination	Unable to sell to DOD, NASA, including Alienation of Agencies	Rapid Expansion; Sudden Success; Labor Shortage	Costs	Shipbuilding
				Precipitating Factors			
Curtiss-Wright	1946–1950			X			
Martin	1947–1949	X		X			
	1952–1953	X			X	X	
Fairchild	1958–1960	X	X	X			
Northrop	1949	X	X	X			
	1956–1959		X	X			
General Dynamics	1947–1949	X		X			
	1957–1962	X					
	1969–1970						X
Republic	1964–1965		X	X			
Douglas	1958–1961	X		X			
	1966	X		X	X	X	
Lockheed	1959–1960	X					
	1969– ?	X	X			X	X
Grumman	1972–1973			X		X	

CONTRACT ROTATION

These results appear to contradict the popular notion of contract rotation, or contract roulette, in which the government is said to spread its business around to all firms. Such a policy would mean that the basis for winning a bid was a lack of business, which would not be an economic or efficient procedure. And it is one which would make "military-industrial complex" sound as though it were collusion. In 1972 Frederic M. Scherer told the Senate that this was Air Force policy in the fifties, implying that it was not before or since.[5] Stekler says the policy was never "clearly articulated or consistently pursued."[6] One difficulty in determining the existence of such an unwritten policy is that there are excellent reasons for awarding a contract to a firm which lacks business: (1) such a company has the capacity to efficiently complete a project, in contrast to an organization that must impose a new order into existing business, which is likely to entail excessive marginal costs; (2) if used judiciously the policy would promote competition; and (3) it may be useful in maintaining mobilization capacity. If these justifications have been used they have not been primary bases for awarding contracts, as is shown by the frequency with which a lack of government business has contributed to corporate crisis. Certainly Curtiss-Wright, Douglas, Fairchild, Martin, and Republic would argue against the existence of contract rotation as a government policy, since they have conspicuously not been beneficiaries of it.

Exit from the aerospace industry through failure is all too easy.

XV

THE INFLUENCE OF THE JET ENGINE
ON THE INDUSTRY

PERFORMANCE OF THE AEROSPACE INDUSTRY

The triumphs and trials of the aerospace industry that are recounted above have ended on sour notes: the failures and near-failures of recent times as the industry entered recession and demobilizational instability. Reflections made in the trough of a cycle should not be unduly influenced by the grim outlook of hard times. Skepticism and pessimism would have been easy to adopt in an assessment of the aerospace industry in the late forties or since the Vietnam War: admiration and optimism would have been easy during and between the Korean and Vietnam wars.

An attempt will be made here to find a middle ground. The industry appears to be basically healthy. Despite a combination of recession and demobilization instability only one company, Grumman, underwent a "normal" business crisis. Lockheed was brought to its knees only by a series of massive blows, and it survives. Boeing, with government business running less than a third of sales in the early seventies, retrenched so successfully that it turned a profit, after taxes, in every year. The industry appears to be in a condition to weather further storms. Like other businesses, it should emerge from adversity in a leaner and tougher condition.

In the sixties two scholars evaluated the performance of the aerospace industry. In 1968 John B. Rae admired it in his book *Climb to Greatness;* although some of the disasters of the sixties were briefly mentioned, his story ended in 1960. This was a time when a highly favorable view of the industry could be taken. In 1965 Herman O. Stekler was critical, concluding that the industry's performance was not outstanding and could be improved.[1]

Both Rae and Stekler were correct. The industry has shown the strength to weather storms, and its accomplishments are impressive. If deterrence has been a success, its achievement has been based partly on the material muscle provided by the aerospace companies. Their hardware has also performed well in our recent military conflicts, and their equipment has won the race to the moon and explored other areas of space. American airliners are the world's standard and bulk large in U.S. exports. In short, the industry's technological accomplishments have met the fantastic demands which have been made. But these achievements have not been attained, with a few exceptions, with the kind of efficiency one expects from American manufacturing. The cause is primarily the government's, for the industry provided the technology that was ordered: technical sophistication regardless of cost. Yet, as has been seen, the industry was overly cooperative in ignoring efficiency.

Fortunately, efficiency is easier to obtain than improved technology. And hard times are the catharsis that cleanses capitalism of the waste that accumulates in prosperity. Therefore, the aerospace industry can do better than it has, and can respond to an order for technology with efficiency.

Within the overall performance of the industry, the advent of jet propulsion has been the dominant technical force.

IMPACT OF JET PROPULSION ON THE NATURE OF AIRCRAFT

Dominating all other facets of jet influence on design has been the geometric increase in unit productivity of aircraft. The jet's greatly increased power-to-weight ratio resulted in such improved distance, time, and payload performance that the airplane has far greater economic and military usefulness than ever before. This obviously benefits the industry.

The kind of aircraft which has most benefited from this improved efficiency has been the civil and military air transport. The jet has made the achievement of mass air transportation possible on a larger scale than the piston airliner could have accomplished. The military transport has provided a major increase in logistics capability and military force mobility for tactical airpower and for armies.

The jet has enabled fighter and attack aircraft to retain their effectiveness. Piston fighters or attack aircraft would have been at a relatively great disadvantage against antiaircraft missiles.

Big bombers have been the least affected by the jet engine. Had they not been made obsolescent by afterburner-jet interceptors armed with missiles and by antiaircraft missiles, they would have been made so in a piston-engine world by the rocket-engined interceptor with missiles and by the same antiaircraft missiles. The German Me 163 rocket interceptor indicated the possibilities for this during the piston-bomber era. The jet engine with afterburner cut off development of rocket engines for aircraft.

The overall result of the jet's impact has been to expand the total market demand for new kinds of aircraft, because of the increased effectiveness of transports and the sustained capability of fighters and attack planes.

The jet engine has spurred development of equipment, adding to aerospace industry sales. The jet provided the ability to lift great weights, so more equipment could be carried; at the same time the higher performance of the jet called for improved navigation and communication equipment.

IMPACT ON MISSILES, SPACE, AND R&D

The rebirth of the rocket engine roughly parallels development of the jet, but production of large jet aircraft preceded that of missiles, except for the V-1 and V-2. Further, larger missiles were not practical until thermonuclear weapons were available in small size. Therefore, the jet engine did not accelerate the basic development of missiles, but only contributed to earlier solution of lesser missile problems. Since space vehicles were a follow-on to the big missile, the relationship between space hardware and jet aircraft is similar to that between the missiles and the jet.

What is important to the aerospace industry is that jet production preceded that of missiles. This changed the "tin benders" into machinists. Had the jet not come along, it would have been far more natural for the automakers to have produced missiles than for the aircraft makers to do so. The auto firms were interested, as we have seen, and they would probably have taken over the business. Therefore, the advent of the jet engine indirectly prepared and enabled the aerospace industry to dominate missile and space development and production, operations which are now a major share of its sales.

The advent of the jet also prepared the industry for its R&D work. Too much had to be learned too soon to rely on NACA, and the industry itself entered R&D perforce. By 1967, without counting Atomic Energy Commission or NASA contracts, defense work occupied one-fifth of America's civilian electrical and mechanical engineers, two-fifths of the physicists outside teaching, and three-fifths of aeronautical engineers.[2] Some benefits besides the jet-missile-space accomplishments have resulted. Research has received more attention compared to development, correcting a long-term American failing. The defense work helped to develop high-speed computers and miniaturization. There were detrimental results as well from the emphasis on defense R&D. The education of scientists and engineers shifted toward more technically sophisticated fields and away from productivity. By 1972 production engineering was not taught in most technical schools. Patent applications in the United States by American citizens declined sharply after 1952, while those filed in this country by foreigners reached almost one-half of the total by 1972.[3]

EFFECT ON AEROSPACE MARKETS AND FINANCES

Aside from the marketing factors already discussed in this chapter, the jet engine created a surge in the market. As the text has shown, reequipment with jet aircraft took two decades: the last major remnants of the piston age, attack aircraft and short-range airliners, died out during the Vietnam War. The replacement of aircraft took place earlier than would have been the case with new piston aircraft models, because the piston aircraft had reached a point of diminishing returns in improvement. Also, since the jet technology had been in its infancy, models became technologically obsolete before they wore out. The peak effects of the reequipping and rapid technological obsolescence were reached during the Korean War. This circumstance should always be considered in connection with that war's mobilization and industrial history.

The surge in markets which was produced probably is now over, and the effect in the future will be fewer sales because of the high performance of the jets. The jet airplane is more rugged and expensive than the piston. It also appears to have now reached diminishing returns in technical improvement, although the advent of the jet age delayed the moment when aeronautics reached such a plateau. Replacement of jet aircraft should be at a lower rate than was the case for piston aircraft, although there may be special cases like the recent major improvements in eliminating smoke and noise from jet engines, which inspired rapid replacement of the dirtier and noisier jetliners. Thus the advent of the jet meant a large acceleration of aircraft sales for two decades, followed by a permanently lower level until there is another major breakthrough in engine efficiency. The durable-goods aerospace industry is, for the most part, selling to a mature market, where replacement should be at a respectable level in our air age.

The reduction in the number of units sold, the increase in capital equipment and handcraft methods required, and the higher costs of inventories for larger, more complex units have caused financial burdens to increase. Therefore, financial needs and risks are much greater for the aerospace industry as a result of the jet.

EFFECTS ON INDIVIDUAL COMPANIES

As might be expected, different firms have taken advantage of the technological revolution to different degrees. As stated before, there must be something more than coincidence in the fact that the most successful aerospace firm since World War II, McDonnell, was a jet-age company. Boeing was, of course, a giant in the piston era; and it obviously mastered jet technology as well. At the other extreme, Grumman faded in the fifties and sixties as the jet age progressed, and Fairchild has not prospered since its success with piston models. Martin never mass-produced a jet airframe of its own design except for its mediocre Matador and Mace guided missiles. Curtiss-Wright's jet designs got nowhere. Thus, of the twelve giant companies, only eight truly mastered and participated in the new technology successfully and on a large scale by the seventies.

For the giants, the jet revolution was an opportunity. Despite external forces and internal inefficiencies which wrought vast changes, Boeing, Douglas, General Dynamics, Lockheed, McDonnell, North American, Northrop, and Republic capitalized on jet technology and maintained U.S. leadership in aerospace production in the period 1945 to 1972.

CONCLUSION

Looking back on the complex story of the United States aerospace industry from 1945 to 1972, one can discern some points which can explain the restoration of American leadership in aviation by the sixties.

There was the bitter experience of battle against effective German and Russian jets. Also it was, for the most part, the same enterprising business managers, scientists, and engineers who gave America leadership in the piston era who were around to repeat their success with the jet engine. They had the requisite skills, means, courage, and motivation to take the necessary risks—they simply carried on. Then, in a country which has natural advantages for air transportation, there was the pressure of economics.

Most important would have to be the manifold competition. Winning the cold war was viewed by Americans as a matter of life or death. We wanted superior technology in order to survive and were willing to pay the cost. There was also the rivalry between the two aerospace military services, which, for a while, was viewed by each as a matter of survival. Then there was the desperate competition between companies. This, too, was for life or death. Thus competition was pervasive and for the highest stakes.

The other nations which contended with America lacked some of the above factors, and they made some major mistakes.

America's leadership in the jet age was not foreordained but earned—forged in the challenge of competition.

NOTES

PREFACE

1. Peter W. Brooks, *The Modern Airliner, Its Origins and Development* (London: Putnam, 1961), pp. 118–19, 137, 141.

CHAPTER I

1. Robin Higham, *Air Power, A Concise History* (New York: St. Martin's Press, 1972), pp. 3–8, 239–46; Higham, "Government, Companies, and National Defense: British Aeronautical Experience, 1918–1945 as the Basis for a Broad Hypothesis," *Business History Review* 39 (Autumn 1965): 323–47.
2. Robert E. Sherwood, *Roosevelt and Hopkins, An Intimate History,* rev. ed. (New York: Harper & Brothers, 1950), p. 100.
3. National Aeronautics and Space Administration, *Fifty Years of Aeronautical Research* (Washington, D.C.: Government Printing Office, 1967), Introduction.

CHAPTER II

1. *Aviation Week* (*Aviation, Aviation Week,* and *Aviation Week and Space Technology* will henceforth be called *Aviation Week*), 19 Oct. 1959, p. 25.

CHAPTER VI

1. Senate Committee on Armed Services, *Hearings, Weapons Systems Acquisition Process* (Washington, D.C.: Government Printing Office, 1972), 92nd Congress, 1st Session, 1971, p. 152.
2. Harold Asher, *Cost-Quantity Relationships in the Airframe Industry,* Study No. R-291 (Santa Monica, Calif.: RAND Corp., 1956).

3. The discussion which follows will concentrate on the Department of Defense. The other large government customer of the aerospace industry, NASA, adopted Defense Department procurement systems and has followed roughly the same fashions in buying at the same times.

4. *Aviation Week*, 19 Mar. 1951, pp. 13–14.

5. *Ibid.*, 8 Sept. 1952, p. 32.

6. *Ibid.*, 14 July 1958, pp. 29–30.

7. Senate *Weapons Acquisition Hearings*, 92nd Congress, 2nd Session, 1972, p. 37.

8. *Aviation Week*, 14 Sept. 1970, p. 28.

9. Richard Austin Smith, *Corporations in Crisis* (Garden City, N.Y.: Doubleday & Co., 1963), pp. 184, 202.

10. *Aviation Week*, 4 Oct. 1965, p. 21.

11. Robert J. Art, *The TFX Decision: McNamara and the Military* (Boston: Little, Brown & Co., 1968). At one point, in the footnote on page 118, Art is puzzled by the Air Council's preference for the Boeing design which was deficient in low-altitude supersonic flight, a property critical to the TFX specifications. However, there should be no surprise that the bomber-minded Air Council chose the Boeing proposal which was stronger in bomber characteristics over that of General Dynamics which was better in fighter qualities. At that time the Navy believed that the "F"-111, the "Edsel convertible," would turn out to be just another strategic bomber, a "B"-111. The F-111 did prove to be too heavy for its proposed roles as an Air Force air-superiority fighter and Navy interceptor, and the aircraft has served mainly in its bomber function.

12. *Aviation Week*, 26 June 1972, p. 15.

13. Senate *Weapons Acquisition Hearings*, 1st Session, p. 19.

14. *Aviation Week*, 10 June 1963, pp. 135, 137–40.

15. Comptroller General of the U.S., *Adverse Effects of Large-Scale Production of Major Weapons before Completion of Development and Testing. Department of the Navy*, 19 Nov. 1970.

16. Stanford Research Institute (SRI), *The Industry-Government Aerospace Relationship*, Vol. I, *Report* (Menlo Park, Calif.: Stanford Research Institute, 1963), p. 34. Joint Economic Committee, Subcommittee on Economy in Government, *Hearings, The Acquisition of Weapons Systems* (Washington, D.C.: Government Printing Office, 1970-1973, 92nd Congress, 1st Session, 1971, Part 3, pp. 859–965.

CHAPTER VII

1. The Electra ultimately may have proven profitable, for it was converted into the highly successful P-3 Orion.

2. Charles J. Kelly, Jr., *The Sky's The Limit: The History of the Airlines* (New York: Coward-McCann, Inc., 1963), p. 168.

3. A clear description of the "prisoner's dilemma" is in Paul A. Samuelson, *Economics*, 8th ed. (New York: McGraw-Hill, 1970), pp. 482–83. A valuable description of similar product strategies is in Laurence J. White, *The Automobile Industry Since 1945* (Cambridge, Mass.: Harvard University Press, 1971), pp. 173, 175.

4. Boeing had expected to break even at 50 aircraft, probably because of the hoped-

for savings from converting a military design. The contemporary and comparable Douglas DC-6 was expected to break even at the more common U.S. airliner level of 300 aircraft.

5. Arthur Reed, *Britain's Aircraft Industry: What Went Right? What Went Wrong?* (London: J. M. Dent & Sons, 1973), p. 3.

6. *Aviation Week*, 19 Oct. 1953, p. 13.

7. The 720 was part of a Boeing program of offering a model for every purse and use, just as General Motors blankets the range of passenger cars. One wag at Boeing suggested the 707/KC-135 family should not be called "Stratoliner" but, rather, "StratoVarious."

8. The one case of satisfactory conversion of the last piston airliners to turbines.

9. *Business Week*, 21 July 1956, p. 170.

10. Dero A. Saunders, "The Airlines Flight from Reality," *Fortune* 53 (Feb. 1956): 91–92.

11. C. R. Smith, "What the Airlines Expect from the 1961 Jet Fleet," *Fortune* 54 (July 1956): 112–13.

12. Because of the propeller, three engines had always been structurally awkward in piston engine aircraft.

13. A factor in jet economy was engine life, or reliability. Time between overhauls for the last piston engines was 2,000 to 2,500 hours, or a flight distance of 750,000 miles. The jets were getting up to 8,000 hours or 4,000,000 miles because of their higher flight speeds.

CHAPTER VIII

1. Tom Alexander, "McNamara's Expensive Economy Plane," *Fortune* 75 (1 June 1967): 90.

2. Letter to author from Lockheed Aircraft Corporation, 23 May 1973. *Aviation Week*, 30 Sept. 1968, p. 13.

3. Senate *Weapons Acquisition Hearings*, 1st Session, pp. 132, 138.

4. *Aviation Week*, 30 June 1952, p. 82; 20 Oct. 1952, p. 17.

5. *Aviation Week*, 16 Nov. 1959, p. 123.

6. Gilbert Burck, "Famine Years for the Arms Makers," *Fortune* 83 (May 1971): 248.

7. Senate *Weapons Acquisition Hearings*, 92nd Congress, 2nd Session, 1972, p. 28.

8. *Aviation Week*, 13 Aug. 1956, p. 33.

9. *Aviation Week*, 2 Aug. 1971, p. 9.

CHAPTER IX

1. Lockheed Annual Report for 1969, p. 3.

2. *Aviation Week*, 27 Aug. 1951, p. 23.

CHAPTER X

1. White, pp. 29, 45–46.

2. *Aviation Week*, 12 Aug. 1963, p. 36.

3. *Newsweek,* 16 Aug. 1965, p. 67.
4. *Business Week,* 25 Nov. 1950, p. 32. Wesley Price, "Merchant of Speed," *Saturday Evening Post,* 19 Feb. 1949, p. 32. This incident raises many interesting questions about aircraft industry costs and practices at the time.
5. Only one jet aircraft was built in numbers, but it was not a Martin design. It was the B-57, an American version of the British Canberra, the only non-U.S. aircraft to go on operations with the Air Force since World War II. Around 400 were built from 1953 to 1956. It has proven to be a productive and long-lived aircraft, as has the whole Canberra line.
6. *Time,* 5 Apr. 1971, p. 82.
7. *Wall Street Journal,* 18 Apr. 1963, p. 8.

CHAPTER XI

1. *Wall Street Journal,* 5 Aug. 1971, p. 24.
2. *Aviation Week,* 17 Sept. 1971, p. 15. *The Arizona Republic,* 9 Mar. 1972, p. 60.
3. A. Ernest Fitzgerald, *The High Priests of Waste* (New York: W. W. Norton, 1972). Joint *Weapons Acquisition Hearings,* 92nd Congress, 2nd Session, 1972, Part 5, p. 1406; 1973, Part 6, pp. 2205–52.
4. Fitzgerald, p. 159.
5. *Aviation Week,* 24 Apr. 1967, pp. 26–27.
6. Senate *Weapons Acquisition Hearings,* 1st Session, p. 161.
7. *The Arizona Republic,* 13 May 1972, p. 17.
8. Martin solved the problems without adding more managers.
9. McNamara and the Air Force and Navy secretaries read the report in detail, analyzed it, and chose General Dynamics as the bid winner.
10. Vincent Davis, *The Admirals' Lobby* (Chapel Hill: University of North Carolina Press, 1967), pp. 307–8.
11. Overall, McNarney may have hurt General Dynamics; it was he who made the decision to build the 880.
12. House Committee on Armed Services, Subcommittee for Special Investigations, *Hearings, Aircraft Production Costs and Profits* (Washington, D.C.: Government Printing Office, 1956), 84th Congress, 2nd Session, 1956, pp. 2639–59.
13. *Aviation Week,* 28 July 1958, p. 58.
14. Quoted in Richard F. Kaufman, *The War Profiteers* (New York: Bobbs-Merrill, 1970), p. 117.
15. *Business Week,* 3 June 1972, pp. 75–76.
16. *Business Week,* 1 Apr. 1972, p. 44.
17. *Wall Street Journal,* 30 Mar. 1972, p. 10.
18. *Aviation Week,* 24 Nov. 1952, p. 17.
19. Fitzgerald, pp. 69–70.
20. R. R. Nelson, *The Economics of Parallel R and D Efforts: A Sequential-Decision Analysis,* RAND Corp. Report No. RM-2482, 12 Nov. 1959.
21. Edgar E. Ulsamer, "The Designers of Dassault: Men Who Take One Step at a Time," *Air Force* 53 (Aug. 1970): 38.
22. Herman O. Stekler, *The Structure and Performance of the Aerospace Industry* (Berkeley: University of California Press, 1965), p. 193; Berkeley Rice, *The C-5A Scandal: An Inside Story of the Military Industrial Complex* (Boston:

Houghton Mifflin, 1971), p. 54; Joint Economic Committee, Subcommittee on Economy in Government, *Hearings, Economics of Military Procurement* (Washington, D.C.: Government Printing Office, 1968), 90th Congress, 2nd Session, 1968, Part 1, p. 160; Senate *Weapons Acquisition Hearings*, 1st Session, p. 146; *ibid.*, p. 244; *ibid.*, p. 215; Joint *Weapons Acquisition Hearings*, 1972, Part 6, p. 2131.

CHAPTER XII

1. A factor in the government's change in policy has been the growing commercial aircraft business and other diversification which should not be publicly financed.
2. Joint *Weapons Acquisition Hearings*, 92nd Congress, 1st Session, 1971, Part 4, pp. 1146.
3. *Aviation Week*, 5 June 1967, p. 79.
4. The result was also a significant reduction in profits as well, for interest on borrowed capital was not allowed as a business expense on defense contracts.
5. Tai Saeng Shin, "A Financial Analysis of the Airframe-Turned Aerospace Industry" (Ph.D. Dissertation, University of Illinois, 1969).
6. *Ibid.*, pp. 134–36, 142–43, 146.
7. William L. Baldwin, *The Structure of the Defense Market 1955–1964* (Durham, N.C.: Duke University Press, 1967), p. 196.
8. They have also been sought for nonfinancial reasons: to gain help in engineering and other resources in attempts by two or more firms to match weakness in one company with strength in another.
9. *Aviation Week*, 20 Nov. 1967, pp. 59, 99, 101, 105.
10. Joint *Procurement Economics Hearings*, Part 1, p. 58.
11. Joint *Weapons Acquisition Hearings*, Part 3, pp. 859–965.
12. *Ibid.*
13. *Ibid.*
14. Allan T. Demaree, "Defense Profits, the Hidden Issues," *Fortune* 80 (1 Aug. 1969): 82, 83. *Aviation Week*, 4 May 1970, p. 55.
15. Senate *Weapons Acquisition Hearings*, 1st Session, p. 133.
16. Gordon R. Conrad and Irving H. Plotkin, "Risk/Return: U.S. Industry Pattern," *Harvard Business Review* 46 (Mar.–Apr. 1968): 91–97.
17. John B. Rae, *Climb to Greatness: The American Aircraft Industry, 1920–1960* (Cambridge, Mass.: The MIT Press, 1968), p. 218.

CHAPTER XIII

1. Stekler, pp. 127–28.
2. Dennis C. Mueller and John E. Tilton, *Research and Development Costs as a Barrier to Entry* (Washington, D.C.: The Brookings Institution, 1970). Reprinted from *The Canadian Journal of Economics/Revue canadienne d' Economique*, Vol. II, No. 4 (Nov. 1969).
3. Merton J. Peck and Frederic M. Scherer, *The Weapons Acquisition Process. An Economic Analysis* (Boston: Graduate School of Business Administration, Harvard University, 1962), pp. 198–99.
4. Senate Armed Services Committee, Preparedness Subcommittee Number 1,

Hearings. Aircraft Procurement. Contract Award of C-119 Cargo Planes by Air Force (Washington, D.C.: Government Printing Office, 1953), 83rd Congress, 1st Session, 1953, p. 113.

CHAPTER XIV

1. Harry S. Truman, *Memoirs,* Vol. 1, *Year of Decisions* (Garden City, N.Y.: Doubleday, 1955), p. 184.
2. *Missiles and Rockets,* 26 June 1961, p. 31.
3. Richard Austin Smith, *Corporations in Crisis,* Chapter 3.
4. *Aviation Week,* 22 Aug. 1955, p. 17.
5. Senate *Weapons Acquisition Hearings,* 1st Session, p. 157.
6. Stekler, p. 199.

CHAPTER XV

1. Rae, pp. 212–19. Stekler, pp. 197, 204.
2. Jacob K. Javits, Charles J. Hitch, and Arthur F. Burns, *The Defense Sector and the American Economy* (New York: New York University Press, 1968), p. 68.
3. J. Herbert Holloman, "Technology in the United States: Issues for the 1970's," *Technology Review* 74 (June 1972): 10, 18, 20.

ACRONYMS

AAF	Army Air Forces
ABM	Antiballistic Missile
ADC	Air Defense Command
AFSC	Air Force Systems Command
AMC	Air Materiel Command
ARDC	Air Research and Development Command
ASW	Antisubmarine Warfare
ATC	Air Transport Command
BOAC	British Overseas Airways Corporation
BuAer	Bureau of Aeronautics
BuOrd	Bureau of Ordnance
CAA	Civil Aeronautics Administration
CAB	Civil Aeronautics Board
CASF	Composite Air Strike Force
Connie	Constellation
Convair	Consolidated Vultee Aircraft Corporation
CPFF	Cost plus fixed fee
CPPC	Cost plus percentage of cost
FAA	Federal Aviation Agency
FBM	Fleet Ballistic Missile
GAO	General Accounting Office
GFAE	Government furnished aircraft equipment
GFE	Government furnished equipment
GFP	Government furnished parts
IATA	International Air Transport Association
ICBM	Intercontinental Ballistic Missile
IRBM	Intermediate Range Ballistic Missile
LMI	Logistics Management Institute
MAC	Military Airlift Command

MDLC	Materiel Development and Logistics Command
MIT	Massachusetts Institute of Technology
MOL	Manned Orbiting Laboratory
NACA	National Advisory Committee for Aeronautics
NASA	National Aeronautics and Space Administration
NATO	North Atlantic Treaty Organization
NATS	Naval Air Transport Service
PEP	Program Evaluation Procedure
PERT	Program Evaluation Review Technique
RAF	Royal Air Force
RAND	Research and Development Corporation
R&D	Research and Development
RDT&E	Research, Development, Test, and Evaluation
RFC	Reconstruction Finance Corporation
SAC	Strategic Air Command
SRAM	Short Range Attack Missile
SST	Supersonic Transport
TAC	Tactical Air Command
TFX	F-111
TPPC	Total Package Procurement Concept
TWA	Trans World Airlines
UMT	Universal Military Training
UN	United Nations
USAF	United States Air Force

ANNOTATED BIBLIOGRAPHY

Considering that aerospace has been the nation's largest industry for nearly all of the past thirty years, surprisingly little has been written about it. Except for a few valuable sources, most useful information must be assembled from fragments scattered through periodicals.

U.S. GOVERNMENT

Government publications applicable to the aerospace industry constitute an enormous field, yet only bits here and there are useful for the historian's broad view. For example, appropriations hearings for a year selected at random, 1963, fill over 1,000 pages for the Department of Defense and almost 5,000 pages for NASA. Consequently, government sources were selected rather than exhausted. The selection was made on the basis of: bibliographies from other useful sources, subject matter, and recognition in periodicals.

Many pertinent General Accounting Office reports are reprinted in the *Hearings* of the Joint Economic Committee.

CONGRESS

Joint Economic Committee
Subcommittee on Economy in Government, *Hearings, Economics of Military Procurement.* Parts 1 and 2, 1968, *Report,* 1969.
Subcommittee on Economy in Government, *Hearings, The Acquisition of Weapons Systems.* Parts 1 and 2, 1970; Parts 3, 4 and 5, 1972; Part 6, 1973. Senator William Proxmire's critical investigations of defense procurement.

SENATE

Committee on Armed Services, *Hearings, Weapons Systems Acquisition Process.*

First and Second Sessions, 1972. A general but searching inquiry into defense procurement.

Preparedness Investigating Subcommittee, *Report. Investigation of the Preparedness Program.* 1952. Criticism of the Korean War mobilization.

Preparedness Subcommittee Number One, *Hearings, Aircraft Procurement. Contract Award of C-119 Cargo Planes by Air Force.* 1953. The inquiry into the Kaiser-Frazer contract.

Subcommittee, *Hearings, Military Procurement.* 1959. Useful for the mechanics of defense procurement.

Subcommittee on the Air Force, *Hearings, Study of Airpower.* 1956. A rambling, lengthy discussion of many aspects of airpower.

HOUSE

Committee on Government Operations
Subcommittee, *Hearings, Navy Jet Aircraft Procurement Program.* 1956. The investigation of F3H procurement.

Committee on Armed Services
Subcommittee for Special Investigations, *Hearings, Aircraft Production Costs and Profits.* 1956. An inquiry made too early to be of great use for the period 1945–1973.

Hearings, Study of AF Contract AF 33 (038)–18503 General Motors Corp.—Buick—Oldsmobile—Pontiac Assembly Division. 1957. Investigation of General Motors' profits in manufacturing F-84Fs.

OTHER GOVERNMENT PUBLICATIONS

Comptroller General, *Adverse Effects of Large-Scale Production of Major Weapons Before Completion of Development and Testing, Department of the Navy.* 1970. Analysis of the effectiveness of concurrent development.

National Aeronautics and Space Administration, *Fifty Years of Aeronautical Research.* 1967. A useful survey.

President's Air Policy Commission, *Survival in the Air Age.* 1948. The Finletter Report.

PRINCIPAL PERIODICALS

Aviation Week and Space Technology (Aviation, Aviation Week), New York, 1916–, Weekly, 1945 through 1972. The principal trade journal. Crammed with key information.

Business Week, New York, 1929–, Weekly, 1946 through 1972. Excellent material on industries and individual firms. Gives a broad view of business.

Flying, New York, 1927–, Monthly, 1946 through 1972. A general aviation publication but occasionally useful for military or commercial aviation.

Fortune, New York, 1930–, Monthly, 1946 through 1972. Excellent material on industries and individual firms.

Newsweek, New York, 1933–, Weekly, 1946 through 1972. Has occasional insights into firms and industries.

Time, New York, 1923–, Weekly, 1946 through 1972. Has occasional insights into firms and industries.

ANNOTATED BIBLIOGRAPHY

U.S. News and World Report, Washington, D.C., 1933–, Weekly, 1946 through 1972. Has informative interviews with key individuals.
Wall Street Journal, New York, 1889–, Monday through Friday, 1958 through 1972. Excellent material on industries, individual firms and government. Gives a broad view of business.

UNPUBLISHED

Alchian, A. A., Arrow, K. J., and Capron, W. M. "An Economic Analysis of the Market for Scientists and Engineers. " RAND Corporation, Research Memorandum RM-2190-RC, 6 June 1958. The title is an accurate description.
Asher, Harold. "Cost-Quantity Relationships in the Airframe Industry." RAND Corporation Study No. R-291, 1956. Details of the learning curve.
Miller, Thomas G., Jr. "Strategies for Survival in the Aerospace Industry." Arthur D. Little, 1964. A well-done study soon outdated by the Vietnam War and airliner technical developments.
Nelson, R. R. "The Economics of Parallel R and D Efforts: A Sequential-Decision Analysis." RAND Corporation No. RM-2482, 12 November 1959. The case for duplication in development.
Stanford Research Institute. "The Industry-Government Aerospace Relationship." Vol. I, "Report." Vol. II, "Supporting Research." SRI Project No. IS-4216. Menlo Park, California, 1963. Contains significant analyses but partly outdated by the end of the McNamara era.

DOCTORAL DISSERTATIONS

Reguero, Miguel Angel. "An Economic Study of the Military Airframe Industry." New York University, 1958. The industry as it was in 1958.
Shin, Tai Saeng. "A Financial Analysis of the Airframe-Turned Aerospace Industry." University of Illinois, 1969. The application of various financial test systems to the industry.
Simonson, Gene Roger. "Economics of the Aircraft Industry." University of Washington, 1959. Shallow.

BOOKS

Aerospace Industries Association of America. *1969 Aerospace Facts and Figures.* Fallbrook, Calif.: Aero Publishers, 1969. Earlier editions: 1953, 1963–68. Best source for assembled statistics.
Armacost, Michael H. *The Politics of Weapons Innovation: The Thor-Jupiter Controversy.* New York: Columbia University Press, 1969. Analysis of procurement decision process in the fifties.
Art, Robert J. *The TFX Decision: McNamara and the Military.* Boston: Little, Brown, 1968. Analysis of the changing of the decision process under McNamara.
Baar, James, and Howard, William E. *Polaris!* New York: Harcourt, Brace, 1960. Journalistic version of the development of the missile.
Baldwin, William L. *The Structure of the Defense Market, 1955–1964.* Durham,

N.C.: Duke University Press, 1967. Analysis of the industry and its market. See also Stekler.

Boeing Company, The. *Pedigree of Champions: Boeing since 1916.* 3rd ed. Seattle, Wash.: The Boeing Company, 1969. Booklet of data on Boeing aircraft.

Brooks, Peter W. *The Modern Airliner: Its Origins and Development.* London: Putnam, 1961. Valuable perspective.

Caidin, Martin. *Boeing 707.* New York: Ballantine Books, 1959. Mostly an operational view.

————. *The Long Arm of America: The Story of the Amazing Hercules Air Assault Transport and Our Revolutionary Global Strike Forces.* New York: E. P. Dutton, 1963. Mostly an operational view.

Chapman, John L. *Atlas: The Story of a Missile.* New York: Harper, 1960. Similar to *Polaris!*

Clayton, James L. *The Economic Impact of the Cold War: Sources and Readings.* New York: Harcourt, Brace and World, 1970. Useful look at a factor of great importance to the aerospace industry.

Craven, Wesley Frank, and Cate, James Lea, eds. *The Army Air Forces In World War II.* Vol. 6, *Men and Planes.* Vol. 7, *Services Around the World.* Chicago: University of Chicago Press, 1955, 1958. Official history with background to this study.

Davies, R. E. G. *A History of the World's Airlines.* London: Oxford University Press, 1964. Detailed account with insights.

Davis, Vincent. *Postwar Defense Policy and the U.S. Navy, 1943–1946.* Chapel Hill: University of North Carolina Press, 1966. Together with the following book, provides understanding of Navy actions since World War II.

————. *The Admirals' Lobby.* Chapel Hill: University of North Carolina Press, 1967.

Day, John S. *Subcontracting Policy in the Airframe Industry.* Boston: Graduate School of Business Administration, Harvard University, 1956. Definitive for its time.

Dempster, Derek D. *The Tale of the Comet.* New York: David McKay, 1959. A popular history.

Fitzgerald, A. Ernest. *The High Priests of Waste.* New York: W. W. Norton. 1972. Impassioned story of a victim of bureaucracy. Excellent account of the mechanics of bureaucracy.

Futrell, Robert Frank. *The United States Air Force in Korea, 1950–1953.* New York: Duell, Sloan and Pearce, 1961. Official history limited to operations.

General Dynamics Corp. *Dynamic America: A History of General Dynamics Corporation and Its Predecessor Companies.* Switzerland: Doubleday, 1960. A picture history.

Hartt, Julian. *The Mighty Thor: Missile in Readiness.* New York: Duell, Sloan and Pearce, 1961. Journalistic.

Heiman, Grover. *Jet Pioneers.* New York: Duell, Sloan and Pearce, 1963. Journalistic.

Hesse, Walter J., and Mumford, Nicholas V. S., Jr. *Jet Propulsion for Aerospace Applications.* 2nd ed. New York: Pitman, 1964. Engineering text.

Higham, Robin. *Air Power: A Concise History.* New York: St. Martin's Press, 1972. Scholarly coverage of all aspects of airpower. Source of the Wave Cycle of Development concept.

Hitch, Charles J. *Decision-Making for Defense.* Berkeley: University of California

Press, 1965. This and the following are rationales for introducing economics into defense management by an architect of the system.

———, and McKean, Roland N. *The Economics of Defense in the Nuclear Age.* Cambridge, Mass.: Harvard University Press, 1960.

Holley, Irving Brinton, Jr. *Buying Aircraft: Materiel Procurement for the Army Air Forces.* Vol. 7 of *Special Studies, United States Army in World War II.* Washington, D.C.: Department of the Army, 1964. Definitive.

Hubler, Richard G. *Big Eight: A Biography of an Airplane.* New York: Duell, Sloan and Pearce, 1960. A popular history of the DC-8.

———. *SAC: The Strategic Air Command.* New York: Duell, Sloan and Pearce, 1958. A popular history.

Hunter, Mel. *Strategic Air Command.* Garden City, N.Y.: Doubleday, 1961. A picture book.

Kaufman, Richard F. *The War Profiteers.* New York: Bobbs-Merrill, 1970. Sensationalist but with useful insights.

Kelly, Charles J., Jr., *The Sky's the Limit: The History of the Airlines.* New York: Coward-McCann, 1963. Useful.

LeMay, Curtis E., with Kantor, MacKinlay. *Mission With LeMay: My Story.* Garden City, N.Y.: Doubleday, 1965. Opinions of the dominant individual in the Air Force in the period of the study.

Lilley, Tom; Hunt, Pearson; Butters, J. Keith; Gilmore, Frank F.; and Lawler, Paul F. *Problems of Accelerating Aircraft Production during World War II.* Boston: Graduate School of Business Administration, Harvard University, 1946. Definitive.

Lockheed Aircraft Corp. *Of Men and Stars: A History of Lockheed Aircraft Corporation.* Lockheed Aircraft Corporation, 1957–1958. Journalistic.

Mansfield, Harold. *Billion Dollar Battle: The Story Behind the "Impossible" 727 Project.* New York: David McKay, 1965. Very detailed popular history.

———. *Vision: The Story of Boeing.* New York: Duell, Sloan and Pearce, 1966. An uncritical, detailed popular history.

Martin, Harold H. *Starlifter: The C-141, Lockheed's High-Speed Flying Truck.* Brattleboro, Vermont: Stephen Greene, 1972. Journalistic.

Maynard, Crosby, ed. *Flight Plan for Tomorrow: The Douglas Story, A Condensed History.* 2nd ed. Santa Monica, Calif.: Douglas Aircraft Company, 1966. Very brief text with data on Douglas' aircraft.

Medaris, J. B. *Countdown for Decision.* New York: Paperback Library, 1961, originally 1960. Army view of the advent of missiles and space.

Melman, Seymour. *Pentagon Capitalism: The Political Economy of War.* New York: McGraw-Hill, 1970. Sensationalist but contains valuable ideas.

Miller, Ronald, and Sawers, David. *The Technical Development of Modern Aviation.* New York: Praeger, 1970. Probing and detailed.

Millis, Walter, with Mansfield, Harvey C., and Stein, Harold. *Arms and the State: Civil-Military Elements in National Policy.* New York: Twentieth Century Fund, 1958. Useful for evaluating postwar national strategy.

Neal, Roy. *Ace in the Hole: The Story of the Minuteman Missile.* Garden City, N.Y.: Doubleday, 1962. Journalistic.

Pace, Dean Francis. *Negotiation and Management of Defense Contracts.* New York: John Wiley and Sons, 1970. Details of the mechanics of contracting with the Defense Department.

Peck, Merton J., and Scherer, Frederic M. *The Weapons Acquisition Process: An*

Economic Analysis. Boston: Graduate School of Business Administration, Harvard University, 1962. Definitive for period covered.

Polmar, Norman. *Aircraft Carriers: A Graphic History of Carrier Aviation and Its Influence on World Events*. Garden City, N.Y.: Doubleday, 1969. The roles and development of carrier aviation.

Proxmire, William. *Report from Wasteland: America's Military-Industrial Complex*. New York: Praeger, 1970. Sensationalist but with valuable insights.

Rae, John B. *Climb to Greatness: The American Aircraft Industry, 1920–1960*. Cambridge, Mass.: The MIT Press, 1968. A scholarly history, but skimpy for the period since World War II.

Reed, Arthur. *Britain's Aircraft Industry: What Went Right? What Went Wrong?* London: J. M. Dent and Sons, 1973. Insights into an industry having similarities to America's. Journalistic.

Rees, Ed. *The Manned Missile: The Story of the B-70*. New York: Duell, Sloan and Pearce, 1960. Brief, journalistic.

Reynolds, Clark G. *The Fast Carriers: The Forging of an Air Navy*. New York: McGraw-Hill, 1968. Evolution of U.S. naval strategy in World War II.

Rice, Berkeley. *The C-5A Scandal: An Inside Story of the Military-Industrial Complex*. Boston: Houghton Mifflin, 1971. Sensationalist.

Richards, Leverett G. *TAC: The Story of the Tactical Air Command*. New York: John Day, 1961. Journalistic. Emphasis is on operations.

Rickenbacker, Edward V. *Rickenbacker*. Greenwich, Conn.: Fawcett, 1969, originally 1967. Views of a key leader in the airline industry.

Ries, John C. *The Management of Defense: Organization and Control of the U.S. Armed Services*. Baltimore, Md.: Johns Hopkins Press, 1964. A criticism of centralization in the Pentagon.

Rogow, Arnold A. *James Forrestal: A Study of Personality, Politics, and Policy*. New York: Macmillan, 1963. Valuable for understanding defense policy in the early postwar years.

Rutkowski, Edwin H. *The Politics of Military Aviation Procurement, 1926–1934: A Study in the Political Assertion of Consensual Values*. Columbus: Ohio State University Press, 1966. Useful as background to subsequent procurement.

Schlaifer, Robert. *Development of Aircraft Engines: Two Studies of Relations between Government and Business* (includes *Development of Aviation Fuels*, by S. D. Heron). Boston: Graduate School of Business Administration, Harvard University, 1950. Definitive on piston and early jet engines.

Schwiebert, Ernest G. *A History of the U.S. Air Force Ballistic Missiles*. New York: Frederick A. Praeger, 1965. Brief early history of ballistic missiles.

Serling, Robert J. *The Electra Story*. Garden City, N.Y.: Doubleday, 1963. Journalistic.

Setright, L. J. K. *The Power to Fly: The Development of the Piston Engine in Aviation*. London: George Allen & Unwin, 1971. Brief but useful.

Schrader, Welman A. *Fifty Years of Flight: A Chronicle of the Aviation Industry in America, 1903–1953*. Cleveland, Ohio: Eaton Manufacturing Company, 1953. Some statistics of worth.

Smith, Perry McCoy. *The Air Force Plans for Peace 1943–1945*. Baltimore, Md.: Johns Hopkins Press, 1970. The best detailed analysis of the views of the Air Force carried into the postwar era.

Smith, Richard Austin. *Corporations in Crisis*. Garden City, N.Y.: Doubleday,

1963. Reprints of *Fortune* magazine articles covering some critical periods for Boeing, Martin, and General Dynamics.

Stekler, Herman O. *The Structure and Performance of the Aerospace Industry.* Berkeley: University of California Press, 1965. Valuable analysis of the industry in the sixties. See also Baldwin.

Stewart, Oliver. *Aviation: The Creative Ideas.* New York: Frederick A. Praeger, 1966. Brief but useful.

Swanborough, F. G. *United States Military Aircraft Since 1909.* London: Putnam, 1963. Aircraft data.

Truman, Harry S. *Memoirs.* Vol. 1, *Year of Decisions.* Vol. 2, *Years of Trial and Hope.* Garden City, N.Y.: Doubleday, 1955–1956. Provides information on postwar defense policy.

Ulanoff, Stanley M. *MATS: The Story of the Military Air Transport Service.* New York: Franklin Watts, 1964. Sketchy.

Wagner, Ray. *American Combat Planes.* Rev. ed. Garden City, N.Y.: Doubleday, 1968. Aircraft data.

Whitnah, Donald R. *Safer Skyways: Federal Control of Aviation, 1926–1966.* Ames, Iowa: Iowa State University Press, 1966. Valuable survey of the role of the FAA in the airline industry.

Who's Who in Aviation, A Directory of Living Men and Women Who Have Contributed to the Growth of Aviation in the United States, 1942–1943. New York: Ziff-Davis Publishing, 1942. This and the following book are somewhat early for this study.

Who's Who in World Aviation and Astronautics. Vol. 2. Washington, D.C.: American Aviation Publications, 1958.

OTHER

Company Annual Reports.
Letter to Author from Lockheed Aircraft Corporation, 23 May 1973.

INDEX

DATE DUE